CHILDREN & BOOKS I

African American Story Books and Activities For All Children

Patricia Buerke Moll, M.A.

Hampton Mae Institute, Tampa, Florida

Photography by Simon's Studios

Second Edition

*Love
Keep the pride growing
Pat Moll
1996*

Dedication

Rosetta Judge

Reverend A. Leon Lowry

First Edition
Printed October, 1991

Second Edition
Printed October, 1994

ISBN 0-9616511-4-8 Perfect Binding
ISBN 0-9616511-5-6 Spiral Binding

Please address your ideas or comments to Patricia Buerke Moll, M.A., Hampton Mae Institute, 4104 Lynn Avenue, Tampa, Florida 33603-3421.

Acknowledgments

Getting to know the children's literature featured in this text has been a challenging and rewarding experience. The work of these authors and illustrators is certainly a beautiful gift for all children.

We sent out questionnaires to the authors and illustrators featured in our text. Some have shared with us their personal feelings and experiences. Learning about them helped to make this book better.

Children throughout the country have had an impact on the materials presented in this book. The children and teachers who agreed to be photographed represent their brothers and sisters well. They are: Amanda Colla, Danielle Colla, Mary Floyd, Tamara Skye Floyd, Bob Gilder, James Hart, Markeshia Haynes, Rosetta Judge, Anthony Ladd, Laura Ladd, Beth Buerke McGuire, Alex James Otten, Brittney Richards, Whittney Richards, and Brandi Timmons.

Simon Rose allowed us to tromp through his studio so he could take our photographs.

Because Mary Floyd agreed to edit my manuscript, you have a book to read. Thanks, Mary.

Final thanks goes to Wilkinson and Associates for our "looks."

Patricia Buerke Moll
September 21, 1991

P. S. Glad you're still on the caravan, RBH, Old Lady and Magoo

Second Edition

Since the first publication in 1991, I have broadened my understanding of the purpose of this book. Dr. Fran Perkins was and is a patient teacher of selection of self-affirming literature. Her chapter "African -American Literature: Sharing the Joy," is a welcome addition to this book. Thank you, Fran.

Thanks go to Jim Trelease and Carol Brunson Phillips for their support of this project.

The artwork in this and the first edition was done by Brenda Flicker and Sara Barry's Kindergarten classes and my Pre-K class at Lockhart Elementary, Tampa, Florida.

Emily Frazier, a California kindergarten teacher, helped me to understand the opportunities for mathematics activities in some of the books presented.

Educators, librarians and book sellers throughout the country helped in making the selection of books more self-affirming with their "have you seen" greeting each time they saw me. Thanks for their continued encouragement and interest.

The twenty-five new books in this edition have black children as their main character and have an author and/or an illustrator of African heritage, which makes this edition more self-affirming than the first edition.

Yes, there will be more volumes (II, III,...).
Want to help?
Have an idea?
Drop me a line.

Patricia Buerke Moll, M.A.
September 10, 1994

P. S. The caravan goes on: with all on board!

The following is a list of jacket illustrations which were produced in this book with permission from their respective publishers:

Jacket Illustrations Continued

Jacket illustration by Catherine Stock from Galimoto by Karen Lynn Williams. Illustrations copyright © 1990 by Catherine Stock. Reproduced by permission of Lothrop, Lee and Shepard Books, a division of William Morrow & Company, Inc., Publisher.

Jacket illustration by James E. Ransome from Do Like Kyla by Angela Johnson. Illustrations copyright © 1990 by James E. Ransome. Reproduced by permission of Orchard Books, Publisher.

Jacket illustration by John Ward from We Keep a Store by Anne Shelby. Illustrations copyright © 1990 by John Ward. Reproduced by permission of Orchard Books, Publisher.

Jacket illustration by David Soman from When I Am Old With You by Angela Johnson. Illustrations copyright © 1990 by David Soman. Reproduced by permission of Orchard Books, Publisher.

Jacket illustration by Floyd Cooper from Grandpa's Face by Eloise Greenfield. Illustrations copyright © 1988 by Floyd Cooper. Reproduced by permission of Philomel Books, a division of Putnam Publishing Group, Publisher.

Jacket illustration by Aliki from A Weed is a Flower by Aliki. Illustrations copyright © 1988 by Aliki. Reproduced by permission of Simon and Schuster, Inc., Publishers.

Jacket illustration by James Ransome from Uncle Jed's Barbershop by Margaret King Mitchell. Illustrations copyright © 1993 by James Ransome. Reproduced by permission of Simon and Schuster, Inc., Publishers.

Jacket illustration by Paul Hunt from Dave and the Tooth Fairy by Verna Allette Wilkins. Illustrations copyright © 1993 by Paul Hunt. Reproduced by permission of Tamarind Limited, Publishers.

Jacket illustration by Lynne Willey from I Don't Eat Toothpaste Anymore! by Karen King. Illustrations copyright © 1993 by Lynne Willey. Reproduced by permission of Tamarind Limited, Publishers.

From Pretend You're a Cat by Jean Marzollo, pictures by Jerry Pinkney. Copyright © 1990 by Jerry Pinkney, pictures. Used by permission of Dial Books for Young Readers, a division of Penguin Books USA Inc.

From Flossie and the Fox by Patricia C. McKissack, pictures by Rachel Isadora. Copyright © 1986 by Rachel Isadora, pictures. Used by permission of Dial Books for Young Readers, a division of Penguin Books USA Inc.

From the Talking Eggs by Robert D. San Souci, pictures by Jerry Pinkney. Copyright © 1989 by Jerry Pinkney, pictures. Used by permission of Dial Books for Young Readers, a division of Penguin Books USA Inc.

From The Tales of Uncle Remus by Julius Lester, illustrated by Jerry Pinkney. Copyright © 1987 by Jerry Pinkney, illustrations. Used by permission of Dial Books for Young Readers, a division of Penguin Books USA Inc.

From The Patchwork Quilt by Valerie Flourney, pictures by Jerry Pinkney. Copyright © 1985 by Jerry Pinkney, pictures. Used by permission of Dial Books for Young Readers, a division of Penguin Books USA Inc.

From Something on My Mind by Nikki Grimes, pictures by Tom Feelings. Copyright © 1978 by Tom Feelings, pictures. Used by permission of Dial Books for Young Readers, a division of Penguin Books USA Inc.

From Why Mosquitoes Buzz in People's Ears by Verna Aardema, illustrations by Leo and Diane Dillon. Copyright © 1975 by Leo and Diane Dillon, illustrations. Used by permission of Dial Books for Young Readers, a division of Penguin Books USA Inc.

From Moja Means One: Swahili Counting Book by Muriel Feelings, pictures by Tom Feelings. Copyright © 1971 by Tom Feelings, pictures. Used by permission of Dial Books for Young Readers, a division of Penguin Books USA Inc.

From Who's In Rabbit's House by Verna Aardema, pictures by Leo and Diane Dillon, Copyright © 1977 by Leo and Diane Dillon, pictures. Used by permission of Dial Books for Young Readers, a division of Penguin Books USA Inc.

From Jambo Means Hello by Muriel Feelings, illustrated by Tom Feelings. Copyright © 1974 by Tom Feelings, illustrations. Used by permission of Dial Books for Young Readers, a division of Penguin Books USA Inc.

From Bringing the Rain to Kapiti Plain by Verna Aardema, illustrated by Beatriz Vidal. Copyright © 1981 by Beatriz Vidal, illustrations. Used by permission of Dial Books for Young Readers, a division of Penguin Books USA Inc.

From Ashanti To Zulu: African Traditions by Margaret Musgrove. Copyright © 1976 by Margaret Musgrove. Used by permission of Dial Books for Young Readers, a division of Penguin Books USA Inc.

Illustrations copyright © 1969 by John Steptoe from Stevie, HarperCollins, Publisher. Reproduced with the approval of the Estate of John Steptoe.

Illustrations copyright © 1988 by John Steptoe from Baby Says, Lothrop, Lee & Shepard Books, a division of William Morrow & Company, Inc., Publisher. Reproduced with the approval of the Estate of John Steptoe.

Illustrations copyright © 1980 by John Steptoe from Daddy is a Monster...Sometimes, HarperCollins, Publishers. Reproduced with the approval of the Estate of John Steptoe.

Illustrations copyright © 1974 by John Steptoe from She Come Bringing Me That Little Baby Girl, written by Eloise Greenfield, HarperCollins, Publishers. Reproduced with the approval of the Estate of John Steptoe.

Illustrations copyright © 1973 by John Steptoe from All Us Come Cross The Water, written by Lucille Clifton, Henry Holt and Company, Inc., Publishers. Reproduced with the approval of the Estate of John Steptoe.

TABLE OF
Contents

Chapter 1: Sharing The Joy   *1*

Chapter 2: Children Love Books   *5*

Chapter 3: Beginner Books   *11*

Sweet Baby Coming   *12*
Feelings
New Babies

The Baby   *14*
A Closer Look at the Words
My Book of Babies
What You Can Make Your Doll Do

My Daddy and I   *16*
Collage of Daddies
Role Play

I Make Music   *18*
Make Music
Let's Do It
Listen and Do

Big Friend, Little Friend   *20*
Big Book of Children
Big Friends, Little Friends
Pudding Painting

Good Night Baby   *22*
Make A Bedtime Book
Put the Baby to Bed
Wash the Baby Dolls

Baby Says   *24*
Dramatize the Story
Baby Talk
Baby Picture and First Word

Bright Eyes, Brown Skin   *26*
We Do What They Do
We Are Beautiful

I Don't Eat Toothpaste Anymore!   *28*
Watch a Baby
Now-I-Can Collage
When I Was a Baby

Truck   *30*
Watching and Talking About Trucks
Cardboard Trucks
Classify Trucks

The Leaving Morning   *32*
How Do I Feel
Good Stuff Free
Write a Letter

Pretend You're A Cat   *34*
What to Do with a Box?
Taped Story
Book Action

The Quilt   *36*
Class Quilt Display and Stories
My Favorite Blanket
Finding a Lost Treasure

Chapter 4: Folklore and Music   *39*

**Shake It To The One
    That You Love The Best**   *40*
Read with Apples on a Stick
Class Rhymes

Apples on a Stick   *41*
The Folklore of Black Children
Learn A New Rhyme
Make Miss Mary Mack

Flossie and the Fox   *42*
Act Out the Story
Classification of Animals
Class Story: Who Is The Teacher?
Change an Animal

Mirandy and Brother Wind   *44*
Cupcakes for a Cakewalk
Cakewalk
Catch Brother Wind

The Talking Eggs   *46*
Magical Animal Collage
Rabbit Dance
Decorate Eggs

**The Tales of Uncle Remus:
    The Adventures of Brer Rabbit**   *48*
Act Out a Tale
Flannel Board and Tapes
Brer Rabbit's Salad
Animal Classification

i

Chapter 5: Family — 51

Do Like Kyla — 52
Copy Cat Puppet Show
Gallery of Children's Friends/Relatives
Kyla Is My Friend

We Keep A Store — 54
Keep Store
Store Signs
My Trip to the Store
Visit a Store in Your Community
Money

Daddy Is A Monster...Sometimes — 56
Act Out the Story
Book About Turning People into Monsters
Monster Puppets

Willie's Not the Hugging Kind — 58
The Hugging Kind
My Favorite Hugs Chart
You Need a Hug
I Love Hugs Headband

She Come Bringing Me That Little Baby Girl — 60
People Who Like Me Book
Big Brother, Big Sister Hats
Make a Gift for a New Baby

Things I Like About Grandma — 62
Draw a Picture
Present for Grandma

When I Am Old With You — 64
Role-Playing Granddaddy and Child
Collage of Granddaddies
Make a Picture for Granddaddy

Everett Anderson's 1-2-3 — 66
Puppet Show
Individual Acceptance of New Parent

Everett Anderson's Nine Month Long — 68
Children's Play
Visit From an Expectant Mother
My Mama Collage

Everett Anderson's Goodbye — 70
Classroom Experiences to Explain Death
Everybody Cries Sometimes

Bigmama's — 72
My Trip
Be an Illustrator
What to Do Chart

My Mama Needs Me — 74
Things I Can Do At Home Poster
Watch a Baby Get a Bath
Give a Baby Doll a Bath
Make Chocolate Chip Cookies

Sam — 76
Act Out the Story
Make a Tart
Things I Can Do By Myself

The Patchwork Quilt — 78
Make a Quilt
Year-Long Class Quilt

Chapter 6: Stories & Poetry — 81

Dave and the Tooth Fairy — 82
Who Lost a Tooth
My Teeth Have Names
What I'll Buy

Ma nDA LA — 84
Tape a Story
Act Out the Illustrations
Shuck and Eat Corn
Mural

Life Doesn't Frighten Me — 86
I'm Not Afraid Of
I am Brave
Pudding Painting

Honey I Love and Other Poems — 88
Make a Book
I Love Headband
Tape Poems
Feelings Picture Collage

I Been There — 90
Children Add to the Story
What I'll See in Outer Space
Real and Pretend
My I Been There Book
Outer Space Reality

Nathaniel Talking — 92
Children's Blues/Rap Books
Expressing Feeling in Movement and
  Oral Language
Group Blues
Class Book of Individual Blues/Rap
Writing Blues/Rap

Mr. Monkey and the Gotcha Bird — 94
Tape Story for Listening Center
You Be a Storyteller
Class Play
Do You Want Mr. Monkey for a Friend?

Half a Moon and One Whole Star — 96
Sleep Book for Each Child
Classroom Sleep Book
Put the Dolls to Sleep

Red Dancing Shoes — 98
My Special Shoes
Shoes for Dancing

ii

Ben's Trumpet   **100**
Jazz and Rhythm Band
Performing "Ben's Trumpet"
Black and White Jazz Collage
Making Instruments

Amazing Grace   **102**
Have a Play
Go See a Performance
Act Out Parts of the Story

Something On My Mind   **104**
Children's Experiences
Feelings Collage
Class Book of Feelings
Writing Down My Feelings

Chapter 7: Black History   **107**

I Am Freedom's Child   **108**
Freedom
Freedom's Child Mural
Freedom Chart

Africa Dream   **110**
Finding Africa
My Dream
Naptime Story

All Us Come Cross the Water   **112**
All Us Come From Posters
African Necklace
Long-Ago Day

Kwanzaa   **114**
Make a Kinara
Cook Sweet Potato Pie
Make Zawadi
Have a Kwanzaa Feast

The Black Snowman   **116**
Make a Kente
Make a Snowman
I Hate Mural

Tar Beach   **118**
Tar Beach Picnic and Flyabout
Quilt Picture
1939 Day

Cornrows   **120**
Braid Children's Hair
Style Show
Class Book and Tape
Learn How to Braid

Follow the Drinking Gourd   **122**
Make the Big Dipper
Act Out the Story

**Book of Black Heroes Vol. 2
Great Women in the Struggle**   **124**
Circle Time
House/Block Area
Dramatic Play
Outside Play

Rosa Parks   **126**
Look at Photos
Act Out Rosa Parks

Harriet Tubman   **127**

Uncle Jed's Barbershop   **128**
I Want to Be
I Wanted to Be
Our Barbershop

**A Weed Is a Flower: The Life of
George Washington Carver**   **130**
Making Decisions
Make Peanut Butter
Draw a Plant

Stop & Go   **132**
Stop Light
Recreate Horse & Car Accident and Solution
Changing the Color of Light
Make a Class Stop Light

**A Picture Book of Martin
Luther King, Jr.**   **134**
Learn "We Shall Overcome"
What's Fair: Civil Rights Poster
Martin Luther King's Life
Peace March

Charlie Parker Played be bop   **136**
Make Instruments
Perform
Listen to a Musical Instrument

The People Could Fly   **138**
Naptime
The People Could Fly
Little Eight John

Dancing With The Indians   **140**
Dancing with the Indians
Making Things Like the Indians
Black Seminoles

**Josephine's 'magination
A Tale of Haiti**   **142**
Make a Doll
Make Cornbread
Market Day

Chapter 8: Friends   **145**

A Cat In Search of a Friend   **146**
On Being Friends
Cat Puppet Show
Flannel Board Story
A Friend in Search of a Cat
Categorizing Attributes of Animals & Friends

A Letter to Amy   **148**
Write and Mail Letters to Friends
Have a Birthday Party
Children Receive an Invitation to an Event
Wind Experiments

iii

Stevie — 150
Tape for the Listening Center
Steptoe Art
Identifying Feelings

Cherries and Cherry Pits — 152
Draw a Story
Grow a Seed
Make a Seed Book
Giant Feast

Me and Neesie — 154
My Best Friend
Imaginary Friend Day

Chilly Stomach — 156
Sexual Abuse
Stuffed Paper Bag Puppet

You Be Me, I'll Be You — 158
Read *Black is Brown is Tan*

Straight Hair, Curly Hair — 160
Book Experiments

Your Skin and Mine — 161
Book Experiments

My Five Senses — 162
My Five Senses Centers
My Body

Chapter 9: African Folktales & Customs — 165

I Am Eyes - - Ni Macho — 166
Large African Animal
Finding Animals
Visit a Zoo

Jafta — 168
Book of Animals and Feelings
Observation of Familar Animals
Identifying African Animals

Jafta's Mother — 170
Dramatize Jafta's Mother
Necklace for Mother

Jafta's Father — 172
Make a Hideout
Make a Drum or Rattle
Present for Father

Mcheshi Goes to the Market — 174
Market Day
Make Hard Boiled Eggs
Visit a Market or Store

Mcheshi Goes to the Game Park — 176
Land Rover Trip
Make a Pair of Binoculars
Learn Animal Names in Kiswahili

Anansi the Spider: A Tale From The Ashanti — 178
Cut and Paste Spiders
Study Spiders
Draw a Spider Book
Tape Story

Why Mosquitoes Buzz in People's Ears — 180
Flannel Board Story on Tape
Models of Animals in the Story
Learn About Mosquitoes
Dramatize the Story

Moja Means One: Swahili Counting Book — 182
Learn Ella Jenkins' Song
Make a Counting Tape
Make a Mankala
Tie-Dye Something to Wear

Who's in Rabbit's House A Masai Tale — 184
Jewelry of the Masai
Papier Mache Mask
Animal Sounds

Jambo Means Hello: Swahili Alphabet Book — 186
Paint in the Feelings Style
African Animal ABC Book
Clay Jar

Bringing the Rain to Kapiti Plain — 188
African Plain Mural
Flannel Board Story and Tape
Cause-and-Effect Relationships

Ashanti to Zulu: African Traditions — 190
Masks
Kye Kye Kula
Living in Africa Day

Authors and Illustrators — 193

Appendix — 219

Index — 230

Additional Books — 234

iv

Chapter I
African American Literature: Sharing the Joy
Dr. Fran Perkins

During my years as an early childhood teacher, I searched for books that reflected my culture and that of the African American children in my classes. Most of the books I found presented African Amercans only in historical settings and stereotypical roles. Only a few books, such as "*The Snowy Day*" and "*Goggles*" by Ezra Jack Keats depicted children in contemporary settings and provided a more diverse view of African American children. My students liked these books, and they did provide a positive image of African American children but the experiences, language, and even the names of the characters were not really culturally representative of African American children.

Fortunately, there has been increased publication and availability of African American literature for all ages to experience the joys this literature holds for readers of all cultures. African American literature is a wonderfully powerful tool for providing experiences that serve as mirrors for the African American child; and the literature can also serve as windows of cultural awareness for the non-African American child.In books such as *I Make Music* and *Honey I Love* by Eloise Greenfield provide children with a variety of settings, family relationships, language (not necessarily dialect), illustrations, and names of characters that are often affirming for the African American child and enlightening to children of all cultures. Therefore, self-affirming literature (that is, literature containing authentic cultural elements) coupled with literature that reflects the lives of all groups of people, is vital to early childhood classrooms.

Some of the benefits gained from incorporating African American literature into early childhood classrooms are the same as those experienced by readers who are exposed to any good literature. Children enjoy listening to and reading exciting books. For African American children, culturally authentic literature can serve as a bridge between young children's culture and their love for books. This connection is critical to children's later interest in school curricula.

As I visit early childhood classrooms and read to children, African American children overwhelmingly express a desire to read and listen to more stories "with people like us in them." When children make personal connections with characters, language, settings and various situations in stories, they are more likely to be drawn into the text and to develop a greater interest in reading. An eight year old boy expressed his interest in African American literature when he told me, "I'm glad you let us read these books because they keep me off my Nintendo. I don't play with my Nintendo ®, hardly. I just read these books." In the words of a younger child, "This story reminds me of my family!" The excitement expressed by this student after reading Faith Ringgold's *Tar Beach* was echoed by others as they requested that I read more books about African Americans. Equally important are the responses I receive from the non African American child. "I didn't know that black people started those kinds of cakewalks a long time ago. Can we have one, too?" This student learned about cakewalks from Patricia McKissack's *Mirandy and Brother Wind*.

African American literature covers a wide range of genres -- board books, picture books, historical and realistic fiction, fantasy, folklore, poetry and nonfiction. The series of board books written by Eloise Greenfield contains a rhythm and rhyme that will excite all toddlers. The illustrations by Jan Spivey Gilchrist provide additional appeal for young children. In previous years, there were virtually no board books written and illustrated by African Americans. Hudson and Ford's *Bright Eyes and Brown Skin* is a perfect example of a book for young children that celebrates the uniqueness of being black. The rhythmic language and the cheerful illustrations highlight the individuality and beauty of each of the toddlers.

There are African American books that can be used in any theme or classroom unit of study. For example, a theme on "family stories" is very easily supported with such books as *Bigmama's* by Donald Crews, *When I'm Old With You* by Angela Johnson, *Aunt Flossie's Hats...(and Crab Cakes Later)* by Elizabeth Fitzgerald Howard and *Mirandy and Brother Wind* by Patricia McKissack. If teachers and students want to engage in a study of poetry, any of Eloise Greenfield's poems or Nikki Giovanni's *Spin a Soft Black Song* could be integrated into the curriculum.

African American literature is also rich in folklore that is ideal for both reading aloud and story telling. Ashley Bryan, a noted author, illustrator and storyteller, has written numerous African folktales with a rhythm and rhyme that captivates audiences of all ages. His *The Dancing Granny,* contains many repetitive lines that encourage children to "shake it to the east...shake it to the west...". Other favorites such as Virginia Hamilton's *The People Could Fly*, a collection of Black American folktales, and Julius Lester's *Uncle Remus* tales are great collections for dramatizing with young children.

Essential to any classroom collection of African American literature are nonfiction texts. There are a variety of biographies and other information books available for young readers. Greenfield's biographies for primary readers, *Rosa Parks* and *Mary McLeod Bethune*, highlight the lives of two well known African American women. The language and pictures interact to produce an inviting story for young children. Additionally, Camille Yarbrough's *Cornrows* combines history and a family story to produce a primary information book. Although this category has traditionally had fewer authentic choices for early childhood classrooms, the recent surge of multicultural literature has provided teachers with numerous possibilities.

Children and Books I is a valuable resource for integrating African American literature into primary programs for all children to enjoy. The books included in this volume were selected primarily for their positive portrayal of African American culture, and their appeal to all children.

Fran Davis Perkins *

Dr. Fran Davis Perkins is an Assistant Professor at the University of Kentucky in the Department of Curriculum and Instruction. She has taught reading and language arts courses, early childhood and elementary practica and children's literature. She also has over nine years experience as a teacher of primary students.

Dr. Perkins' research efforts focus on the role of culturally authentic literature in the literacy development of young children. She is a member of numerous professional organizations and presents nationally on topics such as multicultural literature for children, family literacy, developmentally appropriate practices and the role of culture in literacy development.

Fran and a colleague have developed an extensive bibliography of African American literature for grades K-8. This bibliography has been published in several educational journals. Her other publications include *Whole Language: Putting Theory into Practice* (a monograph); *Author Studies: Profiles in Black; Celebrating African American Authors* and *Literacy in the Inner City.*

Additional Books Our Children Like

CHAPTER TWO

Children Love Books

Children and books go together as naturally as children and ice cream. Children are eager to learn actively with books. They want to see, hear, touch and even taste their favorite books.

Building on these natural instincts, *Children & Books I* offers children extensions of the best of children's African American literature. These extensions will allow children to experience further the rewards that come from reading and being read to.

We have selected books that involve your children, books that help them understand themselves, their friends, their families, books that help them develop skills to solve problems in their world. The books will reach out to your children and they will want to participate in the stories.

We encourage you to allow your children to participate actively in each story, particularly in the early readings. Later, when it has become their own, you will find that they want to hear it read straight through and will be ready to listen quietly.

Because we know - - that young African-American children -- as well as young children in general -- can benefit by experiencing literature in which African American children are the central figures, the special theme of *Children & Books I* is books that feature African American children and/or African language, customs and folktales, or are written/illustrated by an African American.

The books are arranged in general categories: Beginner Books, Folklore and Music, Family, Stories and Poetry, Black History, Friends and African Folktales and Customs. Enjoy the book!

Encouraging Emotional Growth

Any serious study of children's literature should include a reading of Bruno Betelheim's the *Uses of Enchantment: The Meanings and Importance of Fairy Tales*.

Betelheim justifies what you and other early childhood educators practice when you encourage emotional growth in your children through story books.

Although the books he uses as examples are primarily from Euro-American cultures, you will easily translate his theories to children's stories in any culture. His point is that all cultures use stories to teach their children about life.

Use *The New Read-Aloud Handbook* by Jim Trelease to reinforce your own beliefs in reading aloud. It is a must for your reference library. Re-read it from time to time and use it to find ways to encourage your children's caregivers to read aloud to their children.

Developmental Sequence

In each section, the books are arranged in a general developmental sequence. If a book is placed close to the beginning of the section, it can be appreciated by children at an earlier stage of development. Books near the end will be enjoyed more by the children later in their development, after they have experienced the easier stories. The developmental considerations are:

1. Reading of the words

a. How much intense listening is required of the child(ren) to interact with the story? How many words are on each page?

b. What is the length of the total book?

c. Is it necessary to read the entire story to enjoy the book?

d. How independent is each page from the rest of story?

e. Do the pages have a set sequence? Can the book be read forward and backward?

5

f. Can an abbreviated story line be adopted?

g. Generally speaking, how adaptable is the book to getting the children involved with the written story line?

2. Reading of the illustrations.

a. Can the illustrations stand alone?

b. Do they tell the story?

c. Does each illustration tell a story on its own?

d. Can young children make up their own stories from the illustrations?

e. How realistic are the illustrations?

f. How visually appealing to young children are the illustrations?

When all of these considerations were taken into account, the books fell rather easily into our developmental arrangement.

At the same time, it should be emphasized that any of these books can be used with children of any age. The considerations that were used to order the books will be helpful to you when considering how to use books with your particular children.

By making the necessary adjustments, your children can enjoy any book. You know when you are "losing your audience" and it is time to simplify the reading. You can take any book and only look at the pictures, make up your own story, read it forward, read it backward or "read" only the children's favorite pictures and/or words. The more ways you use the book, the more value the book will have for your children.

Books in Your Classroom

Children & Books I is directed toward helping children grow intellectually, emotionally and socially. The extensions suggested for each book follow that particular book.

We have not specified that the activities should fall in particular areas of your classroom. Depending on how your classroom is set up, you will find the most appropriate places to engage your children in the activities. The outdoor activities can also be successfully carried out indoors, and many indoor activities may be taken outside.

We encourage you to adapt the activities to fit the needs of your children. It is the hope of this author that you and your children will experience a wider range of literature and its use because of the books and activities presented in *Children & Books I*.

The importance of books for children is not only in the reading. It is in the involvement of the children, the books and you.

Sources & Criteria

Several sources and criteria were used to select the books.

In our second edition we have substituted books that are more self-affirming for African American children. Most of the new books became available in the last few years.

Dr. Fran Perkins helped this author in the selection of these new books. Her willingness to write Chapter One for *Children and Books I* has strengthened the book's purpose. Helping all children grow and develop through the use of books that use African American children as role models in an African American cultural environment.

•List of books and criteria for evaluation of Augusta Baker of the New York Public Library.

•Both the list and ten ways to analyze children's books from the NAEYC publication, Anti-Bias Curriculum.

•Archie Givens, Sr. collection, Curriculum Guide of Afro-American Literature.

•*The Black Experience in Children's Books,* 1989 Edition, New York Public Library list.

•Coretta Scott King Book Awards.

•The Caldecott Awards list.

•Gloria D. Dickerson's *A Guide to Black Children's Books.*

•Janice E. Hale's *African American Classics for Pre-School Children.*

•Newbery Award Books.

•Books available at the Tampa Public Library and the author's personal collection.

Additional criteria can be found by reading the books in the bibliography. Rely on your own sense of what books you and your children enjoy as a guide to new books for your classroom.

Format

A three-part format is used for each book. In the title box will be found, besides the name of the book, the names of authors and illustrators, information about them, a summary, the publisher and date, and awards the book has received. In the Story Time section for each book, which appears next, you will find the theme of the book and a description of a presentation of the book for your children. The third and final section under the individual books, Extensions, describes ideas you can use to enlarge on the book's theme and message through classroom activities and what cognitive functions the children will use.

Title Box

Title, a bit of information about the author and illustrator and any available anecdote about the book, a summary, the publisher, publication date and awards the book has received.

Title

The title of the book is given first. For ease of access, the books are also indexed by subject, title, author, illustrator and publisher in the back of this book.

Author, Illustrator, Anecdotes

We have made a concerted effort to learn as much as possible about the authors and illustrators of these books. The brief anecdotes printed with the book titles are gems given to this author by the illustrators/authors about a particular book or gleaned from our research.

Further information about these fascinating people, when available, has been included in the Authors and Illustrators section of this book (see Table of Contents). You are encouraged to use this information with your children, making the person who wrote a book and the person who drew or painted the pictures for a book come alive. This will help children to internalize the concept that reading is talk, written down.

That realization also encourages children to write (or to have written down) their own words. When your children dictate to you, call them authors. The children will also begin to recognize and remember authors and illustrators, which adds to the children's self-esteem banks as well as their intellectual banks.

Our authors and illustrators were chosen for the diversity of styles in their presentations. Your children will easily learn to recognize the visual styles and identify the illustrators. The authors represent "reading is talk written down" in the rich variety African-American English styles allow. Your children will delight in hearing these variations and identifying the author. Help your children to value their own language style and a variety of other language styles. Give them the opportunity to experiment, in your art area, with the many media used for visual representation in these books.

By broadening your children's understanding of language and visual expression, you will help them to be more accepting of themselves and others.

African-American children, coming from an oral language and cultural heritage, will further value written language when they learn that some of their favorite books were written and illustrated by African-Americans. This will help all children to expand their concepts of what adult African-Americans do. This information will also help children to become aware of other jobs in the adult world that may be done by all adults.

Summary

The book Summary is not intended to take the place of your pre-reading of the book, but may help you in selecting stories that you know will interest your children or that meet a particular need in your classroom.

Publisher, Date

The editions that we used in developing the extensions are indicated. You can use any edition that you happen to have available.

Story Time

Use of the book during Story Time, including the Theme, Introduction, Reading and children's Response time.

Theme

Theme of the book gives you an indication of when your children can most enjoy the story, based on your experience with them.

Dr. Charles A. Smith believes in helping children grow through books. In his book, *From Wonder to Wisdom,* he discusses eight themes and related concepts. We encourage you to read his book for a further understanding of how to identify the moral imagination of children.

Introduction & Reading

This time is probably already a part of your daily routine. This time should fit into the general atmosphere of your room. Where the children sit needs to be established early so that placement of bodies does not become a distraction from the story. Whether your children sit, stand or lie down is a teacher's personal choice. The children need initial guidance from you as to the rules. Later you need only ask, "Where does your body belong at story time?" The child should be able to make an appropriate response, both verbally and physically.

In the beginning, requiring children to raise their hands before speaking eliminates much noise and confusion. This also discourages children from trying to be the loudest voices. When the children are all talking at once, ask, "What do you do when you want to talk?" Keep repeating the question until a child silently raises his hand.

Call on that child and say, "Thank you for raising your hand, (child's name)." Then hope that the child says, "If you want to talk, raise your hand." If not, then ask the child, "What do you do if you want to talk?" Get the appropriate response. Then allow the child to say his piece.

Raising your hand to talk will become a habit. Next children will recognize the turn-taking habits of conversation, then move into a conversational and/or general response pattern that is manageable.

It is important to maintain an atmosphere in which children feel free to respond to the story and are encouraged to share their ideas and reactions to the story and illustrations. This helps to maintain the children's interest in the story and will encourage shy children to share their ideas.

When your children have settled into the Story Time routine and also have begun to use conversational patterns, raising hands may not be necessary. Spontaneous oral response by the children will begin to fall into a talking, listening, turn-taking conversational style rather than a shouting match. When this happens, the next step becomes staying on the task of reading the story rather than having general conversation.

Children who are having difficulty listening to the story should be placed directly in front of you. This allows you to have good eye contact with that child, and will help a distractible child to maintain interest in the story.

Because you know best the needs of the children in your class, you know best how to use any particular book in your classroom. All or none of our suggestions may be appropriate for your class. Our hope is that *Children & Books I* will identify some new books for you and encourage you to go beyond the reading of those books to children who merely listen quietly.

Books can be ice breakers to talk about a problem that is prominent in your class right now. Under those circumstances, the class discussion is

the task and the book can be put aside for another day. Just because you start reading a book does not mean that you have to finish reading it. The children's needs should be the focus rather than the "reading" of a particular book.

Encourage the children to listen to the rhythm and rhyme of the words, to look at the illustrations and to bring their personal experiences to the book.

After the story belongs to the children from re-reading, they will need or want very little conversation about the book. Rather, they will want the book to be read straight through. Depending on the style of the book, they will want to read it with the teacher and/or tell what is going to happen when the page is turned. The more orally involved the children are in the "reading" of the book, the easier it is for them to make the connection that reading is talk, written down.

Story Time itself can be more involved than reading the book. Depending on the story, puppets, stuffed animals, food, plastic models or other props may be used. The place for the story may also be varied to suit a particular book.

If the story relates to a particular need in your classroom, it may be used as a follow-up activity to the actual experience your children have had, or as an introduction to conversation about a particular topic. Use the Do's and Don'ts in The Read-aloud Handbook, as a further guide to successful reading-aloud experiences with your children. Pass these suggestions on to your children's caregivers.

Response

When the story has been read, encourage children to respond. Use standard, thinking, open-ended questions that require more than a yes-or-no answer:

"What happened when...?"

"Why did...?"

"Why was...?"

"What do you think about...?"

"What was the best part...?"

"What would happen if...?"

"What would you do if...?"

Give the children a chance to personalize the story. They will establish a pattern of reviewing the book for you and themselves.

Augusta Baker, formerly of the New York Public Library, has written an excellent book on storytelling. She will encourage you to memorize stories to tell your children. And the experience of a storyteller is certainly scanty in many a young child's life today. Take any of these books or your own favorites and become a storyteller as well as a book reader.

Extensions

Extension include specific activities, materials needed, suggested ways to do the activities, and the ways in which the children will develop cognitively. The story Extensions are designed around our identified Theme(s) of the book. The Materials lists identifies for you what is needed. Another Thought offers ways to expand on or change the activity. Cognitive Development identifies brain functions or the kinds of thinking skills learned and put to use by the child during a particular activity.

Another Book

Here you will find other books by the author and/or books that relate to this particular theme.

Growing, Learning

Believe in your children's desires to grow and learn. Be sensitive to their needs and adapt these activities to those needs. And, most of all, enjoy with the children the special message that each book gives.

Teacher's Resources:

Strickland, Dorothy S. Ed., (1986), *Listen Children* Bantam, New York

Trelease, Jim,(1994), *Read Aloud Hand Book,* Penguin Books, Inc., New York

Things Our Children Like To Do

9

CHAPTER THREE

Beginner Books

Sweet Baby Coming

The Baby

My Daddy and I

I Make Music

Big Friend, Little Friend

Good Night, Baby

Baby Says

Bright Eyes, Brown Skin

I Don't Eat Toothpaste Anymore

Truck

The Leaving Morning

Pretend You're a Cat

The Quilt

Sweet Baby Coming

Written By Eloise Greenfield

Any time you see a work by this author, take the book and use it with your children. Her words always touch the hearts and minds of children of all ages.

Summary:

A young girl anticipates the birth of a new baby, wondering about the baby and her feelings.

Illustrated by Jan Spivey Gilchrist

An author in her own right, Ms. Gilchrist often teams with Ms. Greenfield. Together they give children gentle, positive messages.

Harper Festival, 1994

STORY TIME

Theme

Waiting for a new baby and wondering what it will be like to have a new baby.

Introduction

1. Board books are designed for small children to handle. Give the book to your toddler and let her look through it.

2. Ask the small group who are interested in the book if they would like you to read it.

3. Gather these children around you in a comfortable spot.

Reading

1. Give the children time to talk about the cover. Depending on the age of your children, let them tell you what they talk about with female caregivers.

2. Ask if anyone knows about a *Sweet Baby Coming*? Read the title of the book.

3. Illustrations and pictures can easily stand alone. You decide which one to "read" first, or whether to combine the two.

4. Be sure to read "I'm going to be a brother" as well as a sister. Your boys will want to be included in the spirit of the book.

5. Also read sweet, sweet baby "sister" for those children who have sisters rather than brothers.

Response

1. On re-reading, allow the time for your children to answer the questions in the book.

2. Be more concerned with the development of the oral language of your children than with finishing the book.

3. Don't be surprised when your children start carrying babies under their clothes. Then they will pull them out and "have a baby." Boys as well as girls will do this. Your children will make the distinction that the mothers have babies. Explain the boys having babies is only "play-play" (pretend).

4. Learn to say the poem with your children.

EXTENSIONS

Feelings

Materials

Pictures of expectant mothers with children, both from magazines and your children, book: *Sweet Baby Coming*.

1. Sit with a small group of your children, the book and the pictures.

2. Encourage your children to talk about how the people in the pictures feel and how your children feel.

3. Talk about how happy most people feel when new babies come. Ask your children to tell you why babies make people happy. Accept as valid your children's responses.

4. Follow your children's mood; don't feel compelled to talk about the negative feelings.

Another Thought

Respect the negative feelings some children have about new babies coming. Use the book to allow these children to express these feelings. Validate these feelings. Re-state them for the child. Comfort the child. Help him identify the feelings. Use another opportunity to explore the positive side of the new baby. In the present, use the time as a comforting, sympathizing time for the child. In the middle of all that understanding, don't be surprised if this "sad child" suddenly pops up and shares a very happy thought about "his new baby coming."

Cognitive Development

Exploring and identifying feelings, life cycles, learning to adjust to change.

New Babies

Materials

Book: *Sweet Baby Coming*

Additional Activities In This Book:

Everett Anderson's Nine Month Long
My Mama Needs Me
She Come Bringing Me That Little Baby Girl

Things Our Children Like To Do

13

The Baby

Written by Monica Greenfield   *Illustrated by Jan Spivey Gilchrist*

New brothers and sisters will love "reading" Monica's words again and again, knowing from personal experiences that "their baby" does these things again and again.

Smiles will appear on the faces of baby lovers everywhere when they see these beautiful illustrations. The expressions on the baby's face are priceless.

Summary:
A new baby's routine becomes a wonderful experience for readers.

Harper Festival, 1994

STORY TIME

Theme

Cycle of a baby's day.

Introduction

1. Sit on the floor with a few children. Be sure that every child can see the pictures.

2. Show the book to your children and wait for their responses.

3. Point to the words with your finger and read the title. Ask what the book is going to be about.

Reading

1. Open the book and wait for the children to respond verbally to each page.

2. If the children do not use the words that are written on the page, read the words. If a child uses the words, reinforce those words by pointing to the printed words.

3. Supply your children with the language for each page. Praise the language they give.

4. Accept each child's explanation of what is happening as valid. Children whose responses are completely inappropriate may need special attention. At another time, re-read the book with that child and consider an evaluation of language skills and emotional development.

Response

1. Let the children take turns holding the book, finding the picture they like and talking about it.

2. Re-read the book and look at the baby's body parts. Let children take turns telling what the baby's body parts are. Example: point to eye and ask, "What is this?" Also let the children show where the body parts are by pointing. Example: "Show me the baby's eyes." "Show me your eyes."

EXTENSIONS

A Closer Look At The Words

Materials

Book: *The Baby*

1. Pair the words by concept and talk with your children about the samenesses and the differences in the words, and what the baby's action means.

2. Pairs:

Kicking	Walking
Crying	Talking
Sleeping	Awake
Eating	Drinking
Yawning	Biting
Stretching	Laying
Sucking	Spitting

3. Example: Kicking/Hitting - "What is the baby doing? Why is the baby kicking?" Help the children find positive reasons for the baby's action. Talk about how the baby tells you what he needs. Help children who give negative motivation to the baby understand the baby is learning to do many things, and that babies are trying to tell others what they want, not trying to be mean.

4. Use the sentence, "When you -----, you -----." Example: "When you stretch, you reach out your hands. When you yawn, you open your mouth wide."

Another Thought

Encourage your children to describe what is happening with both words. Help them see likenesses and differences.

Cognitive Development

Oral expression, visual discrimination, classification, labeling actions, comparisons.

14

What You Can Make Your Doll Do

Materials

Dolls or stuffed animals with long floppy legs, book: *The Baby*.

1. Work with a small group of your children, who have selected dolls or stuffed animals to manipulate.

2. Show one of the pictures in the book and ask the children to make their dolls or animals do what the baby is doing.

3. Let the children take turns selecting a page from the book. Then the child can ask the other children to make their dolls or animals do what the baby is doing on that page.

Another Thought

The children may want to act out what the book babies are doing.

Cognitive Development

Looking at a representation for an action and performing the concrete action, verbal expression, representing body language, identifying own body parts.

Things Our Children Like To Do

My Book of Babies

Materials

Tagboard or posterboard squares (5" x 5"), pre-cut pictures of babies of many races doing things, glue/paste, book: *The Baby*

1. Show a few of your children *The Baby* book and ask them if they would like to make a book.

2. Let each child choose some of the pre-cut pictures. Help the children glue the pictures on the pages. Be sure to put pictures on both sides of the pages. Select one page as a "cover" and write a title chosen by the child.

3. Ask each child what the baby is doing. You write the child's words on the tagboard pages. Write the child's name on the "cover" as the author.

Another Thought

Go to the library and look for more books about babies.

Cognitive Development

Visual representation, oral language, describing actions, eye-hand coordination.

Another Book

Slier, Debbie, (1989), *Little Babies*, Checkerboard Press, New York.

15

My Daddy and I

Written by Eloise Greenfield   *Illustrated by Jan Spivey Gilchrist*

Every father should have this book so they will know what being a "Daddy" is all about. Ms. Greenfield gives us words to learn how to love.

Watercolor images flow together to bond these images to "men" in a gentle caring relationship.

Summary:
A small boy tells of everyday activities with his daddy.

Black Butterfly Children's Books, 1991

STORY TIME

Theme
Being with daddy makes me happy.

16

Introduction
1. Gather a small group of children. Ask them if they know a man or a big boy they like to do things with.
2. Be sensitive to those children in your room who have limited contact with their fathers. Help them find a male in their experience they can do things with.

Reading
1. If indeed, you have many children who have little contact with their fathers, let your children tell you the relationship between the man and the boy on the cover before you read the title.
2. Give your children the opportunity to anticipate what these characters might do.
3. The layout and words will give your children an opening to tell their stories.

Response
1. Eloise Greenfield's words always deserve a reading on their own. Be sure you give your children the opportunity to sit quietly for this listening poem.
2. Have a hug time like the boy and his daddy. Everyone will want to hug someone. Let your children choose who they will hug and who will hug them.

EXTENSIONS

Collage of Daddies

Materials
Magazines and sale catalogs with pictures that reflect your children's physical appearance, scissors, 4' x 4' background paper, glue, book: *My Daddy and I.*

1. Re-read the book. Ask who would like to find pictures of men who would be good daddies.
2. Have your children look through the magazines and catalogs to find pictures they like. Depending on their skill level, they or you can cut out the pictures.
3. Let your children determine where the pictures should be on the background paper.
4. Display this collage of daddies at eye-level so your children can see and talk about "their daddies" in their own time.
5. Your children may want to make their own collage to take home. You can easily do both.
6. This could be a week long project, with a few children working on the collage each day.

Another Thought
Have your children bring in pictures of themselves and their daddies. Put them in a picture album for the children to look at and talk about. Be sure your children understand they can bring in a picture of themselves and anyone they love.

Cognitive Development
Classification, recognizing adult males in many settings, eye-hand coordination, oral language.

Role Play

Materials

Dramatic play materials in your House and Block areas, book: *My Daddy and I.*

1. Re-read the book to a small group of your children. Have props similar to those in the book.

2. Ask who would like to be the daddy and who the child. Let the children choose which page they would like to act out.

3. Also encourage your children to make up their own situations.

4. Role playing is more fun and at this stage more interesting than being in the audience. Children who have "done their bit" may want to go on to other activities. This is certainly permissible. You and the children waiting for a turn are audience enough.

5. Supply the daddies with positive language for your children. "David, thank you for helping me hang up the clothes," etc.

6. An appropriate ending for your role is the hug page. Encourage hugs by giving hugs. Leave the book and your children to continue to play or find another activity.

7. Older children may work well with a director in charge of choosing children's roles.

Another Thought

Girls can easily play parts with daddies. When they want to play mommy roles, extend the idea of the book to include mommies.

Cognitive Development

Dramatic play, bringing a representation to a live role, classification, recall of oral language patterns.

Additional Activities In This Book:

When I am Old With You
Jafta's Father
Things I Like About Grandma

Another Book

Caines, J., (1977), *Daddy,* Harper & Row.

Greenfield, E., *First Pink Light,* (1991) Black Butterfly Children's Books, Publisher, New York,

Jacket illustration copyright (c) 1991, by Jan Spivey Gilchrist used with permission from Black Butterfly Children's Book Publisher.

Things Our Children Like To Do   17

I Make Music

Written by Eloise Greenfield   *Illustrated by Jan Spivey Gilchrist*

Music is made every time Eloise writes.   Children will want to be musical right along with Jan's child.

Summary:
Making music delights this little girl and everyone in her family.

Black Butterfly Children's Books, 1991

STORY TIME

Theme

I make good music.

Introduction

1. Put the book out where a child will pick it up. Make yourself available to the child who picks it up.

2. Give your children the opportunity to say "Would you read me this book, please?" Teach your children several ways to request the reading of a book. Model the sentences they need for the request.

3. After the request has been made, even if the child has just repeated your statement, say "Thank you for asking so nicely."

4. Let the children look through the book. Listen to their explanations of the illustrations.

Reading

1. Eloise Greenfield's words always beg to be said by the listener. And these are no exception.

2. Read a phrase and have your children repeat it.

3. You and your children will easily fall into the music of these words.

4. Don't be shy. Let your bodies enjoy these words.

5. You'll easily re-read this book several times when children request the book.

Response

Encourage your children to relate their personal experiences to each of the illustrations. They have an instrument like that or know someone who does. Or they saw it in a parade or on TV.

EXTENSIONS

Make Music

Materials

Musical instruments in your classroom, book: *I Make Music*.

1. Re-read the book. Ask your children if they would like to play the instruments in the story.

2. Depending on the age of your children and your arrangement of materials, have your children identify an instrument and go and find it in your room.

3. Of course, you could just have the instruments beside you. Have your children look at the illustrations in the book and find the one like it.

4. Have substitutions for the instruments you don't have. Talk about how they are alike and/or different from the pictures in the book.

5. Be sure to have something for every child in the group.

6. Make music. Let the age and experience of your children guide your music. Each child can play his own "song."

7. As your children develop, they will want to play the same song some of the time. Trust your children to develop into "group players." It doesn't have to be self or group. Some time can be spent on each kind of performance.

Another Thought

Find a song with a simple beat. Watch for the children who follow the beat. Help the other children to hear the beat by choosing music with very specific beating sounds. Praise everyone's performance.

Note:

A child who becomes over-stimulated may need to stand with an adult and listen. Then begin to move his body, perhaps clapping his hands then walking. Next, use an instrument, still with an adult buddy. Finally he will move by himself with an adult to give him a positive clue to stay in control of the music rather than letting the music take control of him. Try, "listen and do" so that this child will have an appropriate movement and space for his loud noise and exaggerated body movements.

Cognitive Development

Listening for a musical beat, following a musical beat.

Let's Do It

Materials

Pictures on 5" x 5" cards of children playing instruments, book: *I Make Music*.

1. Gather a few children to play with you.
2. Show the children *I Make Music* and the action pictures. Ask them if they would like to take turns playing the instrument like the children in the pictures.
3. Have the willing children choose a 5" x 5" card picture. You do the action of the picture with them.
4. Let your children take turns choosing a picture, with the whole group doing the action.

Another Thought

Make the book and pictures available for the children to use independently. With older children, let them choose and make their own "Let's Do It" cards. The children could choose from pre-cut pictures or from magazines.

Congnitive Development

Representation, body language, self-esteem, role playing.

Listen and Do

Materials

Your playground equipment, pictures from "Let's Do It" above, book: *I Make Music*.

1. Take the book out on the playground with you.
2. Choose a child to show a picture from the book. Have the child tell his playmates what to do. When they have finished acting, have the child show the picture and tell if they did the right things.
3. With very young children this may turn into "watch me." Then the child is telling and doing. After watching a child perform, you or a child can tell the action. This brings the activity back to a listening skillbuilder.
4. Because you are out on the playground, your children can be noisier and have more space to perform with their bodies. The child we talked about in "Make Music" above will need less guidance to restrain his actions.

Making instruments

See the activities for the following books:

Drum or Rattle - *Jafta's Father*

Blowing Instruments - *Charlie Parker Played be bop*

Jacket Illustration copyright (c) 1991, by Jan Spivey Gilchrist used with permission from Black Butterfly Children's Books, Publisher

Another Book

Crews, Donald (1983), *Parade,* Greenwillow Books, New York.

19

Big Friend, Little Friend

Written by Eloise Greenfield   *Illustrated by Jan Spivey Gilchrist*

If Eloise writes it, children will love it and want to memorize it for their own. All children need friends like these.

Again, Jan sends her own message with her watercolors as she illustrates Greenfield's words.

Summary:
A young boy tells of his adventures with an older child and a younger child.

Black Butterfly Children's Books, 1991

STORY TIME

Theme

Friendship, positive self-image, playing together, learning and teaching.

Introduction

1. Ask, "Who has a friend?" Let children tell about their friends.
2. Show the cover of the book to your children and ask them to tell you about it.
3. Read the title.

Reading

1. Very young children will easily identify with the pictures and want to tell you about their friends.
2. Older children will want to "read" the words and tell about their little friend and big friend experiences.

Reading

1. Encourage your very young children to look at the illustrations and tell who helps them.
2. Ask your older children to look at the illustrations and "read" the words.

Response

1. Have the children tell you which part of the book they liked best. Find that illustration.
2. Examine the illustrations for emotional interaction. Give your children the language for describing these interactions (patience, kindness, loving).

EXTENSIONS

Big Book of Children
Materials

Tagboard (largest size available), roll of butcher paper or brown wrapping paper, scraps of material, yarn, construction paper, scissors, glue, slip rings, rope loops.

1. Ask your children what their favorite things are to do with a friend. Make a list, trying to get two or three children for each activity.
2. Lay a child or children on the paper. Trace the children in a position that will closely resemble someone doing the activity. If the activity is hugging, for example, actually have two children hug each other and trace their outlines.
3. Cut out the silhouette. Glue it on the tagboard.
4. Dress the paper children, add faces and hair using scrap material, yarn, construction paper, markers, crayons. Your children should be involved as much as possible in the cutting, gluing and coloring.
5. Write a label word for each activity. Have children make up titles or make up your own title.
6. Lamination is a must so that your very young children can "read" the book again and again.
7. Bind the book with slip ring or rope loops.

Another Thought

The pictures could be used as posters and hung around the room in appropriate places.

Cognitive Development

Representation of live models and written words, visual perception, eye-hand coordination, verbal expression, written expression.

Big Friend, Little Friend

Materials

Pictures of your children's friends, book: *Big Friend, Little Friend*

1. Send a note home asking for pictures of each child's friends.
2. Re-read *Big Friend, Little Friend*.
3. Encourage your children to tell about the pictures they brought.

Another Thought

In a small group after re-reading the book, let each child tell about their big friends and little friends. Ask about experiences similar to the pictures in the book.

Cognitive Development

Identifying social relationships, comparing real life experiences to visual representations, oral expression, recalling real life events.

Jacket illustration copyright © 1991, by Jan Spivey Gilchrist used with permission from Black Butterfly Children's Books, Publisher.

Pudding Painting

Materials

Pudding mix and milk (or substitute such as shaving cream, fingerpaints, dishwashing liquid,) bowl, clean tabletop, clean hands.

Note: Because we think of friendship and children as a giggly, silly time, you are encouraged to do this activity with whatever mixture you feel comfortable with. The tabletop is suggested because it offers mutual space. Mutual space opens the question of the give and take of space. Pre-plan who paints with whom and be sure to give those children who need a clearly defined space the space they need. This will result in mutual dividing up and sharing of space. Please don't require your children to "share" the space. Each child needs a defined space. The purpose is not for the children to mix their puddings together. If you want two or more children to use the same space, then use a mixture they will not eat.

1. Mix enough pudding to give each child about three tablespoons full. Be sure children have enough room for each child to define his space. Place a lump of pudding in front of each child.
2. Some children may want their pudding in a bowl and a place where they can sit and eat while they are watching the other children. They certainly should be given that choice. Allow them to put their fingers in the bowl.
3. Encourage children to fingerpaint with the pudding. As they are working, help them to tell what they are doing and how it feels.
4. Some children will lose interest quickly. After they clean up, these children should be given some kind of a snack. They may want to watch the others or move on to another activity.
5. You decide whether children can eat the pudding they are fingerpainting with. The children will want to! If you don't want them to eat it, perhaps you should use another material. If your tabletop and their hands are absolutely clean, they shouldn't be harmed by eating it. You be the judge for the potential of germ spreading in your classroom.

Another Thought

If you use fingerpaints, take a sheet of construction paper and press it to the tabletop evenly with your hand. When you lift the paper, you will have a "print" of the child's painting, which can be allowed to dry and be taken home. Help the child to see that her print is a reverse image.

Cognitive Development

Eye-hand coordination, oral expression, spatial orientation, visual perception, emotional expression, positive self-concept.

21

Good Night Baby

By Cheryl Willis Hudson   *Illustrated by George Ford*

Cheryl teaches caregivers, as well as babies, a positive bedtime routine in this story.

Babies and their friends will look and talk about George's illustrations again and again. Lucky for them it's a board book and will last through many readings.

Summary:
Baby gets sleepy, thinks of his day, gets ready for bed and says "good night."

Scholastic, 1992

STORY TIME

Theme
Baby recalling day and bedtime routine.

Introduction
1. Sit with a few children so that everyone can see the pictures.
2. Pass the book around so everyone has a chance to touch the book before it is read.
3. As the book is being passed, read the title and point to the word with your finger.

Reading
1. Position the book so that everyone can see the pictures.
2. Look at the pictures and ask the children what the baby is doing. If there is no verbal response, read the words.
3. As you look at each picture with your children, continue to encourage them to talk about the picture.
4. Very young children are interested in telling you, not listening to other children. Allow the children to come and go from the book reading. Some children may need to wait their turns to talk by walking away. Then when the page is turned, there will be interest in having a turn to talk and the child will come back to the book.

Response
1. These simple illustrations invite conversation about body parts, colors, shapes, as well as the actions of the child.
2. Re-read the book. The members of your small group will change and you will be offered other books to read.

EXTENSIONS

Make a Bedtime Book

Materials
Construction paper, glue, scissors, magazines, crayons/markers, books: *Children & Scissors, Good Night Baby*.

1. This can be a long-term project. Collect each child's page as it is completed. Then put the pages together in book form when they are all completed. Keep reminding the children that they are making a book.
2. You may choose to follow the illustrations and words in the book or let each child make up his own story.
3. Construction paper figures or magazine pictures may be used for the illustrations.
4. Children may want to draw some of the pictures.
5. Focus on one or two pages at a sitting. Using construction paper figures/magazines pictures/ children's drawings, each child can illustrate his page.
6. The words for each page may be written by the child. The child's words can be dictated to an adult or the words can be copies from the text.

Another Thought
On completion of each set of pages, re-read the other completed pages.

If lamination is available to you, this would be a book to laminate. Staple pages together in a construction-paper cover or bind the book.

Cognitive Development
Body language, visual discrimination, representation, oral language.

22

Put the Baby to Bed

Materials

Baby dolls, blanket, bottles, rocking chairs, baby beds, book: *Good Night Baby*.

1. Gather a small group of children or join in a group already in your house area.

2. Ask who would like to put a baby to bed.

3. Encourage your children to tell you what happens at bedtime at their house.

4. Re-read *Good Night Baby*. Ask children if they would like to put a baby to bed like the baby in the book.

5. Have children gather the materials they will need to put the baby to sleep.

6. Praise your children for their gentleness and patience with their babies.

7. Model appropriate language for quieting and relaxing children to put them to sleep.

Another Thought

Have children tell their experiences of watching younger children be put to bed, and tell what happens when they are put to bed.

Cognitive Development

Role playing, oral language, developing a sequence, positive communication of ideas, eye-hand coordination.

Another Book

Hudson, Cheryl Wills, (1992), *Good Morning Baby*, Scholastic, New York

Wash the Baby Dolls

Materials

Your baby dolls, dishwashing soap, wash clothes, nail brushes, small plastic tubs, towels, book: *Good Night Baby*.

1. Re-read with a small group of children. Ask them if they would like to give your doll babies a bath.

2. Ask your children what they will need to give the doll babies a bath. As the children name an item, put that item in front of them. Make sure your children ask for the doll babies they want to wash.

3. Look at the doll babies and talk about whether they are clean or dirty.

4. Set the children up with the materials outside so there is no worry about water spilling. Let them wash the doll babies.

5. Let the children dry the doll babies and put them to bed.

6. Talk about baths before bedtime.

Another Thought

If you have no place of a tub of splashy water, have the children give the bath with a damp cloth. Or a pretend (play-play) bath using a dry cloth can also be fun.

Cognitive Development

Oral language, eye-hand coordination, positive self-esteem, hygiene.

23

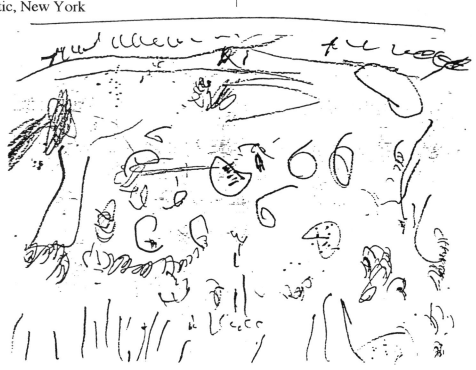

Baby Says

Written and illustrated by John Steptoe

This story , written late in Steptoe's career, shows a growth in his style. The illustrations are as soft and gentle as the big brother in the story. Read and look at his first book, *Stevie*, for comparison and to understand the message he always wanted to give to children.

Summary:
A baby and big brother figure out how to get along.

Lothrop, Lee & Shepherd Books, 1988

STORY TIME

Theme
Family relations, patience, understanding, solving problems, working together.

Introduction
1.   Show the children the cover. Ask them to tell you about babies. What do babies do? How do they act? And so forth.

2.   Ask your children how they think the picture of the baby was made. Did someone draw the baby or did he take a picture with a camera?

Reading
1.   Get the children to predict what will happen to the baby's teddy bear and what the big brother will do.

2.   Have the children predict what will happen next and let the children identify who is talking.

3.   Help your children understand why the big brother is not getting mad. Talk with them about what the baby is trying to tell the big brother.

4.   Ask your children how the baby and the big brother could play together and be happy.

Response
1.   Ask your children to tell you the part of the story they liked best. Turn to that page and ask a child to tell about the emotions in the picture.

2.   Have your children relate their personal experiences to the story.

3.   Ask your children if they think the big brother is always so patient. Do they think sometimes the big brother would just leave the room and not play with the baby? Help them realize the big brother can leave without getting mad at the baby. This big brother can just say, "Baby, I am going to play by myself now."

EXTENSIONS

Baby Picture and First Word

NOTE: Before doing this activity, talk to your parents to be sure that each child has a baby picture and a first word.

Materials
Photos of the children, their first words, construction paper and so forth to decorate a bulletin board.

1.   Ask the children if they would like to bring a picture of themselves to put up on the bulletin board.

2.   For those children who want to participate, ask them to find out the first word anyone remembers them saying. Include "Mommy" and "Daddy," but find out another word, too.

3.   Make a class bulletin board of the pictures and words at a level the children can see.

Another Thought
If you have many children with no early records by caregivers, bring in baby magazines that reflect many races.

Have your children find a picture of a baby. Then let the child decide what his baby's first word will be. Make a class display.

Cognitive Development
Positive self-concept, eye-hand coordination, time, seeing a concept followed through.

Baby Talk

Materials

Your children's favorite materials in the classroom.

1. Ask each child in a small group of children to get her favorite thing in the classroom and come sit with you.

2. Tell the children that everyone is going to pretend he is a baby just learning to talk.

3. You start. Pretend to be a baby who wants to play with one of the children.

4. The children will get the idea. Help them to pair off. Then the two children can try to talk to each other in baby talk.

5. The point is to help the children empathize with young children who have very little language, and to think of ways to help the young child get his point across.

Another Thought

Don't be surprised if some of your children revert to baby talk sometimes during the day. Accept the current need they are expressing and "baby" them.

Cognitive Development

Non-verbal expression, understanding non-verbal language, recalling baby talk, social relations, understanding others' needs.

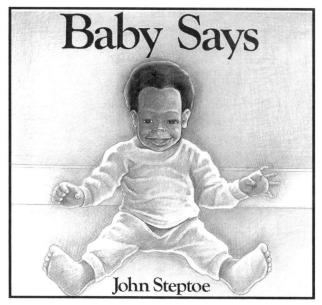

Jacket illustration copyright 1988 by John Steptoe, reprinted with the approval of the Estate of John Steptoe

Dramatize the Story

Materials

Teddy or some other stuffed animal from your room, big blocks or something to make a playpen, toys from your room for the big brother or sister to play with, book: *Baby Says.*

NOTE: Allow even your physically biggest children to play the part of the baby.

1. Working in a small group tell your children that they are going to act out the book.

2. Show your children an illustration from the book. Ask them what they could use from the classroom to make a set like the illustration.

3. After you have set up your stage, choose two children to play out the part. Another child can play the director to show the pages.

4. Your children may incorporate this story into their regular housekeeping play. Help them to realize that, if they are the baby, they must first ask another child to be the big brother or sister. Then both children know the rules and one child will not be surprised at being hit on the back with a teddy bear.

5. Remind your children of the patience the big brother had. Give your children the positive language the big brother can use if he does not want to play. Emphasize that the older child does not have to get mad to move from the younger child.

Another Thought

The children may want to make up their own stories and will invent language for their stories.

Cognitive Development

Role playing, oral language, patience.

Things Our Children Like To Do

25

Bright Eyes, Brown Skin

Written by Cheryl Willis Hudson and Bernette G. Ford   *Illustrated by George Ford*

Response from children of color throughout the world is praise for the sensitivity of these two women's word which help children feel confident. Ms. Hudson is co-owner of Just Us Books.

The Fords collaborated for the first time on this book. Olivia is their daughter. Her father often uses her in his pictures.

Summary:

The words express positive images of children of color while they are busy being children.

Just Us Books, 1979, 1990

STORY TIME

Theme

Children feeling good about who they are and how they look.

Introduction

1. Place this positive self-esteem poem in a learning center. Just Us Books gives common ground for all children to view these happy children with *Bright Eyes, Brown Skin*. We also have role-models for positive behavior in our learning settings.

2. Use the cover illustration to talk about how these children look and feel.

Reading

1. Tell your children this will first be a listening book. They will listen while you read the words and show the pictures.

2. Because your children will identify so easily with the pictures they will want to talk about them. Gently remind them to listen. You are teaching "read-aloud" behaviors.

3. This poem sets the stage for feeling positive about one's self. It deserves a quiet, straight-through reading.

Response

1. Re-read the book and follow your children's lead. Give them the opportunity to tell you what they are thinking.

2. At this reading or on another day, look in the back of the book and find the children's names. Again Just Us Books has given you a tool to help your children to relate personally to the *Bright Eyes, Brown Skin* children. Use it.

3. Using the book children's names relate, the words to the book children. Then encourage your children to relate the words to themselves.

4. On this first experience try to stay focused on the feelings and appearance of the book children.

5. See **"extensions"** to relate to daily routine.

EXTENSIONS

We Do What They Do

Materials

Book: *Bright Eyes, Brown Skin*.

1. Ask your children if they remember where the children on the cover of the book are playing.

2. Tell them that they are ------- (use the name that you use for your kind of setting). Encourage the children to tell you some things they do in their classroom. Ask your children if they think the book children will do those things also.

3. Ask your children, "What is the first thing that happens when you get to school?" (Use your word for school.) Help older children conclude that coming in is the first thing that happens.

4. Show each page and let the children tell you what is happening.

5. Encourage your children to talk about the individual children on the pages, and how happy the children are with themselves.

Another Thought

Let the children choose a page to tell about while they hold the book. Talk about the book children doing things that your children do in your classroom, how the book children feel about themselves and how your children feel about themselves while working.

Cognitive Development

Associating pictures with life experiences, daily routine sequence, oral language.

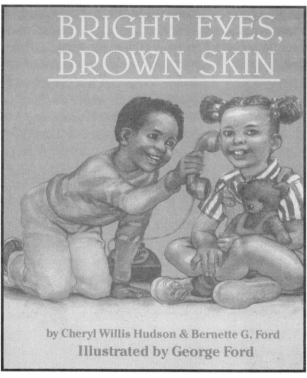

Jacket illustration copyright (c) 1990, George Ford, with permission from Just Us Books, Publisher.

Additional Activities In This Book

My Body
My Five Senses
Straight Hair, Curly Hair
Your Skin and Mine

Another Book

Church, V. (1971), *Colors Around Me*, Afro-American Publishing Company, Illinois.

We Are Beautiful

Materials

Photographs of each child and adult in your setting.

1. Ask caregivers to send in a photo of their child. Take pictures at school or use school pictures.

2. Make a class display of the photos. Photographs can be laminated, which solves the worry of little fingers touching them.

3. Encourage each child to write something positive about how she looks. If the child is reluctant, ask her if you can say something.

4. Be sure the display is at eye-level, or close to it.

5. Model saying positive things about the pictures. Help your children understand they can say something nice about themselves and not have to say something negative about someone else. Because "I'm pretty" you don't have to be "ugly." We can both be wonderful.

Another Thought

Have your children draw self-portraits. Then you might focus more on positive feeling rather than physical characteristics. If you want photos, find children in magazines and catalogs. Talk about their physical characteristics in a positive way.

Cognitive Development

I can be "good" and not make you "bad." Letting other children feel "good" about themselves, while I feel good about myself.

Things Our Children Like To Do

27

I don't eat toothpaste anymore

By Karen King

Illustrated by Lynne Willey

Children will love learning the "new words" of this English author as they brag about themselves.

Every child who sees these illustrations will see the pride in the little girl. Each child will then want to be proud of her own accomplishments.

Summary:
A young girl proudly tells what she can do now and how she did some of those things when she was little.

Tamarind, 1993

28

STORY TIME

Theme

Growing up, learning to do new things. What can I do? Positive self-image.

Introduction

1. Ask your children to tell you something they like to do. Then ask the child who responds if that is something she could do when she was a baby.

2. Read the title of the book. Tell the children this book is about things they do now and the things they used to do when they were babies.

3. Tell your children this book is from England and the children there use different words. Ask them to listen for the new words.

Reading

1. Begin by letting the children tell you what they did as babies.

2. With each "action" be sure to encourage your children to let you know proudly how they do that action now.

Response

1. Ask your children if they know any babies. Then let the child who answers find a page in the book and tell whether the baby he knows can do that. Ask if he can do that action now.

2. Re-read the illustrations and encourage your children to talk about the illustrations.

3. Talk about the words "mum", "tidy-up" and "cuddle". Encourage your children to tell you what words they use for these English words.

EXTENSIONS

Watch a Baby

Materials

Real life babies, friends or siblings of your children or doll babies in your housekeeping center, book: *I don't eat toothpaste anymore.*

1. Re-read *I don't eat toothpaste anymore* and ask your children if they would like to watch babies and see what they can do.

2. Make up some safety rules for your children to interact with the babies: clean hands, soft voices, thinking about what the baby likes (such as being touched, picked up, pulled in a direction).

3. Go to the babies or bring the baby to a small group of your children.

4. Let the children interact softly with the baby.

5. Encourage your children to talk about the baby and to talk to the baby.

Another Thought

As the children watch and touch and talk about the babies, they will want to tell you about when they were babies.

Cognitive Development

Respect for others, oral language, visual discrimination, observation.

Now-I-Can Collage

Materials

Photographs of children, magazine pictures, outdated school supply catalogs, scissors, glue, background paper, pre-cut symbols of accomplishments.

1. Talk with your children about what they like to do. And what they have just learned to do.

2. Depending on the age of your children, you can use photos from your classroom, photos of other children representing your children's accomplishments, or construction-paper symbols representing accomplishments.

3. Baby accomplishments: photos of feeding self, painting colors, walking up steps, doing things represented in *I don't eat toothpaste anymore.*

4. Kid accomplishments: pictures from a magazine or school supply catalog showing a child putting together a puzzle, swinging, jumping rope.

5. Symbols: shoelace for tying one's own shoe, printed name for "reading my name," one's own drawing for being an artist.

6. Let each child decide which of his new skills he wants to paste on the background paper. Then ask the child to tell about the pictures and write down his words.

7. How to use the collages: make individual collages for the children to take home. Display the collages on a class bulletin board at your children's eye level. Laminate the collages back-to-back and make a Now-I-Can big book.

Another Thought

Ask parents to take photos of the new skills children are learning at school. If cameras are not available, send home some 3" x 5" cards and ask parents to write down something new their children have learned. Then let the child tell a small group of children what her card says.

Cognitive Development

Representation, symbolism, visual discrimination, positive self-image, oral language, identifying personal behaviors, pride in one's own accomplishments.

When I Was a Baby

Materials

Furniture and dress-up items from your housekeeping area, book: *I don't eat toothpaste anymore.*

1. Re-read *I don't eat toothpaste anymore* to a small group of children. Ask if they would like to act like babies.

2. Go with the children to the housekeeping area and ask what is in the area that they will need when they act like babies.

3. Ask the children to take turns acting like a baby. Encourage the other children to talk about what the baby wants, needs, is doing.

Another Thought

This activity will probably make some of your children be caregivers to babies. Encourage the caregivers to have positive interaction with the babies. Help them to figure out what the baby needs, to talk to the baby in a gentle, calm voice and understand that the baby needs to learn how to do the right things.

Cognitive Development

Representation, pretending to be someone else, oral language, body language, visual discrimination, social relationships.

29

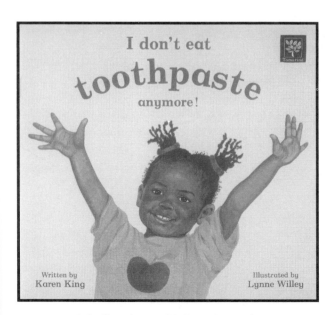

I don't eat **toothpaste** anymore!

Written by
Karen King

Illustrated by
Lynne Willey

Jacket illustration copyright © 1993 by Tamarind, used with permission from Tamarind, Publisher.

Truck

Written and Illustrated by Donald Crews

This is one of Crews' first children's picture books. All of his concept books stimulate children's visual perceptual growth.

Summary:
A truck's journey from loading to unloading.

Caldecott Honor Book   Greenwillow Books, 1980

STORY TIME

Theme
Watching a truck.

Introduction
1. Ask your children to tell you about the cover.
2. Read the title.

Reading
1. Encourage your children to talk about what is happening on each page.
2. Use the illustrations to talk.
3. Children will enjoy talking about the illustrations, and about letters, shapes, numbers, colors and familiar signs.

Response
Re-read the book, allowing the children to "read *Truck*" and talk about the illustrations.

EXTENSIONS

Cut-and-Paste Truck

Pre-cut construction paper, circles, rectangles, squares, scissors, glue, book: *Children & Scissors*.

1. Depending on the age of your children, pre-cut some or all pieces of a truck.
2. Children can paste the pieces of the truck together in a way that pleases them.

Another Thought

Take a long piece of paper and make a truck convoy.

Make a book by pasting trucks on 5" x 5" cards. Use the front and back. Then write the child's name as the title and write a few words on each page at her dictation.

Cognitive Development
Eye-hand coordination, visual discrimination, positive self-image, classification.

Watching And Talking About Trucks

Materials
Trucks that come to your building on a routine basis.

1. Find out the usual schedule of the trucks in your neighborhood.
2. Using safety considerations, watch the trucks that come to your school: food delivery, garbage pickup, mail, package delivery, school supplies and so forth.
3. As the children watch, discuss what is happening. Tell the children the names for the actions as well as the parts of the trucks.

Another Thought

Find out who comes to school or goes home in a truck. Inspect these trucks, encouraging the children to talk about what they see. Give the children the names of the parts of the truck. Ask the parents to talk to their children about the trucks they see around town. Allow the children to tell about these trucks at circle time or during the day.

Cognitive Development
Oral language, visual discrimination, labeling actions and objects, classification.

30

Cardboard Box Trucks

Materials

Cardboard boxes, tempera paint, odd-color paints (free) from paint store, paintbrushes, paint shirts, glue, construction paper.

1.   Ask your children if they would like to make some trucks for your classroom.
2.   The size of the trucks will depend on the size of your storage area. Cardboard boxes that one child can fit in, or long refrigerator boxes that many children can fit in, can be used.
3.   Tape the ends of the box very securely. Lay the box on its side. With the box on its other, large enough for one or more children to fit into. Be sure to allow at least a two-inch edge between the side of the box and the hole. This will help stabilize the box. Also cut smaller holes for hands to go through the sides of the box. The side holes will let the children pick up the box and walk around with it, "driving" the truck.
4.   Paint the box in a way that pleases your children. Construction paper symbols, windows, letters could be pasted on the box. The box could also be painted before cutting.
5.   Encourage your children to make up stories about the trucks.

Another Thought

If you have the space, the children could make traffic signs and make up traffic rules for all of your vehicles to move around your "town." Vehicles other than trucks could be made and all of your "wheeled" vehicles can join the traffic.

Cognitive Development

Representation, eye-hand coordination, oral language, spatial relations.

Another Book

Crews, D., (1989) *Flying,* Greenwillow, New York

Crews, D., (1978) *Freight Train* , Greenwillow, New York

Crews, D., (1984) *School Bus* , Greenwillow, New York

Jacket illustration Copyright © 1980 by Donald Crews, used with permission of Greenwillow Books, a division of William Morrow & Company, Publisher.

31

Classify Trucks

Materials

All the trucks in your room, models, pictures and stories, book: *Truck.*

1.   Show a small group of your children Truck again and get their comments.
2.   Tell the children you want to find out about all of the trucks in your room. Ask them to move around the room quietly and slowly find all the trucks in your room. If no one brings the pictures or books or songs about trucks, ask some questions to remind the children of these things.
3.   Look again at *Truck* and use the illustrations as a guide for classifying your trucks.
4.   Encourage the children to make up their own classifications, using their own labels.

Another Thought

This activity can easily be expanded to include all the vehicles in your room.

Cognitive Development

Classification, visual discrimination, oral language.

The Leaving Morning

Written by Angela Johnson *Illustrations by David Soman*

With a few words, Angela captures the feelings children and their families have when they move.

Your children will enjoy talking about Soman's illustrations.

Summary:
A young boy tells his experiences in getting ready to move away.

Orchard Books, 1992

32

STORY TIME

Theme

What happens when you move away from friends and family.

Introduction

1. Use the cover illustration to set the mood of excitement and sadness that goes with moving.

2. Ask if anyone in the class has moved and listen to their responses.

Reading

1. By using both the words and the illustrations you will be able to get comments from your children for each set of pages.

2. Be sensitive to any child who has just come into your room. This may be a way to get him to open up to the class.

3. Be sure your children understand the family's excitement and anticipation of the new place they are going.

Response

Talk about the lips left on the window. Are they kisses? For whom? Why did he leave them? Accept as valid the responses your children give.

EXTENSIONS

How Do I Feel

Materials

Puppets in your room, book: *The Leaving Morning*.

1. Work with a small group of children. Be sure to have a puppet for each child.

2. Look at each page and ask your children to make the puppet act like the book children.

3. Young children will involve their bodies as well as voices in acting out these feelings. No comment is necessary other than to the puppet.

4. Ask the child how he knows how the puppet feels? Interpreting feelings is a learned skill. Children need to be given the words to describe the feelings as well as to label them.

5. Anger, for instance, can be felt in the stomach, the hands, the feet. Help your children identify the body language of feelings.

Another Thought

Move to your children acting out how the book children feel. Get them to identify how parts of their bodies are involved in the feelings: mouth-smile, arms-hug when happy, etc.

Good Stuff Free

Materials

Children's old things from home, extra old toys, books, stuffed animals, book: *The Leaving Morning*.

1. Re-read *The Leaving Morning*. Talk about what happens when you move. Do you take everything or do you give some things away? Ask your children if they have some old things at home they would like to bring to school to give away. Do some people have garage sales? Would they like to have a give away day?

2. If your children want to have a Good Stuff Free day, send a letter home to your parents. Be sure your children and your parents understand the children are bringing things to give away. Have the parents write a note that this item is a give- away item.

3. On your Good Stuff Free day, sit down with your children and make up giving rules. Your final rule might be that if the owner of a toy wants to take it back home at the end of the day, he can.

4. Put the owner's name on the toy. When the toy changes owners, put the new name on the item. Talk about whether the child is giving it away or just telling the other child to hold it.

5. Be sure to have extra items so everyone has several choices.

6. Talk about how it feels to give away your old stuff.

Another Thought

Find some odd items from friends and bring them for a Good Stuff Free day. Let the children choose something to take home from these items if they did not bring anything.

Cognitive Development

Ownership, giving personal items away, positive self-image.

Another Book

Howard, E.F. (1988), *The Train to Lulu's*, Bradbury, New York .

Write a Letter

Materials

8 1/2" x 11" paper, stamped addressed envelope, book: *The Leaving Morning*.

1. Re-read the book. Talk about people your children know who have moved away; people who your children used to live by, who then moved away; or people your children know who live in another place.

2. Ask your children if they would like to write a letter to these people.

3. Send a letter home asking for an addressed, stamped envelope to the people the child has talked about.

4. You may end up having to send the envelope home to be addressed. Or simply get the address and put it on the envelope yourself.

5. Children who have no one to write to could write to one of your friends or family.

6. Include a note from you about how important it is that the person write back to the child.

7. Put into the envelope a drawing, a painting or anything the child made that can fit .

8. Sit with the children as he dictates what he wants to say (or let him write it).

9. If you have a mail box nearby, go and mail your letters (following school procedures). Or meet your letter carrier in the office.

10. Be sure to give the school's return address so that the children will be sure to receive and share their letters with classmates at school.

11. Keep track of who receives mail. You send a note to those children who have not received anything within 2 weeks.

Another Thought

Go to the post office to mail your letters. Depending on the ages of your children, you may be able to get the "25¢" tour.

Cognitive Development

Remembering people you do not see, recall, using the mail to keep in touch.

Pretend You're A Cat

Written by Jerry Marzollo

Marzollo's poetic story reflects an enthusiastic joy in the antics of children, especially mimicry.

Illustrated by Jerry Pinkney

Pinkney's paintings are of real children, made during an extensive visit with a group at Childrenspace. The girl on the front is his granddaughter. The boy with the chickens is his grandson.

Summary:
Rhymed and illustrated verses ask the reader to act like various familiar animals.

Dial Books for Young Readers, 1990

STORY TIME

Theme

What animals can do. How much fun I can have pretending to be an animal.

Introduction

1. Tell your children that the little girl on the cover of the book is pretending to be an animal. Ask them to guess which animal. Accept all their answers as valid.

2. Read the title and tell your children that the whole book is about children pretending to be different animals. Your children may want to guess at some of the animals that will be in the book. Illustrations on the cover give some clues.

Reading

1. For each animal in the book, the combination of prose, illustrations of animals and illustrations of children pretending to be animals will ensure that your children will be highly motivated to be physically active with this book.

2. So, on the first reading, be sure that each child has plenty of wiggling and acting-out space.

3. Use all three depictions to read to the children. Read the prose. Have the children guess the animal. Show the children the illustration of the animal. Have the children tell how the animal behaves. Show the illustrations of the children. Ask your children to tell you what the book's children are doing, and what animal they might be pretending to be.

Response

1. Use the last illustration of the hibernating child and bear to settle your children into a quiet response time.

2. Giving each child a time to tell, not act out, her favorite animal will help the settling-down process.

3. This is a definite re-read book!

4. Be sure you talk about the details of the illustrations.

EXTENSIONS

What to Do with a Box?

Materials

A cardboard box for every two children doing the activity, book: *Pretend You're a Cat.*

1. Show the page of the chick to a small group of children. Talk with your children about how the book's children used the box.

2. Let your children hatch.

3. Move among your children with the book and talk with them about how they might use the box to be other animals in the book.

4. With safety as your guide, accept as valid all of the ideas your children suggest.

Another Thought

Your children will probably go on to think of new animals and how to use the box. If your children do not think of some new animals, suggest some. Get involved with your children, the box, and pretending to be an animal. Your children will love it!

Cognitive Development

Imagination, body language, oral expression, classification, representation.

Taped Story

NOTE: Because this is an active story, it is a good one to start your tape library.

Materials

Tape recorder, blank tape, book: *Pretend You're a Cat*.

1. Tell your children that you are going to put the story on audio-tape. Talk to them about the procedure you will use so they will know what to do.

From *Pretend You're A Cat* by Jean Marzollo, pictures by Jerry Pinkney. Copyright 1990 by Jerry Pinkney pictures. Used by permission of Dial Books for Young Readers, a division of Penguin Books USA Inc.

2. Read the title and author's and illustrator's names. Let the tape run while you find the cat page. This will give the children time to find the page when they are using the tape on their own.

3. Read the words. Let your children say the name of the animal.

4. Let the children act out the animal.

5. Give a signal for the children to settle quietly, perhaps by showing how that animal goes to sleep. This settling period can also be the signal to turn the page.

6. Make the tape available for the children to listen to independently, after you have taught the use of the tape recorder.

Another Thought

Encourage your children to use your stuffed animals, puppets and plastic model animals while listening to the tape.

Many "broken" telephone answering machines will still play a tape. Ask around and get some for your classroom. An old answering machine could even go home overnight with a child.

Cognitive Development

Following directions, listening, body language, eye-hand coordination, working independently.

Book Action

Materials

Playground, materials from your dress-up box, book: *Pretend You're a Cat*.

1. Ask a small group of children if they would like to go outside and act out the book.

2. Talk with your children about what is available in your room for animal costumes. Gather these things and go outside.

3. Show the children the illustrations. Let the children act out each one, adding their own costumes.

4. Every child could act out each animal or each could choose an animal — or both.

5. The sequence is not important, except that the bear makes a good ending.

Another Thought

Your children will want to add other animals. Encourage them.

Cognitive Development

"Reading" pictures, classification, oral expression, creative thinking, body language.

Things Our Children Like To Do

The Quilt

Written and illustrated by Ann Jonas

The bright squares of a new patchwork quilt metamorphose into life in the colorful paintings by Jonas. Balloons rise, sailboats move across the water, houses lift themselves, gardens grow, and a town with a circus appears as the quilt's owner sleeps in her new grown-up bed.

Summary:
A child's new patchwork quilt recalls old memories and provides new adventures at bedtime.

Greenwillow, 1984

STORY TIME

Theme

Imagination, dreaming, time change, concern for friends, going to sleep.

Introduction

1. Open the book so that your children can see both the front and back covers.
2. Wait for the children's responses. Encourage them to talk about the picture. If no one uses the label "quilt," ask what the little girl has over her head. If no one knows the word "quilt," tell them the word and that *The Quilt* is the name of the story.
3. Be sure the children notice the stuffed dog.

Reading

1. Talk about the title page illustrations and how a quilt is made. If no one has said, ask if anyone has a quilt.
2. Ask your children how they think the little girl feels about getting a new quilt.
3. Have children reflect on what kind of a bed the little girl had before and why her parents would make her a quilt now.
4. Help your children understand that the little girl is falling off to sleep and will dream.
5. Get your children involved in telling the story of the quilt and the hunt for Sally.

Response

1. Re-read the story for a visual discrimination activity.
2. Have the children identify the patches. First look at where the pieces came from, next what the pieces turned into. Also observe the changes in the elephant picture.

3. Examine with your children the morning page. Let your children figure out which patches represent the things that happened in the story.
4. Encourage your children to talk about how the little girl felt when she found Sally.

EXTENSIONS

Class Quilt Display and Stories

Materials

Tempera paints, paintbrushes, newsprint, tape, book: *The Quilt*.

1. Talk with your children about painting a quilt. Show them *The Quilt* illustrations. Talk about the squares and how many different squares there are, and how the squares become part of the story.
2. Ask, "Who would like to paint a square for the quilt?"
3. Let each child paint his own designs.
4. Encourage the child to tell a story about her patch. Write down the story on a 3" x 5" card. Allow the child to tell any story to accompany her quilt patch.
5. Patch the painted squares together with tape and display the quilt. Paste the story of each patch in a corner of that patch.
6. Encourage adults who come to your room to read the children's stories to any child who wants to select stories from the quilt.

Another Thought

Let the children tell their stories on audiotape. Make the tape cassette available for the children's use. You will be surprised at how easily your children will remember which story goes with which patch painting.

Cognitive Development

Creative expression, oral language, visual perception, representation.

My Favorite Blanket

Materials

Each child's own blanket brought from home, book: *The Quilt.*

1. Send a note home to your parents for the child to bring to school a blanket or sheet that he sleeps with.

2. Look at the story to remind the children of the dream that the little girl had. Work with a small group of children.

3. Encourage your children to show their blankets to the other children and tell what the blanket makes them dream about.

Another Thought

Let the children bring anything they sleep with. If the child cannot remember her dreams, encourage her to talk about her bedroom routine. Also talk about how the children settle down to go to sleep and how they make their bodies go to sleep.

Jacket illustration Copyright © 1984 by Ann Jonas, used with permission

Cognitive Development

Sleep habits, oral expression, self-esteem, identifying personal habits and behaviors.

Finding a Lost Treasure

Materials

An item each child values from your classroom, book: *The Quilt.*

1. Sit with a small group of children and talk with them about what they like in the classroom.

2. Show the children *The Quilt* and encourage them to talk about how the little girl felt when she was dreaming about losing Sally.

3. Ask the children if they would like to take turns pretending they had lost their favorite thing in the classroom. Tell them someone will hide the object and they will pretend to look for it in their dreams.

4. Choose an interested child. That child should choose his favorite object to be hidden.

5. Have the child lie down and pretend to sleep.

6. Begin by hiding the object in a very visible place. Tell the child to pretend to be dreaming and walk around the room to find the item. Eyes should be open.

7. When the child finds the item, talk with the group about how it feels when you cannot find something. Talk about how you feel when you find it.

8. Choose another child to sleep and encourage that child to pretend to be worried about finding the object, then be happy when the item is found.

9. This is an exercise in identifying worried and fearful feelings, so the child can learn to have control over those feelings. If the child becomes worried and fearful, then give the child her item and comfort her.

Another Thought

As the children become "good finders," show *The Quilt* again. Talk about how the pictures come out of the patches. Use the word "camouflage" and explain and show that now you will hide the item in a place where it will be camouflaged. Then place it among similar items or before a same-color background.

Cognitive Development

Visual discrimination, identifying personal feelings, acting out feelings, oral expression, possession.

Another Book

Greenfield, Eloise, (1990), *Night on Neighborhood Street*, Dial Books for Young Readers, New York.

37

CHAPTER FOUR

Folklore and Music

Shake It to the One That You Love the Best
Apples on a Stick: The Folklore of Black Children
Flossie and the Fox
Mirandy and Brother Wind
The Talking Eggs
The Tales of Uncle Remus

Shake It To The One That You Love The Best

Collected and adapted by Cheryl Warren Mattox

These songs, loved by children, have been given an easy accompaniment by Mattox.

Summary:

A collection of play songs and lullabies from black musical traditions.

Illustrations by Varnette P. Honeywood and Brenda Joysmith

Honeywood and Joysmith express children's delight in song with their illustrations.

Warren-Mattox Productions, 1989

40

STORY TIME

Theme

Play songs and lullabies from black musical traditions.

Introduction

1. Actually, this is music time. Your children probably know some of these tunes, or at least the words.

2. Your children will be impressed to see their songs and chants in print and to hear them on tape.

Reading

1. Sing the familiar ones, then go on to learn the new ones.

2. Be sure to talk about the illustrations with your children. Some are available in print form and would add to your classroom displays.

Response

Encourage your children to talk about finding their songs and chants in print and on tape.

EXTENSIONS

Read with *Apples on a Stick*

Materials

Tape, tape recorder, books: *Apples on a Stick* and *Shake It to the One That You Love the Best.*

1. "Down Down Baby," "Little Sally Walker," and "Mary Mack" are in both books. Show those pages to your children.

2. Talk about the two very different "Little Sally Walker" illustrations and words..

3. While some children are recording on the tape, let others hold the books and "read" the pages.

Another Thought

Each song or lullaby suggests its own extensions. Memorize, perform, illustrate and share your children's favorites.

Cognitive Development

Reading is talk written down, oral language, recall of information, visual discrimination.

Class Rhymes

Materials

Local rhymes, tape recorder, tape, paper, hole puncher, crayons/markers.

1. Ask your children to say the songs they have learned at home. If possible, have the adult who taught them come to the class and teach your children.

2. Write down the words as the children dictate them. Your children may have difficulty saying the rhyme slowly enough for you to write it down. Tape it and write it down later.

3. These rhymes can then be put into a class book. Or make a book for each child. Encourage your children to draw pictures for each rhyme.

Cognitive Development

Positive self-image, valuing what is taught at home, oral language, seeing one's talk written down.

Another Book

Warren-Mattox Productions has a second book and tape; ask your book store or school supply store.

Apples on a Stick:
The Folklore of Black Children

Collected and edited by Barbara Michels and Bettye White   *Illustrated by Jerry Pinkney*

Michels and White collected these folk poems from children on Houston playgrounds.

Pinkney's drawings of real children will be looked at by your children over and over.

Summary:
A poetry collection from the oral language traditions of children.

Putnam, 1983

STORY TIME

Theme

Rhymes and poetry of black children in Houston, Texas.

Introduction

Your children probably know some of the verses in this book. Tell the children that this book has some of their favorite poems written down.

Reading

1. Look in the index of first lines and read a line familiar to your children. Ask them if they would like you to find it in the book.
2. Read while your children say the familiar rhymes first. Then move to poems you think your children might like to learn.

Response

1. Let the children take turns finding the rhymes they know in the book.
2. As the authors note, seeing their words in print is an important "self-affirmation" for all children. Let the children hold the book and say the rhyme.

EXTENSIONS

Learn a New Rhyme

Materials

Book: *Apples on a Stick*

1. Many of you use circle time to learn rhymes. Try some other places.

2. When walking in a line anywhere:
   Teacher says a line
   Children say a line
   Teacher says two lines
   Children say two lines
   and so on.

3. Of course, the jump rope chants are best learned on the playground.

Make Miss Mary Mack

Materials

Construction paper, scissors, glue, books: *Children & Scissors*, *Apples on a Stick*.

1. Pre-cut the body parts your children are unable to cut.
2. Make your art scrap box available for children to individualize their Marys.

Another Thought

Children & Scissors suggests other cut-and-paste projects. See African-American in index.

Cognitive Development

Representation, eye-hand coordination, visual discrimination.

Another Book

Slier, Deborah, ed. (1991) *Make A Joyful Sound*, Checkerboard Press, New York.

41

Flossie And The Fox

Written by Patricia C. McKissack
McKissack re-tells a story of her grandfather's in his rich, rural South dialect.

Illustrated by Rachel Isadora
The beautiful watercolors by Isadora bring the story colorfully to life.

Summary:
A wily fox, notorious for stealing eggs, meets his match when he encounters a bold little girl in the woods who insists upon proof that he is a fox before she will be frightened.

Dial Books for Young Readers, 1986

STORY TIME

Theme

Humor to solve a problem, positive self-concept.

Introduction

1. The picture on the cover of Flossie with the fox introduces this book very well.

2. Your children will want to tell you about the story.

3. Be sure you read the author's note at the front of the book and tell your children about it.

Reading

1. The style and flow of the language of the text should keep your children's attention. If not, the tale is certainly worth telling through the illustrations and reading some of the text.

2. Each time, ask your children if Flossie will believe the fox.

Response

1. Give your children time to talk about how Flossie used her own brain to trick the fox.

2. This is a re-read story. More of the text can be added as the children become familiar with the story.

3. Use this book for read-aloud and story telling.

EXTENSIONS

Act Out the Story

Materials

Basket of eggs, peach, stuffed animals from your room to represent the animals in the story, book: *Flossie and the Fox.*

1. Review the book with a small group of children. Ask them if they would like to act out the story.

2. Go through the illustrations with your children and decide what you have in your room to use as props. (Teach the word "prop," short for "property," used in the theater.) Decide with the children what you have in your room that can represent each of the animals.

3. Select children to play the roles. If you have more children than roles, ask the children if they can make up some more animal characters.

4. Also select a director to hold the book and keep the sequence of animals in order.

5. The children may want to put their play on for someone else in another class, parents, class visitor.

6. Children are very comfortable with changing roles while practicing a play for an audience. If you have a planned production, the characters for the final performance could be chosen that day.

Another Thought

Puppets could easily be used for the characters. This also will make a good flannel-board story.

Cognitive Development

Role-playing, recalling sequence and relationships, oral language, positive self-image.

Classification of Animals

Materials

All the animals in your room (plastic, stuffed, and puppets), book: *Flossie and the Fox.*

1.. Working with a small group, re-read the comparisons that Flossie made to the fox.

2. Begin by having your children tell you how a fox looks.

42

3. Pass out the animals so that each child has several. Then have them tell you how one of their animals looks like a fox.

4. Once the children begin to compare their animals to foxes, encourage them to talk to each other about their animals.

Another Thought

Your children will understand the concept of two things being similar by having one part in common. Then go to how other animals are alike because of one thing.

Cognitive Development

Oral language, classification, comparison

Class Story: Who Is the Teacher?

Materials

Book: *Flossie and the Fox.*

1. Review *Flossie and the Fox* and talk about how Flossie tricked the fox. Get the children to tell you that Flossie found one thing about another animal that was like the fox. Then she told the fox he was that animal.

2. Tell your class you want them to trick you like Flossie tricked the fox.

3. Start with another adult first. That adult takes the role of Flossie. You are like the fox.

Teacher: I am the teacher (your name).

Adult: No, I don't think so.

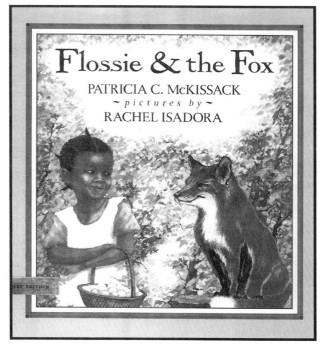

Teacher: I am the teacher. I have a pencil.

Adult: Well, James has a pencil, so you must be James.

Teacher: No, no, no!

4. Go to a child to play the fox role and follow the same procedure. Look at your children's clothes and see what you have that matches color, size, shape, or kind of clothes. The Fox Child will then have to find a child with a similar item and say, "No, you (Teacher) are like (that child) because you have (one thing the same).

Another Thought

After your children understand the game, let them volunteer to play the fox. Be aware of the amount of rejection the fox role gets. Be prepared to soothe feelings and to change children before they have had too much rejection.

Rejection of the adults is funny. Be sure when the children play the role that they continue to understand it is all a joke. Everyone really does know who they are.

Cognitive Development

Role-playing, oral language, observation.

Change an Animal

Materials

Construction paper, scissors, glue, your art scrap box, animals, magazine pictures of animals, books: *Flossie and the Fox, Children & Scissors* .

1. Look at *Flossie and the Fox* with a few children in the art area. Talk with them about how Flossie kept telling the fox he was another animal.

2. Let the children choose to put animals together to make a new animal. Example: Elephant body and legs with a giraffe head and neck.

Another Thought

Looking for ideas? Use ideas from *Children & Scissors*, magazine pictures, and your scrap box. Some children may want to create a whole new animal and even invent a name.

Cognitive Development

Classification, creativity, independent thinking, visual discrimination, and eye-hand coordination.

43

From *Flossie and the Fox* by Patricia C. McKissack, pictures by Rachel Isadora, Copyright © 1986 by Rachel Isadora, pictures. Used by permission of Dial Books for Young Readers, a division of Penguin Books USA, Inc.

Mirandy and Brother Wind

Written by Patricia C. McKissack   *Illustrated by Jerry Pinkney*

McKissack wrote this story based on a family photo of her grandparents as teenagers, before their marriage. They had just won a dance contest (a cakewalk) and been awarded a cake.

Period clothing, quilts, woodpiles, water pumps, barns, cows, chickens, flowering landscapes, lively dancing and a hard-to-catch Brother Wind fill Pinkney's dreamy watercolors of the rural 1900's.

Summary:
To win first prize in the Junior Cakewalk, Mirandy tries to capture the wind to be her partner.

Alfred A. Knopf, 1988

STORY TIME

Theme

Positive self-image, solving problems, social history, setting goals, friendship.

Introduction

1. Show the whole cover of the book and ask the children what they think the story is about.

2. Ask them if they think Mirandy is afraid of Brother Wind.

3. Talk about the author and why she wrote this story.

4. Ask if the children recognize the illustrator from other books they know.

Reading

1. Have the children tell you how the wind feels and how it sounds.

2. Ask the children about how the people are dressed and if this story happened now or a long time ago.

3. Ask what they think Ma Dear means when she says that those who can capture the wind can make the wind do their bidding.

4. During one of your readings of the book, be sure the children have time to talk about the pictures.

5. See if the children can tell you who Ezel wants for his partner.

6. Talk about "conjure" and what it means.

7. Ask children to predict who Mirandy will choose for her partner.

8. Get the children to talk about how Mirandy and Ezel felt when they were dancing.

Response

1. Ask the children what Mirandy did with her wish from Brother Wind.

2. Have the children tell you how they feel when they dance.

3. Encourage the children to talk about what Mirandy did to figure out how to catch Brother Wind.

4. A read-aloud, storytelling book.

EXTENSIONS

Cupcakes for a Cakewalk

Materials

Duncan Hines ® yellow cake mix, three eggs, oil, paper cupcake liners, muffin tin, bowl, measuring cups and spoons, spoon for stirring, oven, icing, sprinkles.

NOTE: This cake mix has never failed us.

1. Explain to the children that the class is going to have a cakewalk. Be sure that they understand that at your cakewalk each child will win a cupcake.

2. Working in a small group, read the recipe on the box and combine the ingredients.

3. Allow the children to do all of the mixing. No tasting after the eggs are added! Explain to your children that raw eggs can carry disease that will be cooked away in the oven.

4. Using the measuring cups, the children can also fill the cupcake liners.

5. After the cupcakes are baked, the children can decorate them.

44

Another Thought

This could be another activity, depending upon how elaborately you want the children to decorate the cakes.

Cognitive Development

Making preparations for a future event, positive self-image, identifying and combining ingredients to make cupcakes, creativity.

Cakewalk

Materials

Cupcakes, juice or milk, record player, records your children like to dance to, chalk square on the floor (at least 4' x 4'), scarves.

1. Have each child choose a partner to dance with around the square.
2. Play music, and let children dance and wave their scarves.
3. Praise all the children for their dancing and present each with a cupcake.
4. Eat cupcakes with juice or milk.

Another Thought

This would be a good parent/senior citizen involvement activity.

Cognitive Development

Auditory perception, self-esteem, self-expression.

Another Book

McKissack, P.C. (1989) *Nettie Jo's Friends*, Knopf. New York.

Catch Brother Wind

Materials

Scarves, ribbons, kites, parachute, windmill (construction paper, stick, crayons, straw, glue, pin).

1. Have the children gather things in your room that they think will blow in the wind.
2. Have available enough things so each child will have something to hold.
3. Another option is to make a windmill for each child from construction paper.
4. On the playground on a windy day, encourage the children to catch Brother Wind.
5. Encourage them to describe what the wind is doing. Be sure to make observations of the natural environment, trees, bushes, sand, leaves, clouds.

Another Thought

On a non-windy day, ask children to remember the windy day and make comparisons.

Cognitive Development

Oral language, creative thinking, visual perception, understanding of natural forces.

Things Our Children Like To Do

45

The Talking Eggs

Written by Robert D. San Souci   *Illustrated by Jerry Pinkney*

A Cinderella-like old Southern tale is re-told in a charming way by San Souci, relating a story of strange creatures and the triumph of good.

The turn-of-the-century South is depicted in Pinkney's pencil, color-pencil, and watercolor illustrations. Children will love his dressed-up rabbits.

Summary:
A Southern folktale in which kind Blanche, following the instructions of an old witch, gains riches while her greedy sister makes fun of the old woman and is duly rewarded.

Dial Books for Young Readers, 1989

STORY TIME

Theme

Respecting and accepting others and their differences, self-esteem, following directions, distinguishing between real and pretend.

Introduction

1. Talk about the characters' style of clothes to give the children a sense that this is a story that people have been telling for a long time.

2. Explain what a folk tale is. Ask the children to tell the names of the folk tales they know.

3. Give the children time to look carefully at the cover illustrations, so they will continue to examine the illustrations throughout the book.

Reading

1. Children will love these illustrations and can tell a very similar story line just from the illustrations. The things they might add will personalize the book for them.

2. Get the children to tell you how the mother treated the girls. Be sensitive to the responses you may get.

3. Help the children distinguish between reality and imagination.

4. If you have read other Pinkney books, talk about those illustrations.

Response

1. Ask your children to tell you why Blanche's eggs turned into things she liked, and Rose's eggs turned into things she did not like.

2. Get children to tell why the Aunty did good things for Blanche and did not do the same things for Rose.

3. Continue to talk to the children and ask them what Rose could have done to have good things happen to her.

4. Encourage the children to talk about why Blanche did not laugh. How did Blanche feel about the things she saw that were different from those she was accustomed to?

5. Talk about looking and listening when you experience new things. Help the children understand that you can learn things and do things and have fun if you don't make fun or get mad at things that are different.

6. Ask the children to tell you about magic.

7. Use for read-aloud and storytelling.

EXTENSIONS

Magical Animal Collage

Materials

Magazine, scissors, glue, paste, markers/crayons/paint, scrap paper, background paper.

1. Each child makes up a magical animal by cutting, pasting, drawing, or painting.

2. Children can choose to use magazine pictures for animal pictures. They can combine pictures or add to them with paint, markers, crayons, or scrap paper.

3. .Each child dictates her animal's magical powers for an adult to write on another sheet of paper.

4. Display collage and story in classroom or hall.

Cognitive Development

Visual perception, imagination.

Rabbit Dance

Materials

Markers, scissors, scrap paper, pre-cut rabbit ears, headband, glue, stapler, dress-up clothes from your room, record player, children's favorite records to dance to.

1. Children make rabbit ears. Encourage children to make their ears unusual, using the scrap paper and markers.
2. .Children dress up from your costume box, putting on rabbit ears.
3. .Children choose songs for the rabbits to dance to.
4. Rabbits dance.

Cognitive Development

Representation, body movement, self-expression.

Another Thought

Allow children to be any animal or person.

Decorate Eggs

Materials

Hard-boiled eggs, egg dye, magazine pictures, glue, plastic or styrofoam eggs, beads, sequins, permanent markers, drawing paper cut into an oval shape, markers, crayons, paints, your art scrap box, book: *The Talking Eggs*.

From *The Talking Eggs* by Robert D. San Souci, pictures by Jerry Pinkney, Copyright © by Jerry Pinkney, pictures. Used by permission of Dial Books for Young Readers, a division of Penguin Books USA Inc.

1. Choose the kinds of materials you want your children to use.
2. With a small group of children, look at the illustrations and recall the story.
3. Help those children who want to make talking eggs to gather the materials they will need.
4. Give your children a time to share their eggs with others.

Another Thought

Use the back of the egg to show what the egg will turn into. The children can draw it or use a magazine picture.

Cognitive Development

Visual discrimination, eye-hand coordination, imagination, pretending to be magical.

Another Thought

Howard. E.F. (1991) *Aunt Flossie's Hats--(and Crab Cakes Later)*. Clarion New York.

Things Our Children Like To Do

47

The Tales of Uncle Remus: The Adventures of Brer Rabbit

As told by Julius Lester

Illustrated by Jerry Pinkney

The first black author whose book was named Newbery Medal Honor Book, Lester writes for children and adults.

Pinkney grew up in a large family, and he always loved drawing people from life. His children in art seem real.

Summary:

African American folk tales of playing tricks and using your wits.

Dial Books for Young Readers, 1987

STORY TIME

48

Theme

Tricksters and humor.

Introduction

1. Be sure to read Augusta Baker's Introduction and Julius Lester's Foreword before you read the tales.
2. Lester's advice is to love the tale. So read and re-read before telling the tales to your children. And choose the ones you love.
3. As Lester suggests, enjoy the tales for their wit and humor.

Reading

1. Can be a read-aloud, or told as a story. If you read, be sure to maintain eye contact with your children.
2. Because the tales are short, re-telling with the children seems a natural.
3. Often the tales lead one into another. Moving on depends on the listening skill of your children.

Response

1. Your children will want to talk about Pinkney's illustrations. They may even want to make up their own tales from the illustrations.
2. Let your children choose the tales to be re-told.

EXTENSIONS

Act Out a Tale

Materials

Clothes from the dress-up area, headbands, masks, book: one of the Uncle Remus books.

1. Choose a tale your children love. Talk about the props you will need. Make and gather them.
2. Decide who will play the parts. The playing of the parts is, of course, the interesting activity. The need for an audience is minimal. Children may choose to come and go until their turns come to play the part.

Another Thought

Children love to perform. Find someone or a group so your children want to perform some of the tales for an audience.

Cognitive Development

Role-playing, planning, oral expression, recalling a sequence.

Flannel Board and Tapes

Materials

Flannel board and figures, tape recorder, tape, book: one of the Uncle Remus books.

1. Talk to your children about which tales they would like to have on a tape. Prepare the figures or work with a small group of children and make the figures.
2. If your children know the tale, let them do the telling. You tell or everybody tells.

From *The Tales of Uncle Remus* by Julius Lester, illustrated by Jerry Pinkney. Copyright © 1987 by Jerry Pinkney, illustrations. Used by permission of Dial Books for Young Readers, a division of Penguin Books USA Inc.

3. Listen to the tape and let your children manipulate the figures.

Another Thought

Encourage your children to make more figures and add tales to the tape.

Cognitive Development

Recall of a sequence, listening skills, eye-hand coordination.

Brer Rabbit's Salad

Materials

Available raw vegetables, lettuce, knives and cutting boards, plate, salad dressing or dip, book: one of the Uncle Remus books.

NOTE: Use safety considerations for knives used by adults and children.

1. Working in a small group, ask your children to recall the things Brer Rabbit likes to eat.
2. Children can wash their hands and then wash the salad makings.
3. Identify all of the food items. Talk about shape, size and color. Talk about how they grow and how Brer Rabbit would get them.

4. Give children an opportunity to prepare at least one of the food items.
5. Put each individual food in a separate container. Each child should be able to select the food he wants for his salad.
6. Encourage — but don't force — your children to taste all of Brer Rabbit's food.

Another Thought

Repeat Brer Rabbit's salad at different times of the year. Grow your own carrots indoors or outdoors.

Cognitive Development

Food preparation, food origins, classification, eye-hand coordination, taste discrimination, visual discrimination, growth from seeds.

Animal Classification

Materials

Animals available in your room (pictures, plastic, stuffed), book: one of the Uncle Remus books.

1. With a small group of children, talk about the animals they know from Uncle Remus.
2. With your children, sort out your classroom animals into Uncle Remus animals and other animals.
3. Identify by name the Uncle Remus animals. Now find different ways to classify these animals: The ones that play tricks, the ones that are big, the ones that are mean, the ones that help Brer Rabbit. Encourage your children to find many different ways to classify the animals.

Another Thought

Include all the animals in the game. Ask children to choose an animal not in the tale. Then have the child tell which group he thinks that animal would be in if he were in the tale.

Cognitive Development

Classification, identification of attributes, visual discrimination, oral language.

Another Book

Lester, Julius (1988) *More Tales of Uncle Remus.* Dial.

Lester, Julius (1990) *Further Tales of Uncle Remus, Dial.*

CHAPTER FIVE

Family

Do Like Kyla
We Keep a Store
Daddy Is a Monster ... Sometimes
Willie's Not the Hugging Kind
She Come Bringing Me That Little Baby Girl
Things I Like About Grandma
When I Am Old With You
Everett Anderson's 1-2-3
Everett Anderson's Nine Month Long
Everett Anderson's Goodbye
Bigmama's
My Mama Needs Me
Sam
The Patchwork Quilt

Do Like Kyla

Written by Angela Johnson

Johnson's first picture book was starred in *School Library Journal* and *Kirkus Review*.

Illustrated by James E. Ransome

Ransome's full-page oil paintings follow the two little girls from breakfast to bedtime.

Summary:

Kyla's little sister wants to do everything all day just like Kyla does.

Orchard Books, 1990

STORY TIME

Theme

Family relations, patience with others, self-esteem, acting on your own ideas, friendship.

Introduction

1. Ask your children who they think the children are on the cover of the book.

2. Encourage them to talk about the family relationship of the children.

3. Talk about what kind of a time the children look like they are having.

4. Children in the tropics or subtropics may have to be told that the children are making angels in the snow.

5. Read the title and see if the children can predict what will happen between the children in the story.

6. Look at the beautiful illustration of the purple boots and ask who the boots belong to and why they are standing together.

Reading

1. After reading the first page, ask the children who is telling the story.

2. Each of the illustrations can invite comments from the children. Encourage their ideas.

3. As you read the book, be receptive to your children's stories about their own relationships with other children (siblings, cousins, friends).

Response

1. Ask your children how they thought the little sister felt when Kyla did just like she did.

2. Look at the cover again and ask the children which part of the story the angels in the snow fit into.

3. Allow the children to relate their own experiences to those of Kyla and her sister.

EXTENSIONS

Copy Cat Puppet Show

Materials

Puppets from your classroom, record player, record: "Copy Cat" by Greg and Steve.

1. Put children into groups of two, each child having a puppet.

2. Let children act out the words of the song, using their puppets.

3. Talk with the children about the fun copy-catting can be for both people. Encourage them to tell you personal stories.

4. Encourage children to make up their own copy cat stories.

Another Thought

Give children the opportunity to be the leader and the copy cat. Encourage children to talk about how they feel in each role.

Cognitive Development

Visual motor perception, eye-hand coordination, right/left brain integration, auditory memory, receptive language (verbal and non-verbal).

Gallery of Children's Friends/Relatives

Materials

Photos from home, drawing paper, magazines, scissors, glue, writing paper, pencils, markers/crayons.

1. Ask each child to bring a picture of a friend or relative. Help children with no pictures to find a picture of someone in a magazine they would like to be their friend. Or have children draw a friend.
2. Have each child dictate a short story about his friend.
3. Make a bulletin board, using the children's pictures and stories.

Another Thought

The gallery can be put into a book and be made available so the children can look at their own and each other's friends as they desire.

Cognitive Development

Visual representation, verbal expression.

Kyla Is My Friend

Materials

Book: *Do Like Kyla*

1. Re-read the book.
2. Talk about what kind of friend Kyla is being.
3. Use the word "patience." Help the children recall when they were a good, patient friend to someone in the room.
4. Talk about how it feels when someone "Copies of Me."
5. Explain what a proud feeling it is for someone to want to be like you.
6. Encourage discussion about how to get the copying person to do something else.

Another Thought

When children in your room say "He's copying of me," remind your children of Kyla and her sister.

Cognitive Development

Identifying personal feelings, respecting other people's feelings.

Jacket illustration copyright © 1990 James E. Ransome, used with permission from Orchard Books

Things Our Children Like To Do

53

Another Book

Caines, Janice (1982) *Just Us Women*, Harper & Row, New York.

We Keep a Store

Written by Anne Shelby   *Illustrated by John Ward*

Shelby grew up in a family of storekeepers. This is her first book for children.

The paintings by Ward for his first picture book show a side of country life that city children will love.

Summary:
A small girl describes some of the many pleasures of running a family country store.

Orchard Books, 1990

STORY TIME

Theme
Family working together, positive self-image.

Introduction
1. Talk with your children about the stores they go to. Ask them if they know who owns the store.
2. Show the cover of the book and tell your children that this story is about this little girl and her family's store.

Reading
1. The illustrations invite conversation. Take time for your children to tell you about the pictures.
2. Help your children identify with the little girl. Ask, "What is she doing and how is she feeling?" Ask "how" and "why" questions.

Response
1. Ask your children to compare this store with the stores where they go shopping.
2. Let them tell you if they would like to have a store like that.

EXTENSIONS

Keep Store
Materials
For store furniture: blocks, furniture from your room, and cardboard boxes, crates, styrofoam packing pieces.

For equipment: cash register (cigar box or toy) with play or real money, paper bags, food containers (meat/vegetable), empty cans, bottles or boxes, plastic food, sturdy real food (oranges, apples, nuts), scoops, scales, price stickers, aprons.

1. Your store can be as simple or as elaborate as you and your children want it to be.
2. Talk to your children about having a store. Encourage them to decide what you have in the room that you can use and what needs to be made or brought in.
3. Parents can be asked to send in empty cans (smooth edges), boxes, bottles, and food trays.
4. Help the children arrange the store in a space that allows other children to work with different activities.
5. Set up positive how-to rules on how the store will be run, who gets to be the checkout clerk, how much a customer will buy, special jobs (bakery-deli clerk, vegetable clerk, butcher, store manager, bag person, candy control, etc.) and any rules you think will be necessary.
6. The "store" may fade away in a few days. Follow the children's lead as to how long the store furniture needs to stay around.

Cognitive Development
Representation, spatial relations, taking turns, visual discrimination, oral language.

54

Store Signs

Materials

Markers/crayons/paints, glue, construction paper, scissors, paintbrushes, newspaper/magazine advertisements, coupons.

1. Ask your children about the signs they see when they go shopping. Talk about what they are for (price, buy me, identification of areas in the store).

2. Gather a group of children waiting for a turn in the store (the extension above), and ask if they would like to make signs for the store.

3. Give each child a piece of construction paper and show him the pictures. Let each child design his own sign.

4. Write down whatever the child dictates to you for his sign.

Cognitive Development

Relating a message, representation, visual discrimination, eye-hand coordination.

My Trip to the Store

Materials

Something a child bought while in a store.

1. Talk to your parents and ask if the children could bring something to school that the child bought at the store.

2. Items might be clothes, food, toy, pencils, pen.

3. Emphasize that you would like the child to hand the money to the clerk and receive the change back.

4. As the children are allowed to buy at the store, give them an opportunity to tell about their experiences and to show the items.

5. Help your children distinguish among grocery stores, department stores, toy stores, and so forth.

Another Thought

Some children may not be allowed to buy at the store. Let them select something in the room that they would like to buy. Then have them talk about what would happen in a real store if they went in to buy it.

Cognitive Development

Recall of events, oral language, positive self-concept, money value.

Visit a Store in Your Community

Materials

Permission slips, camera, emergency cards for children, transportation and so forth.

1. Discuss with your children the kind of store they would like to visit.

2. Contact the store and make arrangements for a visit. Be sure to ask whether they have any giveaways for your children.

3. This visit may well come before you make a class store or even read the book. Then you will know of one store visit that your children can relate to the book and your store-related activities.

4. Make up "do" rules for the behavior to and from the store and while you are in the store.

5. Do some role-playing and have children show how they are going to behave.

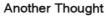

Jacket Illustration copyright ©, 1990, by John Ward, used with permission from Orchard Book.

Another Thought

Make thank-you cards, poster, letter, and send to the store after your visit.

Money

Materials

U.S. coins, small items to buy.

1. Children who are waiting for a turn in the store can buy and sell with real money.

2. Pair children off. Let one be the seller and one be the buyer.

3. Encourage each group of children to set their own prices and system for exchanging money and items.

Another Thought

Make small cards and markers available for the children to make price tags and money.

Cognitive Development

One-to-one correspondence, oral language, role-playing, taking turns, visual discrimination.

Daddy Is a Monster ...Sometimes

Written and illustrated by John Steptoe

Steptoe used the names of his two children in this story, and himself as the occasional "monster" who reacts to their behavior. His paintings are prismatic.

Summary:
A boy and a girl tell about the incidents that can turn their father into a monster.

HarperCollins, 1980

STORY TIME

Theme

Family relations, identifying feelings, positive self-image.

56

Introduction

1. Read the title and ask your children how Daddy can be a monster.

2. Have the children look at the cover and ask them to talk about it. Help the children distinguish between real and imaginary.

3. Show your child the title page and talk with them about why a Daddy would want to be a monster.

Reading

1. Ask your children how these book children feel about their Daddy.

2. See if your children think the book children know what makes their Daddy a monster.

3. Ask your children if the lady in the store knows that Bweela and Javaka had already had ice cream.

4. What do your children think should have happened when Bweela dropped her ice cream?

5. Ask your children how the Daddy felt when the lady bought the ice cream cones for his children.

6. Ask the children about their bedtime and who gets mad at them when they do not want to go to sleep.

Response

1. Let the children tell you about when their Daddy gets mad.

2. Encourage children without fathers to tell about adults or older siblings who get mad at them.

3. Talk about why this Daddy turns into a monster and why the children said "sometimes."

EXTENSIONS

Act Out the Story

Materials

Furniture and household items from your house-keeping area.

1. Tell the children you are going to act out/put on a play about the book.

2. Look at the pictures with your children and let them tell you what props you need from your room.

3. Help the children substitute things you have in the room for what may be in the book but is not available in your room, such as a drum for the trumpet.

4. Choose children to act out the parts of the Daddy and the children.

5. You may want to have different children for each incident.

6. This play can easily move to the children's actual experiences.

Another Thought

Watch your children while in the housekeeping area. If they play "Daddy is a Monster .... Sometimes," give them the language to make the situation have a positive outcome. Teach the Daddy positive language to control his children. Teach the child positive responses to Daddy's anger.

Cognitive Development

Oral expression, body language, representing a fictitious character, recalling a sequence of events.

Books About Turning People into Monsters

Materials

Drawing paper (8-1/2" x 11"), crayons/markers, stapler, book: *Daddy is a Monster ... Sometimes.*

1. Working in a small group, ask the children if they would like to make a book about how they turn their adult caregivers (Mom, Dad, Grandma, and so forth) into monsters.

2. You may have some children who are not secure enough to deal with this activity. Give them the choice of watching and listening or going to another activity.

3. Have the children draw pictures of themselves doing things that turn their adult caregivers into monsters.

4. Each child should then dictate the words for the picture to you. Be sure you include what the child says and what the adult says.

5. Each child should have an opportunity to share his page with the other children.

6. Make a book using the pages. Allow each child the choice of keeping the page or putting it into a book.

7. Laminate the pages and put the book into the class library. Listen to the children as they read the book individually. Be sensitive to their feelings and help the children to identify them. After you have sympathized and laughed with them, give them the positive language to deal with the situation.

Another Thought

Be sensitive to stories your children tell about adults. Emphasize the adult's responsibility to control anger. Help your children believe that they do not deserve mistreatment for being children.

Cognitive Development

Oral expression, recognizing that individual actions bring about consequences, child's power to affect others around him, identifying feelings, accepting responsibility for misdeeds, assigning control of anger as an adult responsibility.

Another Book

Greenfield, Eloise (1991), *First Pink Light,* Black Butterfly Children's Books, New York.

Illustrations Copyright ©1980 by John Steptoe, used with the approval of the Estate of John Steptoe.

Monster Puppets

Materials

Scissors, glue, paper towels, small paper bags, empty toilet paper rolls, sheets of newsprint (one per puppet, to stuff bag), crayons/ markers, cellophane tape, scraps from your art area (see *Children & Scissors*), water colors.

1. Working in a small group, ask the children to tell you about monsters. Lead them to talk about how monsters look.

2. Show the children the scrap art materials you have and get them to tell you how the different pieces could become part of a monster.

3. Pass out the paper bags, the toilet paper rolls, and sheets of newsprint. Help each of the children stuff a bag and attach it to a roll.

4. Encourage the children to cut, paste, draw, paint, until they are pleased with their monsters.

5. The children will spontaneously make their monsters come to life. The group should make rules about how rough to be to someone else's puppet. Talk about how easily the monsters can be destroyed.

Another Thought

A puppet show may evolve. Leave that up to how interactive the children want to be. Perhaps a talent show, where one puppet at a time can show off, would be appropriate for your group. Maybe more — let it come from the children.

Cognitive Development

Visual representation of a monster, eye-hand coordination, creativity, oral language.

57

Willie's Not The Hugging Kind

Written by Joyce Durham Barrett   *Illustrated by Pat Cummings*

Barrett's story can bring tough children along to be open with their emotions.

Cummings often uses family members, pets, and friends as models for her books.

Summary:
Willie doesn't care for hugs but gives himself permission to like them.

HarperCollins, 1989

STORY TIME

Theme

Giving and receiving affection, peer pressure, identifying one's own needs, positive self-image.

Introduction

1. Ask, "Who likes hugs?" Encourage your children to tell hug stories about themselves.
2. Show the cover of the book and ask your children if they think Willie likes hugs.

Reading

1. Young children will listen to a story told about these illustrations.
2. They will also be ready to relate their own experiences to the illustrations.
3. As you read, encourage comments from your children about why Willie's not the hugging kind.

Response

1. Let your children tell you what made Willie decide he wanted to get hugs
2. This is a book to keep on the shelf to read to one or two children who are having a hard time expressing feelings and receiving affection.

58

EXTENSIONS

The Hugging Kind

Materials

Book: *Willie's Not the Hugging Kind*
1. Re-read the book, encouraging your children to personalize the story as you read.
2. Talk about Willie and JoJo's relationship. Discuss Willie's feeling about wanting to be like JoJo.
3. Ask your children why they think JoJo thought hugs were silly.
4. Read page 29 and talk about what Momma meant.
5. Have your children hug an object, then hug a friend. Talk about the difference.
6. Explain for your children their power to make decisions for themselves. Encourage them to talk about Willie using JoJo's brain to decide about getting hugs, and Willie using his own brain to decide about hugs. When was Willie the happiest?
7. In a very familiar and real way, this book encourages children to make their own decisions about their feelings.

Another Thought

Tough children often need permission to receive gentle and caring attention. Willie can help you teach your children the rewards of receiving positive attention. Encourage your children to talk about how Willie could teach JoJo to be the hugging kind.

Cognitive Development

Identifying feelings, expressing opinions, oral language, positive self-concept, identifying peer pressure.

My Favorite Hugs Chart

Materials

Large piece of tagboard for graph, pictures of children (photocopied from school photos), magazine pictures, markers, book: *Willie's Not the Hugging Kind.*

1. Talk through the story. Encourage your children to make comments about the book. Sequence is not particularly important.

2. Make up a class definition of a hug. This could include hugs for happy times, hugs for sad times, hugs from people you like, hugs from people you don't like, animal hugs, hug feelings from a book, a TV program, a movie, loud hugs of sports, quiet hugs.

3. Find some pictures of people hugging. Especially look for the big, strong men of sports hugging.

4. Using your class definitions, make a chart. Put a picture for each kind of hug across the bottom of the chart. Put the picture of each child who likes that kind of hug above the picture.

5. Count the individual children in each group and compare groups with your children. Display it at their eye level.

Another Thought

Children may want to draw or paint their favorite hugs. These illustrations could then be grouped into kinds of hugs.

Cognitive Development

Classification, identifying similar behaviors, oral language, identifying likes, rote counting, set comparison.

You Need a Hug

Materials

Willie's Not the Hugging Kind.

1. Willie can help your children understand a child who will not let anyone get close to him.

2. By talking about Willie, children can begin to see the two sides of receiving love.

3. You will have empathetic children in your class who, with your support, can reach out to a "tough" child.

4. When your "tough" child is having a bad day, remind your children about Willie. Talk about the "tough" child wanting a hug but not knowing how to ask for it.

5. Go to the "tough" child and offer a gentle touch, a lap sit, a hug. Invite another child to help you give the "tough" child some lovin'.

Another Thought

At the same time, teach your children to ask for hugs. Always take the time to give the hug when it is asked for. As you give hugs to your children, they will in turn give hugs to each other.

Cognitive Development

Identifying one's feelings, identifying feelings in others, empathy, expression of feelings, oral language, interpreting body language.

I Love Hugs Headband

Materials

Strips (5" x 23") of construction paper, pre-cut hearts, stars, construction paper, markers/crayons, art scrap box, scissors, glue, books: *Children & Scissors, Willie's Not the Hugging Kind.*

1. Talk again about Willie and his family who liked hugs.

2. Ask who would like to make an "I Like Hugs" Headband. Help a small group of children get set up with materials in the art area.

3. As the children are working, talk about hugs, how to get them, and when and how to give them.

4. Wear the headbands in a parade. Find someone outside your classroom to give your children hugs.

Another Thought

Some children may not want to proclaim publicly their love for hugs. Assure them that their headbands can say and show anything they like.

Cognitive Development

Emotional expression through art, visual discrimination, eye-hand coordination, oral language.

Another Book

Mathis, S. (1991) *Red dog/blue fly: Football poems,* Viking Press.

59

She Come Bringing Me That Little Baby Girl

Written by Eloise Greenfield

Illustrated by John Steptoe

Greenfield's deep understanding of the feelings of young children is exhibited in this story.

With glowing paintings, Steptoe almost tells this bittersweet story without words.

Summary:

A child's disappointment and jealousy over a new baby sister are dispelled as he becomes aware of the importance of his new role as a big brother.

HarperCollins, 1974

STORY TIME

Theme

Accepting a new baby, expressing feelings.

Introduction

1. Kevin will be a welcome relief to children who are having a hard time accepting a new baby in the house.
2. Talk a bit about babies and what they are like. Listen to your children's stories about babies.

Reading

1. Ask your children if they think Kevin wanted a baby sister. Look at the cover and title page illustrations.
2. Read and talk and let your children share their thoughts.
3. Ask your children to predict if Mama will change Kevin's mind about that baby girl.

Response

1. Help your children identify Kevin's feelings.
2. Talk about what happened to make Kevin like his sister.
3. Compare with your children the cover illustration and the last-page illustration.
4. Ask, "Will Kevin ever not want his sister again?" Reassure your children that people do get mad at one another. Then they are happy again, and so it goes.

EXTENSIONS

People Who Like Me Book

Materials

Magazine pictures, personal photos, markers/crayons, scissors, glue, drawing paper, book: *She Come Bringing Me That Little Baby Girl.*

1. With a small group, re-read the book. Talk about Kevin. Did he know people still liked him?
2. Ask your children who they know who likes them. Would they like to make a book about the people who like them?
3. Begin with your children drawing pictures of people who like them, or cutting out of magazines people who they would enjoy being liked by.
4. Later, add any photos parents may send for the book or that you take in the classroom.

Another Thought

The child can dictate a story about each person who likes her.

Cognitive Development

Positive self-concept, identifying feelings in others, eye-hand coordination.

60

Big Brother Big Sister Hats

Materials

Strips for headband, construction paper, your art scrap box, glue, scissors, books: *Children & Scissors, She Come Bringing Me That Little Baby Girl.*

1. Talk with your children about Kevin and how he was feeling.

2. Ask your children to think about what the people in the book could have done to make Kevin feel better. How could they make Kevin feel proud?

3. Talk about what some fathers do to let everyone know that they are new fathers.

4. Ask who would like to pretend to have a new baby. Talk about some ways they could let everyone know they have a new baby.

5. Suggest a hat/headband if none of your children do.

6. Work in small groups with the children who want to make a headband. Write: I AM A BIG (BROTHER / SISTER).

7. Children can wear the headbands around school.

Another Thought

Some children may just want a headband with no message. Or they may want to tell the world about a new pet, grandmother visit, trip, and so forth.

Cognitive Development

Identifying feelings, expressing emotions, eye-hand coordination, positive self-concept.

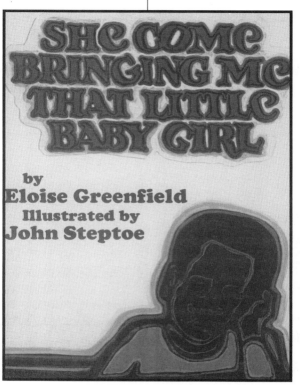

Illustrations Copyright © 1974 by John Steptoe. Used with the approval of the Estate of John Steptoe.

Make a Gift for a New Baby

Materials

Flannel, scrap material, Stitch Witchery, iron, drawing paper, paints, paintbrushes, markers/crayons, colorful magazine pictures, black and white paper.

1. The important learning for the child is that she has something of value to give to a new baby. The actual gift is secondary. The act of giving and the feeling of being important and needed are what the child is learning.

2. A small flannel blanket with a patch ironed on is a simple gift to make. See *The Patchwork Quilt* for instructions.

3. Paint or draw a picture or card for the new baby. Child dictates message and teacher writes his words on the card.

4. Make a mobile or wall decoration for the baby to look at. Cut any shape from a colorful magazine page and outline the shape in black marker. Children choose some shapes and fold the picture into an accordion. The shape could be a butterfly, flowers, or abstract. Have enough so that the children can make one to keep and one to give away.

Another Thought

Black and white shapes and designs are also important for babies to see. Encourage your children to include some.

Cognitive Development

Positive self-image, giving to others, eye-hand coordination, seeing one's oral language written down.

Another Book

Caines, J. (1973) *Abby,* Harper & Row, New York.

61

Things I Like About Grandma

Written and Illustrated by Francine Haskins

Be sure to find the dolls in the illustrations. Francine is a doll maker.

Summary:
A granddaughter tells about the wonderful everyday activities she does with her special grandma.

Children's Book Press, 1992

STORY TIME

Theme

Grandma and Granddaughter's special relationship of teaching, telling, giving and bonding.

Introduction

1. Listen to your children tell about their grandmas. Find out what name each child has for her grandma.

2. Show the cover of the book and encourage comment.

3. This book can easily turn into a "my grandma and me" conversation. You have to decide how much listening and how much talking you want for the first reading.

Reading

1. On first reading, you may want to have a small group of children so that everyone can see the illustrations.

2. The illustrations are full of interesting things and your children may want to show you what appeals to their eyes.

3. This is definitely a book where the words or the illustrations can capture your children's attention.

4. On re-read, you can establish "we are just going to listen to the words this time." As children comment, gently remind them this time it is a listening story.

Response

1. Follow your children's lead. Probably they will want to tell about their own grandmas.

2. Be sensitive to those children who have limited experiences with their grandmas. Help them remember someone they know that does special things with and for them.

3. If a child feels she has no one who is like "grandma," you should certainly follow-up and find someone, even someone at school. Everyone needs someone whom they think is happy they are alive.

EXTENSIONS

Draw Grandma

Materials

Drawing paper, markers/crayons, book: *Things I Like About Grandma*.

1. Again, the book will inspire your children to tell you about their grandmas.

2. Ask your children to draw about grandma. Depending on the level of skill, you will get a variety of pictures. Accept all of them as valid.

3. Have the child dictate (or do her own writing) about his grandma. The words and pictures need not be related.

4. Make a class display on an eye-level bulletin board.

Another Thought

Put the drawings into a book. Read the book at story time. Display the book on the children's book shelf.

Cognitive Development

Verbal expression, relating feelings about a particular person, eye-hand coordination, creativity.

Present for Grandma

Materials

Magnetic strip 2" x 4" (approximately), wallet-sized photograph, white contact paper, scissors, permanent fine line markers, clear packing tape.

1. We found a flat magnetic strip with an advertisement on it. The merchant gave us enough for each child to have one.

2. We covered his advertisement with white contact paper. (This will peel off easily to allow the child to try many drawings: see #4.)

3. Mark off where the photo will be on the magnet. Encourage your children to draw in the remaining space.

4. The first time children use new materials they like to experiment. For this reason, allow your children to have practice drawings using the markers on the contact paper. They may want to use their first drawing. But give them the opportunity to do several different drawings and choose the one they like best.

5. Put the photo in place and cover the entire magnet with wide clear packing tape.

6. Wrapping paper can easily be made using another of the child's drawings on an 8 1/2" x 11" sheet of paper.

7. What happens to this gift should be the child's decision, even if he decides to keep it for himself. (Each child could make two – one for giving and one for keeping.)

Another Book

Greenfield, Eloise (1980), *Grandma's Joy*, Philomel, New York.

Haskins, Francine (1991), *I Remember 121*, Children's Book Press, San Francisco.

Jacket Illustration copyright (c) 1991, by Francine Haskins, used with permission from Children's Book Press, Publisher.

Another Thought

If photos are not available, grandmas will be delighted with the drawings. Be sensitive to those children who need a "grandma" figure. Help them identify an adult who would enjoy getting a present from them.

Cognitive Development

Making a present for someone who cares about you, eye-hand coordination, creativity, exploring new materials.

Things Our Children Like To Do

63

When I Am Old With You

Written by Angela Johnson   *Illustrated by David Soman*

Do Like Kyla is another of Johnson's books that show her understanding of youthful human nature.

Soman and Johnson also collaborated on *Tell Me a Story, Mama* — the *School Library Journal's* Best Book of the Year in 1989.

Summary:

A child imagines being old with Granddaddy and joining him in such activities as playing cards all day, visiting the ocean, eating bacon on the porch.

Orchard Books, 1990

STORY TIME

Theme

Pride in having a grandfather family relationship.

64 Introduction

The cover of this book is its best introduction. Encourage your children to talk about the cover. Let them tell you who the people are.

Reading

1. For each set of pages, allow time for your children to bring their personal experiences to what is happening.

2. Help your children understand what the child means by "When I am old with you." Each child may have her own idea. Accept it as valid.

Response

1. Let your children take turns holding the book and telling about their favorite set of pages. They may relate it to something they did with someone special.

2. On re-reading the book, show the title page illustration and ask your children to tell you about the dogs. Help them relate which dog belongs to the child and which to the Granddaddy. Then be sure they continue to follow the dogs through the story.

EXTENSIONS

Make a Picture of Granddaddy

Materials

Paints, paintbrushes, crayons/markers, water colors, construction paper, fingerpaints, fingerpaint paper, book: *When I Am Old With You.*

1. During circle time, help children remember the book about the Granddaddy.

2. Ask them if they would like to make a picture for their granddaddies or someone else's granddaddy or someone they know. Explain that you will take turns in the art area making the pictures, and that everyone might not start his picture today.

3. It is easier for setup to stick to paints, but it would be nice if the child had free choices in the art area of what to use to make her picture.

Another Thought

Encourage each child to dictate a message to go along with the picture. Ask parents to supply an addressed, stamped envelope, and mail the picture/letter from school or a nearby mailbox.

Cognitive Development

Role-playing, appreciation of age differences, oral language, visual discrimination, positive self-concept, family relationships.

Collage of Granddaddies

Materials

Photos of your children's grandfathers (laminate each photo individually), or magazine pictures of possible grandfathers.

1. Depending on your class, you could use photos of granddaddies and other men special to your children. Or, if you have only a few children who have photos of their grandfathers, make a pretend collage and let your children choose pictures of men they think would be good granddaddies.

2. Be sure to talk to parents before you start the collage so you'll know which of the themes to use.

3. With either theme, you can have the children dictate things about their granddaddies (real or pretend) to put beside the pictures.

4. Be sure to display the mural at eye level to encourage the children to talk about it.

Another Thought

The mural could have a grandparents theme or a grandmothers theme.

Cognitive Development

Representation, recalling good times, positive self-image, oral language, seeing your work written down.

Things Our Children Like To Do

Jacket Illustration Copyright © 1990 by David Soman, used with permission from Orchard Books, New York.

65

Role-Playing Granddaddy and Child

Materials

Dress-up clothes and props from your room, book: *When I Am Old With You.*

1. Book in hand, ask a few children if they would like to act out the pictures in the book.

2. Re-read the book. For each set of pictures, collect the items from your room that you might use as props.

3. Let the children choose which pages to act out rather than trying to do all of the pictures in order.

4. Children may want to take turns acting out the same scene again and again.

5. Encourage children to talk about how older people walk and talk. Then help them try to walk and talk the same way.

Another Thought

Your children may just want to play Grandparent and Grandchild in your House Area. Make the book available when this happens.

Cognitive Development

Visual discrimination, creativity, eye-hand co-ordination, positive self-image, giving to others.

Another Book

Igus, Toyomi (1992) *When I Was Little*, Just Us Books, Inc. Orange, N.J.

Additional Activities In This Book

Things I Like About Grandma
The Patchwork Quilt

Everett Anderson's 1-2-3

Written by Lucille Clifton   *Illustrated by Ann Grifalconi*

An award-winning poet, Clifton is author of many books.

Grifalconi has illustrated 30 books, including this series.

Summary:
A boy learns with some difficulty to accept a new father.

Holt, Rhinehart and Winston, 1977

66

STORY TIME

Theme

Accepting a new father, respecting children's feelings.

Introduction

1. Read the title and ask your children what they think Everett Anderson is counting.
2. Explain that he is trying to figure out how many people he likes to be with.

Reading

1. Your children may have developed their listening skills sufficiently to listen to the entire book. A straight-through reading will help them to relate to Everett Anderson's growing acceptance of Mr. Perry.
2. Other children may need to relate orally to each page on the first reading, bringing their own experiences to the page. On re-reading, children will listen to more pages in a row.
3. Be sure to help your children see how the illustrations and the words convey the same feelings.

Response

1. Talk about the passing of time in the book. Discuss how the idea of Mr. Perry marrying Everett Anderson's Mom took a long time for Everett to accept.
2. Explore with your children the feelings Everett had and how he came to change his mind.

EXTENSIONS

Puppet Show

Materials

Puppets available in your room, numerals 1, 2, 3, book: *Everett Anderson's 1-2-3*.

1. Look through the book again with your children. Ask if they would like to have a puppet show about being one, two, or three people together.
2. Gather the puppets in your room, the numerals 1, 2, and 3, and a small group of children.
3. Let the children decide which numeral they will tell a story about. The child may choose to act out a page from the book or make up his own story.
4. Continue to help your children think about when and why it is fun to be a certain number, and when and why it is not fun to be a certain number.

Another Thought

A child chooses to do a puppet show alone or chooses to invite other children to help put on the show. Talk about the advantages and disadvantages of each choice. The discussion should not be the focus of the activity. Rather, occasional comments or questions by the teachers will help children verbalize their thinking, why they choose to be by themselves or why they choose to ask other children. Accept as valid their reasoning.

Cognitive Development

Social interaction, assessing the feelings of being alone or being with other children, oral language, control of hands and body.

Individual Acceptance of New Parent

Materials

Book: *Everett Anderson's 1-2-3.*

1. As you become aware of a child in your room who is getting a new parent, use the book as a resource. Read and talk about the book with the child.

2. Talk to the present parent about the book and encourage her to read it to her child, and to talk abut the feeling Everett Anderson and her child both have.

3. Encourage the parent to accept as valid any feelings her child might express. Help the parent show the child how to grow to be a family.

Another Thought

The new parent should also read the book with the child. He also needs to accept the child's feelings as valid. The new parent should also relate to Mr. Perry and how Mr. Perry handle's Everett's feelings.

Cognitive Development

Identifying feelings in others, relating those feelings to yourself, expressing one's feelings, oral development.

Things Our Children Like To Do

Another Book

Caines, J. (1973) *Abby,* Harper & Row, New York.

Clifton, L. (1970) *Some of the Days of Everett Anderson,* Holt Rinehart & Winston, New York.

67

Everett Anderson's Nine Month Long

Written by Lucille Clifton

Clifton is an award-winning poet and author and has written many children's books.

Illustrated by Ann Grifalconi

Grifalconi is both a writer/illustrator and collaborator as artist with other writers.

Summary:

Little boy waits while his mother and new father have a baby.

Holt, Rhinehart and Winston, 1978

STORY TIME

Theme

Life cycle, time passing, family unity, identifying feelings.

Introduction

1. If you have read *Everett Anderson's 1-2-3,* talk with your children about Everett Anderson. Encourage your children to tell about him and his family.

2. Ask your children to guess what will happen to him next. Accept as valid what your children predict.

3. When someone says, "get a baby," show the book cover and read the title.

4. Ask your children what Everett is thinking about.

Reading

1. Because your children know Everett, they may be content to listen to what happens to him.

2. Accept your children's comments as the story evolves.

3. Connect the illustrations and words as telling about the same feelings.

Response

1. Let the children take turns showing a page in the book and telling about how Everett feels.

2. Help your children understand the feelings Everett had at seven. Talk with your children about how they feel when they do not know if people will still like them.

3. Your children who are anticipating a new baby will want to hold onto this book. As with *Everett Anderson's 1-2-3,* it should be shared with the child's parents.

EXTENSIONS

Children's Play

Materials

Your housekeeping area.

1. Don't be surprised when everyone (including the boys) start having babies.

2. The needs of your children in each classroom vary. How you meet those needs should be a reflection of who you are as a person. The important role for you to play is to be positive and accepting. If you are uncomfortable with having babies born in your classroom, redirect your children in a positive way to take the mother to the hospital to have her baby. Then change the scene to everyone waiting for the baby to be born. You can avoid the physical birth scene and still let the children act out the anticipation and the excitement of the doctor showing off the newborn baby.

3. On the other hand, children's daily life exposure to babies being born can produce a rather lively delivery room.

4. Be sure to clarify in a positive way any misinformation the children may be acting out, such as boys having babies.

Another Thought

You may note this is not a planned extension. These comments are to help you to interact with your children when and if they include having babies in their play.

Cognitive Development

Role playing, oral language, sequence of events, sex education.

68

Visit From An Expectant Mother

Materials

Expectant mom, stethoscope, books: *Everett Anderson's Nine Month Long* and any books showing how babies grow and develop.

1. Talk with someone you know who is going to have a baby. Explain to her how curious your children will be about her, how open their questions will be. Find someone you think can be open and warm and caring with your children and their questions.

2. If the woman is a parent of one of your children, let the child introduce her mother at circle time. Otherwise, you will tell about your friend.

3. Give a little time for the woman and your children to exchange comments during circle time. Move on to your worktime/playtime, and tell the children she wants to work/play with them.

4. By being a part of the children's independent time, the woman will belong to the children. They then will be able to ask private questions and get individual attention from her.

Another Thought

Ask the expectant mom to read *Everett Anderson's Nine Month Long* and *Sweet Baby Coming*.

Cognitive Development

Sex education, oral language, body language, visual discrimination, caring for future generations.

Additional Activities In This Book

Sweet Baby Coming
The Baby

My Mama Collage

Materials

Pictures of children and their mommas, maybe some of the mother when she was pregnant, markers/pens, drawing paper, magazine pictures, book: *Everett Anderson's Nine Month Long.*

1. Re-read the book and ask the children if they would like to make a collage of themselves and their mothers.
2. Send home a note asking for a picture of the mom and the child and of the mom pregnant.
3. Some children may choose to draw a picture of themselves and their mothers.
4. Or you may want to let the children select magazine pictures of mothers expecting, mothers and babies, and/or mothers with children.

Another Thought

Children who are not living with their mothers should be encouraged to be a part of the activity by bringing a picture of themselves and their caregivers. They could draw pictures of themselves and their mothers or caregivers. Help your other children to be respectful of these children and their feelings.

Cognitive Development

Representation, oral language, visual discrimination.

Another Book

Clifton, L (1974) *Everett Anderson's Year.* Holt Rinehart & Winston, New York.

69

Everett Anderson's Goodbye

Written by Lucille Clifton

Clifton has written many books in addition to the Everett Anderson series.

Illustrated by Ann Grifalconi

Grifalconi's soft pencil drawings complement the text in mood and help children understand.

Summary:

A little boy comes to grips with his father's death, through denial, anger, bargaining, depression, and acceptance.

Holt, Rhinehart and Winston, 1983

STORY TIME

Theme

Stages of grief, circle of life.

Introduction

1. Your children now have a book friend named Everett Anderson. Ask them to tell you about him.

2. When someone remembers about his Daddy dying, show the cover of the book and ask your children to tell you about it.

3. Read the title and ask, "Who will Everett say goodbye to and why?"

Reading

1. Your children can almost tell you the story from the illustrations.

2. If you are reading the book, read the five stages of grief and explain that everyone feels like that when someone dies. Tell your children that the story will tell them what the words mean.

3. As you read about each stage, encourage your children to talk about the hows and whys of Everett's feelings.

4. Children in your room who have had a mother or father die may be hesitant to talk about it in a group. Seek these children out for a quiet reading.

5. Talk with the child's caregiver about reading this book with the child. It could be a good avenue for the child and the adult to talk to each other about the person who died.

Response

1. Ask your children if Everett will always love his Daddy.

2. Re-read the last two pages and ask your children to tell you what the words mean. Accept as valid what they tell you.

3. Talk with your children about Everett's feelings. Help the children understand that Everett knows he will always love his father and his father will always love him. Then ask, "If he knows about all that love, do your children think Everett can be a happier boy?"

EXTENSIONS

Everybody Cries Sometimes

Materials

Record: "Everybody Cries Sometimes"

1. Learn the song in circle time.

2. Use the song to comfort children throughout your day.

Cognitive Development

Identifying and accepting feelings.

NOTE: See "Sources" for ordering information.

Classroom Experiences to Explain Death

Materials

Books: *Everett Anderson's Goodbye, The Dead Bird,* and other books you have about dying.

1. Throughout the year, your class will encounter animals, insects, and perhaps people who die. Use these experiences to help your children understand the cycle of life.

2. Showing respect for a dead animal/insect by giving it a funeral can help children also learn to respect the cycle of life.

3. Be sure to help your children identify their feelings during these experiences.

4. Don't be surprised when your children dig up the buried animal or insect in a few days to see what has happened to it. Bring it inside and look at it under the microscope or with a magnifying glass.

5. Ask your local librarian about books on the cycle of life and add those you like to your class library.

Another Thought

Follow your children's lead during work/play. Answer questions and correct any misinformation.

Cognitive Development

Life and death as a part of the daily routine, identifying feelings, oral expression.

NOTE: These three books can be used as a series or individually to help children identify, express, and feel control of, very basic human emotions. You and your children will be more sensitive, caring people through their use.

Another Book

Greenfield, E. (1988) *Grandpa's Face*, Philomel-Putnam, New York.

Walker, Alice, *To Hell With Dying,* Harcourt Brace, Jovanovich.

Things Our Children Like To Do

71

Bigmama's

Written and Illustrated by Donald Crews

By sharing these wonderful memories of his own Bigmama, Crews gives children an opportunity to experience the fun and excitement of a farm. This is a book children will love to return to, as Crews loved to return to his Bigmama's each summer.

Summary:
Crews recalls his summer adventures with family and friends at his grandmother's farm.

Greenwillow Books, 1991

STORY TIME

Theme

72   Summer at Bigmama's for young Donald Crews.

Introduction

1. The cover easily introduces this book for you. Your children will be full of comments.
2. Identify the train windows for them.

Reading

1. On first reading, young listeners will want to tell what's happening from the pictures.
2. On second reading or with older listeners, the text may be read in part and, on further readings, more text may be added.
3. The illustrations and the text give children information about the past. Wait for children's responses.
4. Help your children understand the children in the story are checking out Bigmama's to be sure everything is just as they remember it.

Response

1. Your children will want to tell you about the pictures they like best. Give them the opportunity to relate their personal experiences to the story.
2. Each illustration is a story in itself. Use them for answers to questions your children have about living on a farm long ago.
3. Be sure to show the photo of Crews and his family.

EXTENSIONS

My Trip

Materials

Children's photographs, book: *Bigmama's*

1. Send letters home to ask parents for pictures of trips your children have made.
2. In a small group, recall *Bigmama's* and the excitement of a trip.
3. Encourage your children to talk about their trip and show their photographs.

Another Thought

Using *Bigmama's* as an introduction, encourage a small group of children to tell about any adventure they have had outside their homes. (Trip to grocery store, mall, church, etc.)

Cognitive Development

Oral language, positive self-concept, recall of past events, visual representation.

Be an Illustrator

Materials

Drawing paper, markers/crayons, paints, book: *Bigmama's*

1. Show your children the photograph of Donald Crews and his family at *Bigmama's* to a small group of children.

2. Let the children tell you about their favorite illustration in the book.

3. Talk about becoming an artist/illustrator.

4. Ask your children if they would like to draw a picture of a trip they have taken, their family or something they would like to do.

5. Older children may want to make a series of pictures.

6. Be sure and write text for the drawing from your children's oral descriptions of their art work.

Jacket illustration Copyright © 1991 by Donald Crews, used with permission from Greenwillow Books, a division of William Morrow & Company, Publisher.

Another Thought

Provide pictures of places in your community for very young children. Let them choose a place to go to and write down their dictation.

Cognitive Development

Positive self-image, career planning, eye-hand coordination, visual perception, oral language.

Another Book

Crews, Donald, (1978), *Freight Train*, Greenwillow, New York.

Pinkney, Gloria Jean, (1992), *Back Home*, Dial, New York.

What to do Chart

Materials

Large tagboard, name/symbol/picture of each child in the room, symbol of each activity.

1. Although all of your children can be represented on the chart, work with one small group at a time to allow plenty of verbal exchange among your children.

2. Talk about the activities on the farm.

3. Let each child choose one activity he would like to do on the farm. Place that child's symbol on the chart for that job.

Another Thought

When the members of the group finish choosing their jobs, count and compare sizes of groups that choose each job.

Cognitive Development

Identifying activities on a farm, making decisions, rote counting, one-to-one correspondence, comparing sizes of groups, oral language, visual discrimination.

Things Our Children Like To Do

73

My Mama Needs Me

Written by Mildred Pitts Walter   *Illustrated by Pat Cummings*

While spending time visiting baby clinics in preparation for writing this story, Walter learned that a child can help a newborn's appetite by rubbing the top of its ear, as the little boy does in this story.

Cummings often uses family as models. She puts a lot of detail into her drawings, "surprises" she calls them, to draw children into the story and personalize it for them. This book has flowers, butterflies, stripes.

Summary:

Jason wants to help, but isn't sure his mama needs him after she brings home a new baby.

Lothrop, Lee and Shepard Books, 1983

STORY TIME

Theme

Self-esteem, family relations, sibling rivalry, identifying feelings, adjustment to a new baby.

Introduction

1. Read the title of the book, show the title page, and ask the children what they think the book is about.

2. Encourage the children to tell their experiences of a new baby coming home from the hospital.

Reading

1. After reading the story, ask your children why Jason did not stay and eat the cookies. And ask if he wished he had stayed and eaten some.

2. Talk about how Jason felt when he thought nobody needed him.

3. Give the children the opportunity to talk about breast feeding and bottle feeding.

4. Ask what Jason did to make the baby start nursing again. See if any of your children know that trick.

5. Be sure to get the children's comments on these illustrations.

6. Ask how Jason felt when he finally had a job to do for the baby.

7. Talk about Jason saying, "My Mama needs me," and what he needed to have from his Mama.

Response

1. Help children identify the feelings of love Jason had for the new baby and the sad feelings he had because he was not sure his mother needed him any more.

2. Encourage children with younger siblings to talk about how they feel about their siblings.

EXTENSIONS

Things I Can Do At Home Poster

Materials

Drawing paper (8-1/2" x 11"), magazine pictures, scissors, glue, crayons/markers, photographs of child, construction paper, book: *My Mama Needs Me*

1. Working in a small group, show the children *My Mama Needs Me*. Ask them to tell you what jobs they do at home.

2. Each child can make an illustration of something they do at home. The children can draw, paste magazine pictures, paste construction paper figures onto the page. If available, home or school photographs of the children can be used.

3. The child dictates to the adult what job he is doing.

4. Children show their home jobs and tell about them.

5. All of the illustrations are placed on a poster board or a bulletin board. Encourage children to look at the board and find new jobs they can do at home.

Another Thought

Use the board for caregivers to share ideas for home jobs for their children.

Cognitive Development

Positive self-concept, family relations, assessment of one's skills, solving problems.

74

Watch a Baby Get a Bath

Materials

Mother with a baby, bathtub, and other items used for giving baby a bath.

1. Invite a mother, related to one of your children if possible, into the classroom to give her baby a bath.

2. Seat the children where they will all have a good view.

3. As the baby gets his bath, identify which things children can help with, and which things they should be patient and watch.

4. If the mother is willing to let the children hold the baby, ask the children what Jason finally got to do with the baby. Then take turns holding the baby. The sibling should go first if he wants to.

Cognitive Development

Importance of cleanliness, sequence of taking a bath, items used for giving baby a bath, positive self-image, how to be useful, patience.

Give a Baby Doll a Bath

Materials

Small plastic tubs, dolls from your housekeeping area, soap, wash cloths, towels.

1. Gather children in a small group. It would be good if you have a doll and tub for each child or at least for each two children.

2. Encourage the children to talk about the live baby they saw being washed. Or talk about what happens when they take a bath themselves.

3. Watch the children washing their dolls. Encourage them to talk about what they are doing. And let them tell you safety rules about holding onto the baby and where the baby's head should be.

4. Be sure the babies get their rock from Jason when the bath is finished.

5. Throughout the bathing time, help children to substitute positive language for negative scolding.

Cognitive Development

Safety rules for bath, sequence of bath-giving, items needed for a baby's bath, positive self-concept, oral expression.

Make Chocolate Chip Cookies

Materials

Chocolate chip cookie mix, ingredients listed on package, bowl, fork, spoon, cookie sheet, oven, cooling racks, recipe on chart paper.

1. Ask the children what Jason's mother said about playing with his friends. Then talk about how he felt because he did not eat any of the cookies.

2. See if the children would like to pretend to be Jason and have another chance for cookies.

3. Work in small groups, so that all of the children can be involved in the preparing.

4. Read the recipe on the package. (Or you may have prepared a large chart of the recipe for the children to read.) Assign jobs to the children or ask for volunteers.

5. As the ingredients are added, talk about their texture, form (dry or wet), color. As they are blended, talk about the physical changes that are taking place. Allow children to taste the ingredients whenever possible.

NOTE: If your recipe includes an egg, do not let the children taste the dough after the egg is added. Explain to them that raw eggs can carry disease that will be cooked away in the oven.

6. Be sure each child has the opportunity to put some cookies on the cookie sheet.

7. Note the size of the cookies, and use the term "expand" when the cookies come out of the oven.

Another Thought

Let someone pretend to be Mrs. Luby and offer the cookies to Jason. Have Jason tell how his mama needed him and what he did for the baby.

MY MAMA NEEDS ME
by
Mildred Pitts Walter
pictures by Pat Cummings

Jacket Illustration Copyright ©1983 by Pat Cummings, used with permission from Lothrop, Lee and Shepard Books Publisher, New York.

Cognitive Development

All work and no play makes Jack a dull boy, sequence of ingredients, understanding expansion, observation of natural changes in ingredients, measuring ingredients, concept of liquid and solid.

75

Sam

Written by Ann Herbert Scott

Shimin's drawings are sensitive to the child's problems.

Illustrated by Symeon Shimin

Most of Scott's story ideas come as gifts from children.

Summary:
Sam can't find anybody at home to play with. Everybody tells him to stop touching their stuff. Only when he cries do the members of his family realize that he needs them.

McGraw Hill Book Company, 1967

STORY TIME

Theme

Being too little, family relationships, value of family members.

76

Introduction

The book jacket or inside illustrations set the mood for the book with your children. Ask them to tell how Sam feels and why.

Reading

1. The picture of Sam standing on his head will give your children many things to talk about. Be sure to ask if Sam is sad now.

2. As Sam goes to each of his family members, have your children predict what will happen and how Sam feels.

3. Have your children tell you how Sam's family felt when he cried.

Response

1. Ask your children if Sam was a cry-baby. Encourage them to talk about how it feels when someone calls you a cry-baby, and why Sam's family did not call him a cry-baby.

2. Talk with your children about what else Sam could have done so he would not be sad. Play with his toys, draw, find a friend, ask one of his family members if he could just sit and watch them, tell someone how sad he was feeling.

EXTENSIONS

Act Out The Story

Materials

Items from your housekeeping area, newspaper, doll, book: *Sam*

1. Because Sam's experience is usual for young children, acting out the story is a must.

2. Re-read *Sam* and ask who would like to act out the story.

3. Have the children identify the characters and you choose children for the parts. Depending on who wants to be an actor, the roles could change from boy to girl or girl to boy.

4. Now talk with the children about the props they will need. Most of the items can be found in your classroom. Your children may want to choose what they were playing with when Sam comes along rather than the items in the book.

5. Choose a director to turn the pages in the book. This will help the children follow the story line.

6. Encourage the children to express the emotions of their characters. Identify how each person felt in the story and let the children practice the feelings.

7. The play does not need an audience other than an adult helping. The children may choose to do another activity, then come back and play a part.

Another Thought

The play can comfortably be adapted to meet the needs of the children in your classroom. The adult and child roles can represent the people in any child's household.

The end of the play could change so that, instead of crying, Sam uses words to let his family know how he feels.

Cognitive Development

Identifying feelings, expressing emotions, empathy with feelings of others, representation.

Make a Tart

Materials

Individual tart pans, tart filling, ready-made piecrust dough or your favorite recipe using cooking oil, cold milk, flour, water, salt, rolling pin, individual mixing bowls.

1. Let your children measure and mix the dough.

2. By using jam like Sam did, it is easy to give children a choice of fillings.

3. When no oven is available, make a graham-cracker crust. Use butter/margarine, sugar, crushed graham crackers or other cookies. Look on the side of the graham cracker box for a recipe.

4. If tart pans are too expensive, use canned biscuits. Give each child a biscuit. Let the child shape the biscuit by pinching. Have the child put his thumbs in the center of the biscuit. He uses his fingers to support the sides. Remind the child to be careful not to break through the bottom of the biscuit. Now the child chooses a jam to put in the hole. Follow the directions on the can to bake.

Another Thought

Cook in a small group. When children know they will have a day to cook, they do not all have to cook on the same day. By cooking the same thing several days in a row, the cooking children will get to be involved in the preparation. Your other children may come as observers. They can be reassured that their turn will come by telling them when their cooking day will be. Children may even choose to delay cooking for another activity when they are sure that their turn will come.

Cognitive Development

Positive self-esteem, scientific observation and description, following a sequence, delaying gratification.

Things I Can Do By Myself

Materials

Toy catalogs, school supply catalogs, scissors, glue, background paper, book: *Sam.*

1. Talk about why Sam was sad. Ask your children if they know how to do things by themselves.

2. Encourage your children to talk about what they like to do by themselves.

3. Make the catalogs available to a small group of children. Tell them they can find pictures of things they can do by themselves.

4. Help your children cut and paste their pictures onto the background paper.

Another Thought

This may turn into a "Things I'd Like To Have" collage.

Cognitive Development

Identifying personal skills, positive self-esteem, eye-hand coordination.

Things Our Children Like To Do

Another Book

Pinkney, B. (1994) *Max Found Two Sticks,* Simon & Schuster.

77

The Patchwork Quilt

Written by Valerie Flourney

First she was an editor like her twin sister Vanessa; now Flourney writes children's books.

Illustrated by Jerry Pinkney

Pinkney won the 1986 Coretta Scott King Award for these illustrations.

Summary:
The family art of quilt-making is passed on from grandmother to granddaughter.

Winner of Ezra Jack Keats, New Writer, and Christopher awards.   Dial, 1985

STORY TIME

Theme

Family values, learning from others, planning, time, a thing worth doing is worth doing well, lasting relationships, carrying on traditions.

Introduction

1. Encourage the children to tell you about the cover of the book.

2. Ask about who the people are, what they are looking at. Ask, "Does anyone have a quilt at your house? Who made the quilt? What do you do with a quilt?"

Reading

1. Talk with the children about the Grandmother's comment that old ways of doing things are sometimes forgotten.

2. Help the children realize that the story in the book goes on for a year. Get the children to relate personally to each season. Point out that making a quilt was long job, and that it took working for a long time.

3. Discuss with the children why it was important for Tanya to continue to work on the quilt while her Grandmother was sick.

4. Ask your children who they think will get to keep the quilt.

Response

1. Encourage individual children to tell why Tanya got to keep the quilt.

2. Remind children that Grandma had said that sometimes people forget old ways of doing things. Ask them if the quilt was an old way and if it was forgotten. Ask also if they think, when Tanya is grown up, she will show someone how to make a quilt.

3. Have individual children tell about the "old ways" in their families.

EXTENSIONS

Make a Quilt

Materials

Each child brings a small blanket from home or a yard of flannel material for a backing, scrap material from home or pre-cut squares of different-patterned fabrics, Stitch Witchery or other cloth bonding material, irons, cloth-cutting scissors, book: *The Patchwork Quilt*.

1. Review the book with your children. Ask if anyone would like to make a quilt. Talk about what you will need.

2. Talk with your parents about a suitable "blanket" or backing for the children to use. If you decide to use new material, ask at the fabric store about what they have that would do. If you get the manager interested in your project, she may donate the material or at least give you an "educational" discount.

3. Explain to your children that some quilts are made from old pieces of cloth, like the one in the story, and that some are made from new pieces of cloth.

4. Encourage grandmothers or other relatives or friends to come in and help the children make their quilts.

5. The children should understand that it will be necessary to take turns while making the quilt, and that everyone will get a turn.

78

6. If your children cut their own pieces, be sure they use cloth-cutting scissors, with adult supervision.

7. Each child can lay out his squares in a pattern that pleases him.

8. Have an adult supervise bonding the pieces onto the backing. The cloth bonding material has directions for cutting and ironing it on.

Another Thought

If you have the available womanpower, sewing the patches on the backing after they have been bonded would make a more permanent quilt.

Cognitive Development

Planning a project and completing it, visual discrimination, eye-hand coordination, spatial relations.

From *The Patchwork Quilt* by Valerie Flournoy, pictures by Jerry Pinkney. Copyright © 1985 by Jerry Pinkney, pictures. Used by permission of Dial Books for Young Readers, a division of Penguin Books USA, Inc.

Another Book

Greenfield, E. (1993) *William and the Good Old Days*, HarperCollins, New York

Year-Long Class Quilt

Materials

Class-made pictures of events in the class throughout the year, wall space, book: *The Patchwork Quilt*.

1. Re-read the book, paying particular attention to the passage of time.

2. Ask your children if they would like to make a paper quilt that will show what happens in your room all year long.

3. Your first squares could have a picture drawn on the square by each child. Print the child's name next to the picture.

4. As events take place in the class, add them to your quilt.

5. Review the year by talking about the quilt from time to time.

Another Thought

Space is the problem in displaying the quilt. Some teachers use the space above their bulletin boards. They make a straight line (time line) around the room. This does not produce a square quilt and it is not at eye level, but in many classrooms it can be very workable.

Cognitive Development

Recording special events, recalling events in sequential order, oral language, visual discrimination, eye-hand coordination.

NOTE: See *The Quilt*, and *When I Am Old With You* for more related activities.

Things Our Children Like To Do

CHAPTER SIX
Stories & Poetry

Dave and the Tooth Fairy
MA nDA LA
Life Doesn't Frighten Me
Honey I Love
I Been There
Nathaniel Talking
Mr. Monkey and the Gotcha Bird
Half a Moon and One Whole Star
Red Dancing Shoes
Ben's Trumpet
Amazing Grace
Something On My Mind

Dave and the Tooth Fairy

Written by Verna Allette Wilkins   *Illustrated by Paul Hunt*

In England, Verna found few books with black children as the main character. So she set about writing and publishing them herself.

An artist living in England shows the magic of this story in his paintings.

Summary:
Dave has lost his fallen-out tooth. He wants the tooth fairy to come, so he must find his tooth or another tooth. The tooth fairy finds something, too.

Tamarind Ltd., 1993

STORY TIME

Theme
Solving problems, a child's perspective.

Introduction
1. Give your children the opportunity to talk about the cover. Encourage them to think of many stories that might be in this book.

2. Read the title. Expect your children to have tooth stories of their own. Swapping tooth stories may become the activity.

3. Some children may not believe in the tooth fairy because of the beliefs of their adult caregivers. Be sensitive to these children and their need to be supported in their beliefs. A simple "children don't have to believe in the tooth fairy" may satisfy all your children. Certainly, you would not require children to listen under these circumstances.

4. For most children, the magic of the tooth fairy is delightful and full of wonder. Those children will be eager to listen to the story.

Reading
1. Because the story has a new twist, a straight through reading may hold your children's attention.

2. Of course, if your children want to make comments along the way, listen.

3. The story has so many parts, it can easily become a conversation, so you must decide how close to stay to the story line.

Response
1. Talk about the illustrations. Every one begs for language from your children.

2. Zizwe and his wheelchair is a gift. It allows your children to experience two boys that are friends. One happens to be in a wheelchair. Talk with your children about their personal experiences with people who use wheelchairs "to move about" (English phrase).

3. There is the dilemma of Dave taking granddad's teeth. Be sure to explore it with your children: how granddad felt and if he got mad. Why did he take Dave to the kite store? Accept as valid your children's responses.

4. Then we have the tooth fairy: liking her job, but wanting a new one. Talk about how to change jobs. Do you just quit the first one?

5. As stated earlier, this story has many angles. You'll have to re-read it many times to use all its wealth.

EXTENSIONS

Who lost a tooth?

Materials
Poster board with children's names and names of teeth marked as a chart to check off lost teeth, book: *Dave and the Tooth Fairy*. (See the appendix for our chart and the names of the teeth.)

1. Re-read the book. Show your children the chart.

2. Mark off on the chart when each child loses a tooth and when the permanent tooth arrives.

82

3. Children worry about getting a new tooth. So we have provided a place on your chart to mark the new tooth coming in. This tells the child you believe she will get a new tooth.

4. Remember to chart the teeth children have already lost and are now permanent.

5. We tell our children losing a tooth means you are growing up.

6. Help the child who has lost no teeth anticipate and know everyone grows in their own time and way.

7. My experience says never pull or help a child pull a tooth. Call your school nurse or the child's caregiver if it looks like an emergency. Most children will come to you with tooth in hand.

Another Thought

Let each child count the number of teeth she has on her jaws. Accept as valid any number the child counts. Make a graph of "how I lost my deciduous tooth," (pulled it, it fell out, sneezed it out, etc.).

Cognitive Development

Using a chart, recognizing changes in one's body.

My Teeth Have Names

Materials

3" x 5" cards, markers, chart and pictures from the appendix.

1. Make cards with pictures of the teeth, and show them to your children.

2. Teach the words for the teeth that fall out: "temporary", "deciduous", "milk teeth" and the word "permanent" for the new teeth.

3. Help your children learn the names for their individual teeth.

Another Thought

Each time someone loses a tooth, match it to the cards to learn the name of that tooth.

Cognitive Development

Classification, oral language.

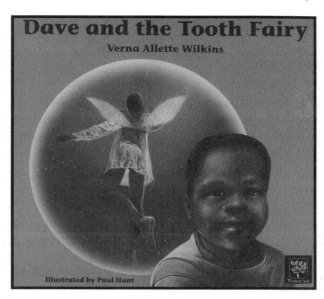

Jacket illustration copyright (c) 1993, by Tamarind, used with permission from Tamarind, Publisher.

What I'll Buy   83

Materials

Catalogs, scissors, glue, background paper, book: *Dave and the Tooth Fairy*.

1. Re-read the story, and talk about what Dave bought with his money.

2. Ask children if they would like to pretend they lost a tooth and got lots of money from the tooth fairy.

3. Pass out the catalogs so that your children can find items they would like to buy.

4. Your children can cut or tear out these pictures or you can do it for them.

5. Glue the pictures onto the background paper.

Another Thought

In a small group, encourage your children to tell about what they decided to buy with their tooth money. Display the collages at the children's eye level for further conversations.

Cognitive Development

Making decisions, pretending, eye-hand coordinations, oral language.

MA nDA LA

Written by Arnold Adoff   *Illustrated by Emily McCully*

Adoff enjoys word sounds and word play, and children enjoy those with him as you read the book.

McCully has illustrated many books for children as well as books for older readers.

Summary:
In Adoff's idiom, MA is "mother," DA is "father," n is "and," LA is "singing," HA is "laughing," RA is "cheering," NA is "sighing," and AH is "feeling good" in a celebration of family and life.

HarperCollins, 1971

STORY TIME

Theme

Family working together, fun with words, cycle of life, how words get meaning.

Introduction

1. Show your children the book cover. Encourage them to tell you about it.

2. Talk with your children about words and tell them that people make up the sounds of words. Tell them about Arnold Adoff and how he likes to play with words.

3. Read the title and tell the children that Adoff made those special sounds stand for something. Translate the words of the title from the information in the summary above.

Reading

1. The illustrations tell the story beautifully. You'll have to decide whether to read the pictures first or translate the words or read the rhythm of the words. All three are important presentations of this book.

2. Your children can easily relate to this African lifestyle through their conversation about the pictures.

Response

1. Re-read the written words and keep the chant of the words as you read.

2. Encourage beginning readers to read Adoff's language.

EXTENSIONS

Tape a Story

Materials

Tape, tape recorder, book: *MA nDA LA*.

1. Ask a group of children if they would like to tape the story.

2. You read the words on the page and then have your children repeat the same words.

3. The number of words you read will depend on how many times you have re-read the book with your children. You may only read one line for the children to repeat. If they know the story well, they can easily repeat a longer stretch.

Another Thought

Re-do the tape several times, increasing the number of words the children repeat. Eventually the children will be able to "read" the words for the tape themselves.

Cognitive Development

Short-term memory, oral expression, appreciating the rhythm of language.

Act Out the Illustrations

Materials

Items from your dress-up box, book: *MA nDA LA*.

1. Working in a small group, ask the children if they would like to act out the story.
2. Let your children decide what they need and can use from your room to act out the story.
3. Choose a child to be director. Then choose children to play the roles. You may want to have a different set of children for each page or section of illustrations.

Another Thought

After you have the body language for the illustrations, combine them with the words and their rhythm. Now the children have made up their own finger (body) play.

Cognitive Development

Representation using body language, recalling a sequence of events, creative dramatics.

MA nDA LA

by Arnold Adoff

pictures by Emily McCully

Jacket illustration Copyright © 1970 by Emily McCully, used with permission from HarperCollins Publishers.

Shuck and Eat Corn

Materials

Corn in husks, big pot, stove, margarine, paper plates, book: *MA nDA LA*.

1. Pass out ears of corn, still in their husks, to a small group of children.
2. Ask your children if any have shucked corn. Let experienced children demonstrate.
3. Point out the husk of the corn, the corn silk, the kernels, and the cob. Be sure to tell them that each kernel has its own individual piece of silk leading to the top. Then let everybody shuck an ear of corn.
4. Boil the corn, butter, and eat it.

Another Thought

After the corn husks dry thoroughly, make cornhusk dolls like those in *Josephine's 'magination*.

Cognitive Development

Appreciation of processes involved in preparation of food, eye-hand coordination, oral language, identification of parts of an ear of corn.

Mural

Materials

Sheet of white paper 3' x 10', tempera paints, brushes, book: *MA nDA LA*.

1. Re-read the illustrations. Let the children tell you what they see.
2. Rely on the vivid color and the basic shapes to tell your children what to paint.
3. If the children are not concerned with a sky-land line, don't you be.
4. Let the children take what they enjoy from the book's illustrations to the mural.
5. You may even get some surprise visitors painted into the mural.

Another Thought

If your children have not painted on a space this large , they will first need a sheet to explore with paints. Then start with a new sheet to paint this mural.

Cognitive Development

Observation of painting style, color perception, eye-hand coordination.

Life Doesn't Frighten Me

Written by Maya Angelou

One of Angelou's poems from 1978. She composed and read a poem for the inaugural swearing in ceremony of President Bill Clinton, January 1993.

Paintings by Jean-Michel Basquiat

Basquiat drew incessantly as a child. His works will stir children's imaginations to draw with the same love of expression.

Summary:
Describes common fears and the courage to conquer them.

Stewart, Tabori & Chang, 1993

STORY TIME

Theme

You have the courage to walk through life.

Introduction

1. This poem and these paintings are so powerful, they can easily be used separately, as well as together.

2. Your children will be eager to tell you about the painting on the cover.

3. Read the title. Tell your children this is a poem about being brave and courageous.

Reading

1. Your children will listen to the words and want to comment. You'll have to decide how much conversation you want on first reading.

2. Watch your children as they straighten up their bodies to let you know how brave and strong they are.

Response

1. Your children will want to tell you what they are not afraid of.

2. Also, they will want a closer look at the paintings.

EXTENSIONS

I'm Not Afraid Of

Materials

Tempera paint and brushes, butcher paper, paint shirts, book: *Life Doesn't Frighten Me.*

1. Re-read the book. Ask who would like to paint "I'm not afraid of" pictures.

2. Talk about how many of Jean-Michel's paintings were on walls or big spaces.

3. Tape a 10' to 12' long piece of butcher paper to the wall or a fence.

4. Help (4) children set up paint and get on shirts. Explain to the other children that everyone will have a turn to paint.

5. If this is your children's first experience with a large space, they may paint only to cover the paper. Their verbal expression while painting will make this a total "I'm brave" experience.

6. Give them other opportunities to paint an "I'm not afraid" picture.

7. As you can tell, it will take several days to give everyone a turn to paint.

8. Follow your children's lead as to what should be done with the paintings. Some will be finished as soon as they put down their brushes. Other children may want to take the paintings home.

Another Thought

If you have the display room, put up the paintings, then sit in front of them. Re-read the book and ask your children if they have a poem about their painting. Accept as valid any words the child wants you to write down, even if they have no relation to Maya Angelou's poem. Let the children give dictations about their painting in a place that pleases them.

Cognitive Development

Self-expression, eye-hand coordination, spatial relationship, creativity.

I Am Brave

Materials

3" x 5" index cards, with each child's name written on one, pen, book: *Life Doesn't Frighten Me.*

1. Re-read the book to a small group.

2. Encourage your children to relate to the words. Talk about courage.

3. Let them tell you what doesn't frighten them. Use the word "brave" when responding to their comments.

4. Write down what the child says on his card.

5. Talk to the children about what to do with the words. Make a class book, put them with paintings, take them home or throw them away.

Another Thought

Older children may want to read the book themselves and write their own words. These could be displayed or put into a class book.

Cognitive Development

Self-assurance, identifying courage and braveness, oral expression of feelings.

Pudding Painting

Materials

Pudding mix and milk, bowl (or substitute, such as shaving cream) fingerpaints, dishwashing liquid, clean tabletop, clean hands, book: *Life Doesn't Frighten Me*. You may be more comfortable giving each child a new plastic tray and letting them paint in the tray with their fingers. You make the decision about germ-spreading in your classroom.

For further instructions, see *Big Friend, Little Friend*, page 20.

Note: Because we think this book will encourage your children to express their emotions, you are encouraged to do this activity. Use whatever mixture you feel comfortable with. The tabletop is suggested because it offers large space. Pre-plan who paints with whom and be sure to give those children who need a clearly defined space the space they need. This will result in mutual sharing of space. Please don't require your children to "share" the space.

Another Book

Bryan, A. (1992) *Sing to the Sun,* HarperCollins, New York.

Drawing by Jermaine Gosa, age 5

Honey, I Love and Other Poems

Written by Eloise Greenfield

In Greenfield's first book of poems, she gives children "words to love, to grow on." The rhythmic verses all celebrate love and a feeling of being loved by family, friends, neighbors.

Summary:

A book of poetry for young children

A Reading Rainbow Book

Illustrated by Diane and Leo Dillon

The Dillons studied children's art for this book. Pencil drawings show confident children, graffiti shows their lively work.

HarperCollins, 1978

STORY TIME

Theme

Positive self-image.

Introduction

1. Ask your children to tell the group about things they love.
2. Show the cover of *Honey, I Love,* and encourage your children to talk about the child on the cover and the things that child might love.

Reading

1. Read the title of the book and wait for your children to settle down.
2. Decide how much of the poem your children can listen to without responding. Talk about having a listening time. Encourage them to make their own pictures in their minds as you read.

Response

1. Each of the poems should be reacted to individually.
2. Use the book as a resource in your daily routine. Use it to respond to the questions and actions of your children.
3. Memorize these poems with your children.

EXTENSIONS

Make A Book

See *Nathaniel Talking* and *Something On My Mind.*

I Love Headband

Materials

Magazines, newspapers, flyers, school supply catalogs, headband strip, glue, scissors, staples, crayons/markers.

1. Read *Honey, I Love* poem, and let your children tell you what they love.
2. In a small group, let your children find pictures of things they love. Depending on the skill level of the children, you or they can cut out the pictures.
3. Children then glue pictures on the headband strip in an arrangement that pleases them.
4. Children may want to add their own drawings to their headbands.

Another Thought

Have a parade to other classrooms or the office. Let the children tell about their hats.

Cognitive Development

Expressing positive feelings, visual discrimination, eye-hand coordination.

88

Tape Poems

Materials

Tape, tape recorder, book: *Honey, I Love.*

1. Collect a small group of children and review the book.
2. Read each poem. Then have your children tell about the illustrations on that page.
3. Let your children decide what sound to use to signal the turning of the page.
4. Make the book and tape available for individual use at the listening center.

Another Thought

Use the tape at naptime. Encourage your children to make pictures in their minds.

Cognitive Development

Listening skills, relating pictures to words.

Feelings Picture Collage

Materials

Magazines, background paper (8-1/2" x 11"), personal photos of children, children's drawings, markers/crayons, scissors, glue.

1. The collage can have a single emotion or be a collection of emotions.
2. Children glue their individual pictures on a background paper. Children's drawings can be added.
3. Children show their pictures and tell about them.
4. These words can become poems.
5. Write down the children's poems.

Another Thought

Encourage children to say "poems" while looking at the collage.

Each child could make his own picture to take home.

Cognitive Development

Using creative activity to express feelings.
See *Story Stretchers* (page 222).

Things Our Children Like To Do

89

Another Book

Morninghouse, Sundaira, *Nightfeathers* (1989) Open Hand Publishing Inc., Seattle, WA.

I Been There

Conceived by Northern J. Calloway   *Written by Carol Hall*   *Illustrated by Sammis McLean*

Calloway (David on "Sesame Street") had the original idea for this book.

Hall is a songwriter. She won an Emmy for "Free to Be ... You and Me."

McLean is a film producer who loves science fiction and fantasy movies.

Summary:
A little boy takes a rocket trip to the moon.

Doubleday, 1982

STORY TIME

Theme

Science fiction trip to the moon, imagination, improvising.

Introduction

1. Have your children tell you about TV cartoons they watch. Discuss whether they are real or play, made up in someone's head.

2. Ask them if they know about David on "Sesame Street." Tell them he made up this story and then got Carol Hall to write down the words and Sammis McLean to draw the pictures.

3. Read the title and let the children guess where the little boy goes in the book.

Reading

1. Let your children tell you about outer space.

2. Make the point that there are now black astronauts. The book was written in the past.

3. Listen for children's comments about what is in outer space.

4. Allow your children to spread their arms and feel the wind on their ears.

5. The illustrations will draw the children into the fantasy. Let them comment.

Response

1. Ask your children if the little boy could say, "I been there."

2. Discuss with your children why and how the story changed so quickly sometimes.

3. Be sure to show that the frog jumping sequence begins with the title page and ends with the final illustration in the book.

EXTENSIONS

Children Add to the Story

Materials

Book: *I Been There*

1. Sit down with a small group of children. Talk with them about how the boy made up his own story. Tell your children you want to hear how they would tell the story.

2. Begin reading on the page where the boy becomes his own rocket.

3. Depending on the age of your children, you may want to read the text or just look at the pictures.

4. Accept as valid any tale a child wants to tell you. Some may follow the story line. Some may relate to one item in an illustration. Some may amaze you with their imaginative powers.

5. The important element is that the child is considering other possibilities for the story.

Cognitive Development

Imagination, considering other possibilities, oral expressiveness, sequencing events.

90

What I'll See in Outer Space

Materials

Construction paper, paper rolls, your art scrap box, scissors, glue, tape, books: *I Been There, Children & Scissors*

1. Show the children the gorilla-bat. Ask them if they would like to create their own outer-space creatures.

2. Encourage your children to make a creature. Children may need help in finding a piece for the body and figuring out how to tape and glue the pieces together.

3. Give each child an opportunity to tell the other children about her creature.

Cognitive Development

Oral language, eye-hand coordination, expression of imaginative ideas.

Real and Pretend

Materials

Collection of plastic animals, puppets, stuffed animals, pictures of animals available in your room (with at least one for each child) book: *I Been There.*

1. Put all the animals in one pile or box and gather a small group of children around them.

2. Show your children the gorilla-bat and talk about whether he is real or pretend (play-play).

3. Give each child an animal. Let the child decide whether her animal is real or pretend.

4. Help children find realistic reasons to decide about the animals. Does it eat? Does it breathe? Can you see one at the zoo? And so forth.

5. Also talk about your class' toy animals being models or representations of living or pretend animals.

6. This could be a center or station activity in the future. You might want to use only small plastic animals.

Cognitive Development

Classification, real/pretend distinctions.

My "I Been There" Book

Materials

Pictures of places your children would like to go. Pictures of modes of transportation, 8-1/2" x 11" paper, crayons/markers, book: *I Been There.*

1. Ask your children, "Where are some places you would like to go?" Write them down. Contact a travel agent for pictures. Look in magazines and newspapers. Write to the attractions.

2. When you have all of your pictures, re-read *I Been There.* Again, ask your children where they would like to go.

3. Small groups of children working with an adult can select the pictures of where they want to go.

4. Children can then make their own *I Been There* book. They can draw and paste pictures of how to get there, what to do when they get there, and getting back home.

5. Remind the children of how the boy made up pretend things when he was in outer space.

6. The children may want to dictate their stories for you to write down.

Cognitive Development

Expressing desires, visual discrimination, eye-hand coordination, wishing.

Outer Space Reality

Materials

Gather some space books from the library. NASA will send you pictures of the astronauts (especially ask for black astronauts). See *Children & Scissors* (Shuttle and Rockets).

1. With the real astronaut materials, let the children dictate true stories about space. They can decorate the pages with the space materials or their own drawings.

2. Nearly realistic shuttles and rockets can be made following the directions in *Children & Scissors.*

Cognitive Development

Oral language, eye-hand coordination, imagination, learning the difference between real and pretend, positive self-image, seeing one's words written down (which affirms that reading is talk written down).

91

Nathaniel Talking

Written by Eloise Greenfield   *Illustrated by Jan Spivey Gilchrist*

Greenfield has written many books for children. She catches the rhythm as Nathaniel raps that rap.

In charming pencil drawings, Gilchrist shows a serious child and his relatives, teachers, and friends.

Summary:

Nathaniel raps rhythmically about his life, the people around him, and his future.

Black Butterfly Children's Books, 1988

STORY TIME

Theme

Positive self-worth, sharing feelings of self with others, considering the behavior of others, self-expression of emotional states.

Introduction

1. Talk to the children about Nathaniel. Label his words as blues and rap. Then explain that with the blues/rap, Nathaniel can tell about how he feels and thinks about himself and others.

2. Ask the children what they think Nathaniel might rap about in blues words.

Reading

1. Begin with blues on a subject you have heard your children talking about. You decide how many raps to read in one sitting.

2. After a blues/rap is read, encourage your children to relate their own similar experiences.

3. Show the illustrations to the children both before and after reading the blues/rap. Be responsive to the children's comments.

Response

1. As you did during the reading, allow children time to comment and identify personally with individual blues/raps.

2. Ask the children to identify the content of a blues/rap by looking at its picture.

EXTENSIONS

Children's Blues/Rap Books

Materials

Paper (8-1/2" x 11"), markers/crayons, manila envelopes to store raps, book covers, book: *Nathaniel Talking*.

1. Read the book with the children and encourage them to make up their own blues. Children may prefer to follow the 12-beat blues or any rhythm they prefer.

2. Encourage each child to make up a rap/blues.

3. Write down the child's words.

4. Children draw pictures to go with their blues/rap.

5. Keep the pages for the child. Add more raps on other days. When you have several, put them inside a cover to make a book for the child. Call it "(Child's name) Talking."

Another Thought

Use popular rap or blues music as background for the child's rap/blues and tape-record his creations.

Cognitive Development

Putting value on one's own feelings, identifying and expressing feelings, understanding the rhythm of language, positive self-image.

Expressing Feeling in Movement and Oral Language

Materials

Microphone (block that looks like a microphone, recycled microphone, working microphone), tape player, radio as an amplifier.

1. Re-read a few of Nathaniel's blues/raps. Ask the children if they would like to say their own blues/raps.
2. Children gather in a small group and take turns standing, dancing, and saying their blues/raps.
3. This may be a one-time experience using a pretend microphone (wooden block).
4. Use the amplifier system to make the activity more lively.
5. Use a tape recorder to tape the blues/raps for listening to another time. Or use a camcorder if you have one.

Another Thought

The permanent transcription of your children's blues/raps, whether written or taped, may be more important to you than to them. Follow their lead and allow them to create for the moment. If you encourage these activities, they may well ask you to write them down or tape them.

Cognitive Development

Spontaneous expression of feelings and ideas, positive self-image, oral language, body language.

Group Blues

Materials

Lined chart paper, markers/crayons.

1. Select a topic. It could be one of Nathaniel's or one made up by the class.
2. Individual children dictate lines of the blues/rap while the adult writes down the words.
3. Children take turns adding to lines and adding lines.
4. Children then use crayons to illustrate the blues/rap on the same chart paper or an additional sheet.

Another Thought

Blues/rap can then be displayed and, as new sheets are written down, they can be laminated and bound into a class book.

Cognitive Development

Expressing feelings, creativity, feeling and expressing rhythm, oral expression.

Class Book of Individual Blues/Rap

Materials

Lined chart paper, markers/crayons, photos, magazine pictures.

1. Each child makes up his own blues and the adult writes it down for him.
2. Each child illustrates his own blues/rap. Personal photos, class photo, favorite pictures from magazines can enhance the illustrations.
3. Each child's blues/rap is collected and laminated and bound in a class book.

Another Thought

Each child makes his own book.

Cognitive Development

Valuing one's own feelings.

Writing Blues/Rap

Materials

Unlined paper (8'1/2" x 11"), spiral-bound unlined notebook, markers/pencils/crayons.

1. Each child makes up her own blues/rap.
2. An adult writes down the child's words.

Another Thought

If the child is expressing the words and doing the writing, attention should be given to the expression, not the neatness or grammar. Let the right brain do its work. The left brain may later want to make corrections, but this interruption will only slow the flow of creativity at first. Little will be gained by pointing out errors in spelling and/or grammar. Preoccupations with this left-brain work may be a sign to you that the child needs help in expressing feelings.

Cognitive Development

Expressing feelings in word pictures.

93

Mr. Monkey and the Gotcha Bird

Written by Walter Dean Myers

Myers writes about the black experience. His hobbies are photography, the flute, and word games with his children.

Illustrated by Leslie Morrill

Morrill has illustrated numerous books. The *Cassey Valentine* series is one of his most popular works.

Summary:

Monkey tricks animals to be meals for bird, then tricks the bird so he cannot eat the monkey.

Delacorte Press, 1982

94

STORY TIME

Theme

Imagination, problem-solving, understanding what other people want, playing with language, predicting outcomes, learning to tell stories, trusting others.

Introduction

1. Show your children the jacket of the book and read the title. Ask them to tell you what they see.
2. Talk about what might happen in the story and if they think the two animals will be friends.
3. Alert the children that the story will use sentences in a different way than the way most of the children do.
4. Be sure to tell the children how the story was made up.

Reading

1. Ask your children who the woman is.
2. Have children predict what will happen to Monkey.
3. With each new meal for the Gotcha Bird, allow children to talk about how Monkey will trick the new animal.
4. Let the children tell you why Monkey decides on a lion for Gotcha Bird to eat.

Response

1. Ask your children if they think Mr. Lion would ever find a supper for Monkey.
2. Talk about why Monkey found supper for Mr. Lion. Ask your children if they think Monkey found Mr. Lion supper to be his friend.
3. Ask your children who they thought was the smartest animal. Encourage them to tell you why.

EXTENSIONS

Tape Story for Listening Center

Materials

Tape recorder, taped story, small plastic animals to represent the animals in the story, book: *Mr. Monkey and the Gotcha Bird*. You may also want a figure for the storyteller.

1. When re-reading the story as a listening story, tape the reading. Have someone make a noise each time the page is turned.
2. Make the tape, the book, and small plastic animals available at the listening center.
3. As a small group or as individuals, children make use of the materials.

Another Thought

After the children know the story, let them make a story tape by following the illustrations and their imaginations.

Cognitive Development

Auditory perception, representation of fictional characters, manipulation of models and tape recorder, positive self-esteem.

You Be a Storyteller

Materials

Brightly colored clothes, skirt, shirt, pants, apron, book: *Mr. Monkey and the Gotcha Bird.*

1. Meet with a small group of your children. Remind them that Walter Dean Myers made up this story.

2. Encourage them to put on the storyteller's clothes.

3. Give each child a chance to tell a story. Accept any story, even a telling of something that happened to the child.

4. Encourage children who make up fictional stories. Identify these stories as stories like the Gotcha Bird. Help children to understand that they control what happens in their stories.

5. As the children choose to play the storyteller themselves, their stories will expand and get more complicated.

6. After building some confidence, the children will want to tell the whole class. Eventually some of your children may want to tell other classes.

Cognitive Development

Oral expression, planning a sequence of events, creativity, dramatic expression, controlling of events

Class Play

Materials

Feathers in a headband, tail (rope) for Monkey, box for turtle's shell, masks for all the animals, clothes for the storyteller, string, clothes, furniture and plants from your room for props, book: *Mr. Monkey and the Gotcha Bird.*

1. The play could easily have more than one of each animal so more children can be included.

2. Talk to the children about how the animals look. Ask them what things you already have in your classroom to use for costumes.

3. Supplement the animals by making masks from paper plates, paper bags, or using headbands (see *Children & Scissors*).

4. While the children are making their costumes, encourage them to re-tell the story so they will memorize the sequence of animals.

5. Gather those children wanting to put on the play. Help the storyteller keep the children within the bounds of the story.

6. Acting in the play is really more important than acting for an audience (except for adult viewers). A willing audience would be appreciated by the actors. If you are doing this activity at free/work time, children may choose to come and go as audience members. Your actors may choose to perform for your whole class or even other classes.

7. Children can easily switch roles from performance to performance. If the children are enthusiastic about the play, you may want to perform it for parents. The less regimentation you require of your children, the more comfortable they will be at the parent performance.

Another Thought

The play could easily be done with puppets from your room or puppets made as an art activity (see *Children & Scissors*).

Cognitive Development

Oral expression, body language, dramatic expression, recalling sequence of events, recalling written language, positive self-esteem, recreation.

Do You Want Mr. Monkey for a Friend?

Materials

Book: *Mr. Monkey and the Gotcha Bird*

1. Talking with children in a small group, ask who would want Mr. Monkey for a friend. Encourage the children to talk about what they think about Mr. Monkey.

2. Use the illustrations from the book to explore how and why Monkey uses each animal.

3. Allow children to come to their own conclusions about what Monkey did. This clever, fun story can tell you a lot about your children's feelings of empathy. Rather than moralizing, accept each child's conclusions as valid for him.

Another Thought

Take advantage of future events in your classroom to show children that using people for your own ends is not always the happiest solution.

Cognitive Development

Understanding, trust, being a friend, ways to get out of trouble, oral expression.

Another Book

Myers, Walter Dean, *Dragon Takes A Wife*

95

Half a Moon and One Whole Star

Written by Crescent Dragonwagon   *Illustrated by Jerry Pinkney*

Sleepy time is the focus of Dragonwagon's text for a book that will help children go from day into evening or naps.

The warmth of Pinkney's illustrations has brought him honor after honor. His work is exhibited in many museums.

Summary:
A little girl cycles into sleep.

Coretta Scott King Award for Illustration   Macmillan, 1986

STORY TIME

Theme

Safety during sleep, rhythms of life, positive self-image, controlling one's body.

Introduction

1. If your children know other Jerry Pinkney books, ask them who drew these pictures.

2. Have the children tell about the cover illustration and relate it to their going to sleep.

3. Read the title and ask if it is a good name for a book about sleeping.

Reading

1. These words create such mental pictures that you may want to have just a listening reading of the words. The children would then create their own pictures. This may be done page by page, following the lead of the children as to when to show the illustrations.

2. Pinkney's illustrations easily lend themselves to children's comments about related experiences.

3. Sleep is viewed by many children as another separation. Use this book to ease those fears by helping your children feel its smooth, strong, safe, predictable rhythms.

Response

1. Listen to children's comments about what goes on around them when they go to sleep.

2. Talk about Susan and how she could go to sleep when all those things were going on around her.

EXTENSIONS

Sleep Book for Each Child

Materials

Construction paper, magazines, scissors, markers, crayons, glue.

1. Working in small groups, ask children to identify what they hear at their houses at bedtime. Write their comments down.

2. Also have them dictate the things they know that happen while they are sleeping.

3. Children can then draw pictures, find magazine pictures, or cut construction paper pictures to illustrate their words.

4. Depending on your adult-to-child ratio, you may want this to be a project that takes several days to complete.

Another Thought

Let each child decide on a title for his book.

Cognitive Development

Representing one's environment, eye-hand coordination, dictating a story.

Classroom Sleep Book

Materials

Chart paper, magazine pictures, markers, construction paper, glue, scissors, photographs of your children sleeping (individually or as a group).

1. As a large group, have the children make up the sequence of events for your class naptime. Write each event on one page of chart paper.

2. Working in small groups, illustrate one page at a time. Use magazine pictures, construction paper forms, children's drawings and photos to illustrate the words as a central focus.

3. Also allow the children to draw and write on the pages as they like.

Another Thought

When the book is completed, read it with the children as part of the naptime ritual. Done in the beginning of the year, it may help to soothe the reluctant to sleep.

Cognitive Development

School is a safe place to sleep, representation, eye-hand coordination, sleep routine at school.

Another Book

Gilchrist, Jan Spivey (1993), *Indigo and Moonlight Gold,* Black Butterfly Children's Books, New York.

Jacket illustration Copyright © 1986 by Jerry Pinkney, used with permission from MacMillan Children's Books Publisher, New York.

Put the Dolls to Sleep

Materials

Furniture, dolls, stuffed toys you have in your blocks area.

1. While the children are in your housekeeping area, remind them of *Half a Moon and One Whole Star.*

2. Encourage the children to talk to their potential sleepers about the noises and goings-on in the classroom.

3. If necessary, supply the words for the children to talk their sleepers to sleep.

Another Thought

Make the book available for use in your housekeeping area

Cognitive Development

Soothing and relaxing someone to sleep, solving problems, self-esteem.

Things Our Children Like To Do

97

Red Dancing Shoes

Written by Denise Lewis Patrick

Paintings by James E. Ransone

Denise brings her strong family feelings to this story.

Children will be pleased to meet the beautiful characters.

Summary:

A pair of new red dancing shoes become magical until... Happy ending of course.

Tambourine Books, 1993

98

STORY TIME

Theme

Feeling so good, something happens, a friend helps get things back of track.

Introduction

1. Ask who likes to dance and does anyone have special shoes to dance.

2. Hold out the book so as to show the fromt and back covers.

3. Your children will want to continue on with the story rather than have a conversation about a particular instance.

Response

1. "How did she feel when?", questions work easily with this story.

2. Emphasize how Aunt Nen helped to clean the shoes rather than fussing about getting them dirty. Aunt Nen understood how her neice felt.

EXTENSIONS

My Special Shoes

Materials

Everyone in the classes, a dancing record, book: Red Dancing Shoe

1. Re-read the story with a small group.

2. Give each child who wants to, an opportunity to tell a story about her shoes. Accept as valid each child's story.

3. Review your rules for dancing. Put the music on and dance.

Another thought

Give individual children an opportunity to dance by themselves.

Cognitive Development

Classification, positive self-esteem, music and movement, oral expression.

Shoes for Dancing

Materials

Tap shoes, ballet shoes, toe shoes, clogging shoes, any others you know about, book: *Red Dancing Shoes*.

1. Re-read the book. Ask what made the red shoes dancing shoes.

2. Show the shoes you have gathered that are dance shoes. Perhaps some of your children can bring theirs to school.

3. Talk about the shoes. Help your children to understand the difference between shoes that are made to dance a particular dance and dancing in shoes.

Another Thought

Look in the yellow pages and find someone who sells dancing shoes. Ask them to send you a catalog. Look at the shoes with your children. Make a poster and display at eye level.

Cognitive Development

Labeling, classification, oral language.

Additional Books

Bullard, Brian (1992), *I Can Dance*, Putnam, New York.

Lotz, Karen E., *Can't Sit Still*, (1993) Dutton Children's Books, New York.

99

Ben's Trumpet

Written and illustrated by Rachel Isadora

A ballerina-turned-writer/artist who loves music, Isadora wrote and illustrated this book because the topic is close to her heart.

Summary:
A little boy enjoys learning music on an old man's jazz trumpet.

Caldecott Honor Book, 1980   Greenwillow, 1979

NOTE: Perhaps you should listen to some jazz recordings before you read the book to your children.

STORY TIME

100

Theme
Having a dream, loving jazz.

Introduction
1. Ask your children if any of them know what a trumpet is.
2. Show the jacket cover, read the title, and get comments from your children about the man and the little boy. Ask which figure they think is Ben.

Reading
1. The illustrations are so striking that, on first reading, you almost have to choose whether to talk about the illustrations, read the story as a listening story, or go at a slow pace and get lost in the words and illustrations.
2. Ask questions about how Ben feels throughout the story.
3. Also let the children tell you whether the story is a "now" story or an "old-time" story, and how they know.

Response
1. Talk about the illustrations and ask if they look like music. Identify the music as jazz.
2. Re-read the story, just looking and talking about the illustrations.
3. Encourage the children to talk about why Ben kept playing his trumpet.
4. Ask the children why the man let Ben play his trumpet.

EXTENSIONS

Jazz and Rhythm Band

Materials

The rhythm band instruments from your classroom, jazz record (from your local library), trumpet, book: *Ben's Trumpet, Charlie Parker Plays Be Bop.*

1. Find a jazz lover among your friends and invite her to your classroom. If she can't come, have a talk with her about jazz and get her to suggest a record to use with your children.
2. Show your children the book. Ask if they remember the name of the kind of music Ben liked.
3. Play a short (2 minutes) track of jazz. Move your bodies with the music.
4. Pass out the rhythm band instruments. Talk to the children about playing softly enough so they can still hear the music.
5. Play the short jazz track while the children keep the beat with their instruments.
6. After playing, encourage the children to talk about how the music feels and sounds.

Another Thought

As this noisy activity will fill the entire room, involve as many children as possible. Encourage those who want to be audience members, showing them how to nod their heads, clap their hands, tap their feet, or wiggle their toes to the beat.

Cognitive Development

Music appreciation, auditory discrimination, eye-hand coordination, musical rhythm and expression, verbal expression.

Performing "Ben's Trumpet"

Materials

Jazz record, rhythm band instruments, clothes from your housekeeping area, a trumpet, book: *Ben's Trumpet.*

1. Gather a small group of children who are interested in acting out the book.
2. Talk with your children about what you have in your room to act out the story. Get them to find something to improvise the trumpet.
3. Look at your rhythm band instruments and the musical instruments in the story. Have the children find substitute instruments. Let the number of children who want to perform determine the number of people and the kind of instruments in the band.
4. Choose a director to use the book to keep the play line similar to the story line.

Another Thought

Some children may want to dance or parade. Encourage these additional dimensions.

Cognitive Development

Role playing, dramatizing the written word, recalling sequences of events, identifying feelings.

Black and White Jazz Collage

Materials

Background paper (black and white), pre-cut shapes similar to those in the illustrations, scissors, glue, scraps from your art box, white chalk, black markers, white crayon, jazz record, book: *Children & Scissors* .

1. Look at the illustrations again with your children. Encourage them to talk about the pictures and describe them in any way they like.
2. Ask the children if they would like to make a Jazz Collage. Gather those children who are interested into a small group.
3. Play your jazz record and give each child background paper, scissors, and glue.
4. The children should have easy access to the materials, choosing what they would like to include on their collages.

Jacket illustration copyright ©1979 by Rachel Isadora with permission from William Morrow & Company, New York, Publisher.

5. Continue to talk with the children about how the music makes them feel, and making the collage look like the music.

Another Thought

Make the art materials and record available for individual use. Use music as a background for other art activities in the future.

Cognitive Development

Visual discrimination, creative expression, auditory discrimination, eye-hand coordination, oral expression.

Making Instruments

Materials

Paper tubes (toilet paper, paper towels and so forth), cans, plastic bottles, small boxes, construction paper, bells, string, newspaper strips, papier mache, your art scrap box, book: *Ben's Trumpet.*

1. Talk about *Ben's Trumpet* with your children. Ask each child if he would like to make a musical instrument of his own. Encourage the children to talk about what kind of instruments they would like.
2. Show the children the tubes, boxes, cans and bottles. Let each child choose an object that will be the base for his instrument.
3. Giving the children easy access to the materials, allow them to decorate their instruments.
4. If you use papier mache to change the shape of the base, allow at least one day's drying time.
5. Each child can name his instrument. He may invent a whole new name.
6. The instruments can be as simple or as complex as wanted. With help from you, your children will continue to create real and imaginary instruments. You can relate the present instrument to their past experience with Ben.

Cognitive Development

Imagination, representation, creative expression, eye-hand coordination, planning.

Another Book

Walker, M (1980) *Ty's One-Man Band,* Four Winds, New York

Amazing Grace

Written by Mary Hoffman

Mary knows all about girls. She has three daughters who musts keep her constantly entertained.

Illustrations by Caroline Binch

Using her watercolor techniques, Caroline beautifully illustrates the many shades of African Americans.

Summary:

Grace loves to act out different roles. She is eager to play the part of Peter Pan at school. With the support of her family and her own enthusiasm, she has the ability to earn the part.

Dial Books for Young Readers, 1991

STORY TIME

Theme

Believing in yourself, family support, gaining the respect of your classmates.

Introduction

1. Grace's warm smile introduces herself to your children.

2. Ask your children why they think she is so happy.

Reading

1. Your children will want to tell a story about each page. Listen to them.

2. Use the pictures on the title page to talk about acting out parts or "play-play".

3. Encourage your children to "act out" the characters along with Grace.

4. Discuss the reasons children gave Grace when they tell her she cannot be Peter Pan. The age and social experience of your children should be considered. Be sure you are listening to the children's reactions rather than giving a lecture on fairness. A more complex discussion might come after the reading of the book.

5. If your children become very interested in the question of who can be Peter Pan, put the book aside to finish later. Allow your children to express their views.

Response

1. Explore with your children all the feelings that are expressed in the story. Be sure to include the feelings of the other children and Grace's family.

2. Your children will want to tell you about the roles they like to play.

3. If you are really brave, you'll talk about opposite gender roles. The idea, it seems to this author, is to help the children realize they can pretend (play-play) to be the opposite role. At the same time, they remain the gender they were born.

Most of your children will be comfortable with this idea. Talk with the parents of those children who are confused by playing gender roles and living gender roles. Some children may think their clothes make their gender. These children need to understand they remain the gender they were born, even when they play the opposite gender.

EXTENSIONS

Have A Play

Materials

Dress up clothes and props available in your classroom. You may want to ask your children to bring items from home.

1. For very young children, take your cue from Grace. Let your children be anything they want to be.

2. With a small group at your centers/work time, encourage children to play out their individual parts. They need not be related in any way.

3. Allow the audience to come and go. Focus your attention on the present actor rather than making an audience pay attention.

Another Thought

Circle time could be used for a few children to act out parts. Make a chart so that children can take turns during the week to play out their parts.

Go See A Performance

Materials

Information about a play in your area, book: *Amazing Grace*.

1. Re-read the book; ask your children if they would like to see a play.

2. Share the information you have about the play.

3. Young children like to know what will happen on non-routine days. Start with when they get to school and what will happen each step of the way: arrive at school, eat breakfast, go to the bathroom, get name tags, decide what adults they will be responsible to, etc., and continue until you arrive back at school. Then tell the first activity they will do at school.

4. Make up rules for behavior at the play. Role play these rules. Decide ahead of time about bathroom privileges, at the play.

5. Follow the field trip procedures for your setting.

Another Thought

Find another class that is putting on a play and ask if you can be the audience. Call your local volunteer groups and see who is available to come to your room and perform.

Cognitive Development

Passive listening skills, anticipation of events, practicing appropriate behavior and dress.

Act Out Parts of the Story

Materials

Phones in your room, toys in your room, book: *Amazing Grace*.

1. Gather a few children who would like to act out their favorite part of the book.

2. Re-read the story and let the children tell you which part they liked best.

3. Talk about what pages they will need to act out that part.

4. Watch the children act out their part. Talk about the feelings of each part. If no one acts out the exclusion part, wait for another time to talk about and act out Grace's feelings.

5. Your children may come and go from your group: being interested in playing a part, but having no interest in staying to be part of the audience.

Another Thought

Giving children an opportunity to play out these feelings will help them to identify and be in control of their own feelings.

Cognitive Development

Role-playing, expressing anger, pleasure, oral language.

Another Book

Johnson, D. (1992) *The Best Bug to Be*, Macmillan, New York

103

Something On My Mind

Words by Nikki Grimes   *Illustrated by Tom Feelings*

Feelings gave Grimes access to a number of drawings and asked her to write poems to go with them. Grimes said that she stuck copies up all over her place, around the bed and on the floor. She got to know the children well before writing.

While most children's books are written and then illustrated, in this case Feelings asked Grimes to select a group of his drawings and, as it were, illustrate the art with poetry. She studied the paintings intensively before writing the story.

Summary:
Some pictures of feelings, with poems for young children.

Dial Books for Young Readers, 1978

STORY TIME

Theme

Self-expression, self-worth, value of one's own feelings.

Introduction

1. Talk with your children about "thinking." Relate how you think about things to *Something On My Mind*.
2. Encourage your children to tell each other about the things they think about.
3. Show the book cover and ask the children to tell you how the children look when they are thinking. Have children show you how they look when they are thinking.

Reading

1. One poem may be all your class needs to hear at a sitting. Use the poems to meet the needs of your classroom.
2. Help your children relate to and interact with these poems.
3. These illustrations beg to be talked about. You may be surprised at how easily your children will relate to them.

Response

1. Talk about Tom Feelings and how his illustrations (what he draws) can tell stories about what people are thinking and feeling.
2. Let children tell you how they think Nikki Grimes makes up the words and why she would want to put them in a book.
3. Discuss whether the thinking up of the words or drawing of what people feel would come first.

4. Use individual poems to talk about things that happen in your classroom.

EXTENSIONS

Children's Experiences

Materials

Book: *Something On My Mind*

Children's worries and fears are real. Listen to your children. When one wants a friend, talks about bad words, wants to live somewhere else, needs to cry, or has any other need that is reflected in these poems, go get the book and read the poem to the child. Then ask the child if she would like to tell about the way she feels. Also see if the child would like you to write down her feelings (words).

Cognitive Development

Identifying one's feelings, oral language, expressing feelings to others.

Feelings Collage

Materials

Posters, pictures, photographs of people which clearly show emotions, crayons/markers, chalk, drawing paper, background paper, glue, book: *Something On My Mind*.

1. Review the illustrations in *Something On My Mind*.
2. Working in a small group, let the children look at and talk about the pictures you have available.
3. Decide whether you will make a class collage or if each child will make an individual collage, or if a group of children will make a single collage for an emotion.

104

4. Let children choose pictures to paste on the collage.

5. Some children may want to add their own drawings to the collage.

Another Thought

Display collage at eye level and encourage children to talk about it throughout the day. Use the collage for the children to look at emotions, then go to the painting easel and paint how that picture feels.

Cognitive Development

Visual discrimination, identifying feelings, eye-hand coordination.

Class Book of Feelings

Materials

Pictures of people, crayons/ markers, construction paper, glue, book: *Something On My Mind*.

1. Look through the book again and get your children to respond. Ask them if they would like to make a class book that shows what they are thinking about.

2. Work in a small group, looking at the pictures you have gathered.

3. As children find a picture that they like, ask them to tell you about it and write down their words.

4. Have the child glue the picture beside the words.

5. Allow the child to draw and "write" on his page.

6. Laminate the pages back-to-back, make a front and back cover, and put the pages in a book.

Another Thought

Read your class book as a group and tape it. Make the book and tape available in the listening center. Help individual children make their own books. Both the class book and the children's books can be added to over a period of time.

Cognitive Development

Visual discrimination, oral language, eye-hand coordination, identifying feelings, expressing feelings.

From Something on My Mind, by Nikki Grimes, pictures by Tom Feelings, Copyright (1978) by Tom Feelings, pictures. Used by permission of Dial Books for Young Readers, a division of Penguin Books USA Inc.

Writing Down My Feelings

Materials

Note pad, 8-1/2" x 11" sheet of paper or a card, pencil/pen, book: *Something On My Mind*, or other similar books.

1. During your daily routine, as you interact with your children, make a habit of giving them the opportunity to write down how they are feeling and thinking.

2. At a moment that does not disrupt the child's play, ask the child if she would like you to write down what she is thinking about.

3. Write the words exactly as the child dictates them to you. The child may want to do some "writing" for herself.

4. These words could be displayed in the classroom, collected in a book for the child, or sent home that day.

Another Thought

Use this technique to help children sort out their feelings of having no one to play with, pride in completing a puzzle, settling a dispute, planning for future events.

Cognitive Development

Oral language, expressing one's thinking, seeing one's thoughts being written down.

Note:

Thinking or inner language develops in children; they don't just have it. Young children (under six years) need to learn oral language then "thinking:" will come.

Another Book

Feelings, Tom, (1993) *Soul Looks Back in Wonder*. Dial Books

Grimes, Nikki, (1993) *From A Child's Heart*, Just Us Books, Orange. New Jersey.

CHAPTER SEVEN
Black History

I Am Freedom's Child

Africa Dream

All Us Come Cross the Water

The Black Snowman

Tar Beach

Cornrows

Kwanzaa

Follow the Drinking Gourd

Rosa Parks

Harriet Tubman

Book of Black Heroes: Great Women in the Struggle

Uncle Jed's Barbershop

A Weed Is A Flower: The Life of George Washington Carver

Stop and Go

A Picture Book of Martin Luther King Jr.

Charlie Parker

Dancing with the Indians

Josephine's 'magination: A Tale of Haiti

I Am Freedom's Child

Written by Bill Martin, Jr.   *Paintings by Symeon Shimin*   *Lettering by Ray Barber*

With his writing, Martin helps children to feel free and to be friends, regardless of color. Shimin's paintings of young children show a happy, carefree relationship among them.

The large lettering by Barber will make the story easy to read for many youngsters.

Summary:
A child likes himself, and learns to like others and the differences among them because all people are freedom's children.

Bowman, 1970

STORY TIME

Theme

I like me, you like you, we can like each other.

Introduction

1. The history of America is freedom, and the history of black America is moving toward that freedom. *I Am Freedom's Child* is a good beginning for young children to have an idea of what freedom is.

2. Begin by asking your children what they think freedom means.

3. At some point, be sure that your children know this book is written by the author of *Brown Bear Brown Bear*.

Reading

1. The combination of text and illustration gives the feeling of freedom to your children. A straight read-through with your children listening is very appropriate for this book.

2. Your children will be cheering at the final page.

Response

1. Re-read and talk about the illustrations.

2. Encourage your children to tell how they feel when they see and hear the book, and how the children in the book feel.

3. Talk again about the word "freedom."

EXTENSIONS

Freedom

Materials

Book: *I Am Freedom's Child*

1. Re-read the book to a small group of children. Ask them to tell you about freedom.

2. Talk about liking yourself. Show the illustration and encourage your children to tell why the children in the book like themselves. Then give your children an opportunity to tell why they like themselves.

3. Move on to the illustration showing that the other child likes himself, too. Explore with your children the feeling that it is okay for everyone to like themselves. Remember some things each child has done, how that child was proud, and how the class could also be proud.

4. Next talk about how your children are different (size, age, likes, dislikes, siblings, race, religion, language). Some children will be able to tell why they like these differences in the other children. Accept those likes as valid.

5. Remind the children about interaction in your classroom. Have them tell you when the classroom is a happy place. Help them to understand when each child is happy. When each child is following the class rules, when no one is trying to be the boss of everything, then everyone is free to be happy in the classroom.

6. Talk again about freedom, and what freedom means in your classroom.

Another Thought

Self-respect and respect for the rights of others are what we teach every day in our classrooms. Help your children relate your class atmosphere to freedom.

Cognitive Development

Assessing one's positive behaviors, ability to be proud of someone else, recognizing that differences can be positive, beginning to understand freedom, logical thinking, oral language, visual discrimination.

Freedom's Child Mural

Materials

Paint, paintbrushes, markers/crayons, construction paper, scissors, glue, 3' x 10' background paper, book: *I Am Freedom's Child.*

1. Re-read the book to your children. Ask if they would like to make a class mural about being free.
2. Work indiv-idually or in small groups. Each child should choose how he would like to make a picture of himself (paint, draw, cut and paste).
3. Arrange the pictures on the mural. Be sure each child's picture has plenty of space. Place the mural where your children can talk about it. Encourage them to talk about liking oneself, the positive differences, and liking others.

Cognitive Development

Positive self-image, respect for others, freedom requiring mutual respect, visual documentation, eye-hand coordination.

Freedom Chart

Materials

Tagboard, outdated school supply catalogs, construction paper, scissors, glue, crayons/markers, book: *I Am Freedom's Child.*

1. Re-read the book and ask your children if they would like to make a Freedom Chart. The chart would show what your children like to choose to do in the classroom.
2. Talk with a small group of children about freedom and being able to choose what you want to do.
3. Children decide how to show their choices, with photographs or drawings.
4. Divide your chart into the areas of your classroom. Place the child's choice in the area it is stored. Also write the child's name next to the item.
5. Count first how many children choose to play in each area. Then count how many children choose a particular item.
6. Counting and comparing will show the children the need for rules so that everyone can have a turn.
7. Talk about the freedom to choose to play somewhere, then the responsibility of respecting the other children after you get there.

Another Thought

Laminate pictures of the most popular items in your class. Working with a small group, let each child choose his favorite item and place it in the proper area on a chart. Count and compare sizes of groups for individual items and areas. Make it available for children to use independently.

Cognitive Development

Making choices, respecting others' choices, one-to-one correspondence, comparison of sets, understanding the need for rules.

Africa Dream

Written by Eloise Greenfield

Greenfield takes an American child on a dream journey with her evocative words of long-ago African relatives.

Illustrated by Carole Byard

Black children long for the land of their ancestors and Byard takes them to Africa with beautiful, dreamy drawings.

Summary:

A black child's dreams are filled with the images of the people and places of Africa.

Coretta Scott King Award

Thomas Y. Crowel, 1977

STORY TIME

Theme

African heritage, recognizing your past, positive self-image, becoming a part of the passing of time, pride in your ancestors, respect for the feelings of others.

Introduction

1. Show your children the book jacket and ask them what the child is doing. Ask them what you do when you know someone is sleeping.

2. Wait for the children to settle quietly. Tell them they must listen very quietly because we want to see the child's Africa Dream.

Reading

Read the book slowly and softly, quietly reminding the children not to waken the sleeping child.

Response

1. First, allow the children to make general responses.

2. Ask the children about the words as well as the illustrations.

3. Talk to the children about Africa. Ask whether it is a place anyone could go or if it is only a dream place.

4. Ask what Greenfield means when she writes about Africa long ago.

5. Encourage your children to tell you which place in the book they would like to go.

6. Let the children tell you why the child wanted to go to Africa.

EXTENSIONS

Finding Africa

Materials

World map or globe, picture of the earth with a view of Africa (see Appendix for how to get a black-and-white NASA satellite view of Africa), book: *Africa Dream.*

1. Re-read the story to examine its content and illustrations. Show the children where they live, and where Africa is, on the map.

2. Ask the children why they think the child dreamed about Africa. How would the child know about Africa?

3. Let the children talk about any other places someone has told them about.

4. On your globe, show your children the Atlantic Ocean.

5. Talk about what long-ago Africa means.

6. Have the children look at the illustrations and tell what else may have been in the marketplace and where pearls come from.

7. Talk about the strange words and the tall stone buildings.

8. Ask the children who they think will be in the village and what they will look like.

9. Remind the children that the child is dreaming and ask why the long-ago people look like people she knows.

10. Talk about a new-old friend and what it means.

11. Encourage the children to tell you how the child felt in Africa and why the child felt that way.

Another Thought

Show the children a cutout of the African continent and see if they can find it on a globe, map, or satellite photo.

Cognitive Development

Learning about maps and globes, Africa. Self-esteem, feeling of being part of a line of people reaching back into antiquity.

My Dream

Materials

Sheets of white tagboard, crayons/markers, pictures from magazines and travel agents, book: *Africa Dream.*

1. Prepare for this activity by finding out as much family history as the parents of your children know. Get the parents involved in helping the children have some knowledge of their family history. (Suggested parent letter and questionnaire are in the Appendix.)
2. Talk with your children about ancestors. Tell them that everyone has ancestors, and they are going to find out about some of theirs.
3. Encourage your children to talk with the people in their house about long-ago relatives.
4. Using the questionnaires and the children's experiences with relatives, provide the children with copies of photographs, pre-cut magazine and travel brochure photographs.
5. Re-read *Africa Dream.*
6. Let the children arrange the photographs on tagboard and add their own drawings for their dream posters.
7. Children can dictate their dreams to an adult.

Another Thought

Your class or a small group of children may become very involved in this project. The result may be books of the children's family histories.

Of course, some families will have more knowledge of their family histories than others. Every child's history should be valued. If all the child knows is that he lives in your city, make that important. Help him find it on the map and call it his city. You can find photographs of local scenes in the newspaper for him to add to his poster.

The child may want more on his poster. *Africa Dream* is a dream. Encourage the child to dream about his long-ago relatives. Then the child can draw and paste whatever pictures he would like. This applies to all of your children's posters.

Your children will gain a sense of self-pride knowing about their relatives. Because they value their own history, they can then be interested in and value the other children's histories.

Cognitive Development

Positive self-image, sense of history, family relationships, visual discrimination, oral expression, recall of information.

NOTE: Look at the *I Been There* story activity for more ideas.

Naptime Story

Materials

Your children's dream posters, book: *Africa Dream.*

1. When your children are settled on their mats, tell them you are going to read *Africa Dream.*
2. After reading the story, tell your children to make pictures in their minds of their dream posters. (Your class arrangement may allow each child to have a view of his poster.)
3. Tell them if they keep still and keep thinking of their posters, they will dream about them.

Another Thought

For more naptime ideas, look at the discussion of *Ten, Nine, Eight* and *Half A Moon and One Whole Star.*

Cognitive Development

Relaxation skills, listening skills, mental imagery, concentration, controlling sleep habits.

Things Our Children Like To Do

111

All Us Come Cross the Water

Written by Lucille Clifton

Clifton is a mother of six and writes to the heart of "who are my ancestors".

Illustrated by John Steptoe

The unique illustrations of Steptoe give life to a boy and his surroundings.

A youngster of African heritage tries to learn where he is from — a continent, a country, or a people.

Holt, Rhinehart and Winston, 1973

STORY TIME

Theme

Personal roots, pride in heritage, positive self-concept, family relations, solving social problems.

Introduction

1. Show the children the whole book cover and ask them to tell you about it.
2. Help them to understand the connection between the title and the illustration.
3. Help your children recall *Africa Dream* and Dream Poster, and how they found out about their family history.

Reading

1. Your first reading may be only a telling of Steptoe's illustrations. Use your children's experience with *Africa Dream* to help them decide what Ujamaa (Jim) is thinking about and why he acts the way he does.
2. Use some of Clifton's words to make the point of each illustration.
3. .If you have read *Sam*, help the children remember how he felt when his family did not pay attention to him. Also talk about how Ujamaa solved that problem.
4. On re-readings, include more and more of the text.
5. Help your children understand Ujamaa's pride in standing for all of the people who came from Africa.

Response

1. Ask your children what Ujamaa's problem was. How did he solve it?
2. Talk about why Ujamaa had two names. Let your children tell you about their school names and their family names, baby names, or nicknames.

All Us Come From Posters

Materials

Child's completed poster (see *Africa Dream* for instructions), book: *All Us Come Cross the Water*.

1. Working in a small group, re-read the book.
2. For each page, find a child who had a similar experience when finding out about his long-ago relatives.
3. Encourage the children to talk about who they know that talks to them about long-ago relatives and who does not.
4. Talk about storytellers and how there have always been storytellers to help people remember and know about long ago. This is true no matter where your long-ago relatives lived.

Cognitive Development

Positive self-image, oral expression, understanding of history, problem solving.

African Necklace

Materials

Pre-cut African continent, black for background piece; cut a second continent in three pieces — one part yellow, one part red, one part green; beads to be strung (macaroni, clay, glass); cord, yarn or string; your scrap box.

1. Show your children the continent of Africa on a map, and tell them that you are going to make a necklace. Remind them of *All Us Come Cross the Water*.

2. Let a small group of children work in the art area.

3. Fit the three colored pieces of Africa together.

4. Glue the pieces on the black background shape. The children may want to add to the shape from the scrap box.

5. String the beads and Africa on the necklace.

6. Your children may need help in getting the map in the middle of the cord.

7. A child who does not want to make a necklace may make a headband or another project.

Another Thought

A long-wearing necklace could be made by laminating the African continent and making clay beads. See *Mudworks*.

Cognitive Development

Visual discrimination, representation, eye-hand coordination, oral language.

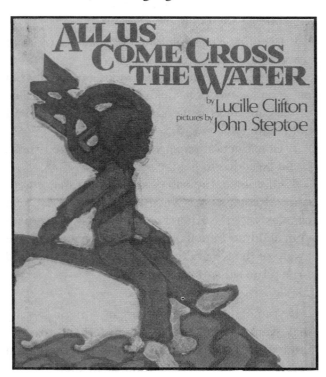

All Us Come Cross The Water, illustration copyright © (1973) by John Steptoe, with permission of the Estate of John Steptoe.

Long-Ago Day

Materials

Senior citizens, children's relatives, book with pictures of many kinds of immigrants.

1. This is another opportunity to have older Americans in your classroom.

2. Talk with your children about who told them stories about their long-ago relatives. Ask if they would like to invite these people to the classroom.

3. Let the children make an invitation to Long-Ago Day. You should also write a letter explaining the day.

4. Relatives may want to bring a family favorite dish. Encourage each relative to bring something the children can eat or touch. Ask for something that was brought from across the water if available, or something that was made or bought here but originally came from across the water.

5. Begin with a short circle time. Then set up the relatives around the room so that your children can visit the people they find interesting.

6. Eating may take place as a large group. Or the children could go from person to person and nibble.

Another Thought

For children who have no one to come, find a resource person in your school to represent those children. Be sure to take pictures.

Cognitive Development

Oral history, visual discrimination, oral language, positive self-concept.

Things Our Children Like To Do

113

Kwanzaa

By Deborah M. Newton Chocolate   *Illustrated by Melodye Rosales*

In the spirit of binding today's children with the heritage of their ancestors, Ms. Chocolate has written her first book.

This is the first book Ms. Rosales has illustrated about African-American experiences. She has illustrated children's literature for many years.

Summary:
A young boy explains the meaning of Kwanzaa. He tells the events of his household over the seven day celebration.

Children's Press Chicago, 1990

STORY TIME

Theme
Pride in the customs and values of your ancestors. Following, learning and adapting traditions.

Introduction
1. No matter what the age of the child with whom you are sharing this book, the cover illustration is the perfect introduction.

2. Listen to your children's comments about the cover, allowing them to relate their interest and experience to the actions of the young boy.

3. You may have some children in your class whose families celebrate Kwanzaa. This can bring life to the story.

4. Lighting candles is a part of many kinds of ceremonies. Be sensitive to the cultural experiences of your children. Help them to relate to the children in this book.

Reading
Young children will be interested in the picture story. They will easily tell what's happening in their own words. You can add factual information by reading part of the text, or simply by telling the essential part of the text.

Response

1. Encourage your children to relate their own family experiences to the Kwanzaa celebration.

2. At the same time, help your children understand that Kwanzaa is a special celebration of its own.

EXTENSIONS

Make a Kinara
Materials

Piece of wood 2"x2"x10"; permanent fine line markers; soda bottle caps, spray painted: 3 red, 3 green, 1 black candle for each child; hot glue gun or wood glue; book: *Kwanzaa*.

Note: Construction paper tube candles could be made. Wax candles should be the responsibility of the child's parent at home.

1. Encourage each child to decorate her piece of wood with the fine line markers.

2. Glue the candle holders (soda bottle caps) in place on the wooden stick. (Leave the flat surface of the caps and the wood unpainted; the glue will hold better.)

3. Construction paper candles or painted sticks could be added to get the total effect.

4. Of course, fire safety should be a major concern. "Rules" about when and where to use real candles with the Kinara should be discussed with your children. Parents should intentionally be made aware of the Kinara that goes home with the child from a fire safety aspect.

Another Thought

If your children are not African-American, they may want to adapt the Kinara to reflect their cultural roots. Encourage them to relate important ceremonies that include candles in their experience. Help them make a candle holder they can use at home with their families.

Cognitive Development

Using a concrete object to represent feelings and ideas, eye-hand coordination, fire safety rules.

Cook Sweet Potato Pie

Materials

1 pint boiled and mashed sweet potatoes, 4 eggs, 1 cup cream, 1 cup butter, 1 cup brown sugar, 1 tbsp. allspice, pie crust, 3 bowls, fork, potato masher, electric beater.

1. Pre-heat oven, talk about the changes that will take place in the ingredients.

2. Your children may be skilled enough with knives or peelers to peel and cut the sweet potato, then boil until soft. Or have one store-grown sweet potato for the children to handle, and used canned sweet potatoes to make the pie.

3. Using an electric mixer or hand masher, the children should be able to mash up the potatoes.

4. Give children turns at cracking the eggs and beating them with a fork.

5. In another bowl, have a child cream the butter and sugar together. Then add 1 cup cream.

6. Another child can combine all the ingredients together in one bowl.

7. Pour into a prepared pie crust and cook for about 35 minutes at 350^0.

8. Be sure to make enough pies for everyone to have a piece.

Another Thought

Cook other traditional African foods with your children. Recipes are available in cookbooks at your library.

Cognitive Development

Appreciating unusual foods, pride in foods of one's culture, chemical changes in ingredients, visual perception, oral language.

Make Zawadi

NOTE: Look in the African Folktales & Customs and the Family chapters for directions to make other gifts.

Materials

White cotton cloth 18"x36", crayons, white drawing paper 18"x12", iron, newsprint.

1. Ask who would like to make a scarf.

2. Children can draw a heavy crayon picture/design on the white drawing paper. Encourage the children to make heavy, dark lines.

3. Print the drawing on the cloth by using a hot iron.

4. Put down newsprint, lay down the white cloth, then place the drawing face down on the white cloth. Iron the drawing paper for about 10 seconds.

5. Depending on how heavy the crayon marks are, you may be able to make 3 prints to fill up the cloth. Or the child may need to make 3 drawings to fill the cloth.

Another Thought

Your children may want to keep this "present." So make two: one to keep and one to give away.

Cognitive Development

Eye-hand coordination, visual discrimination, positive self-esteem, pleasure of giving to others.

Have a Kwanzaa Feast

Materials

Foods from your children's homes.

1. Talk to your parents. Ask who cooks collard greens, black-eyed peas, cornbread, fried chicken, sweet potato pie, peach cobbler, rice pudding, carrot cake, fruit salad or other African dishes.

2. Depending on your cooking equipment, the parents could help their children cook at school or bring the food prepared from home.

3. Let the children light their mishumaa saba (seven candles).

4. Enjoy the food and fellowship.

5. Look in the African Folktales & Customs Chapter for activities your children can share with their families.

Another Thought

If your families are unable to come to school, have a feast just with your children.

Cognitive Development

Respect for African-American culture.

Additional Books

Cedric McClester, *Kwanzaa*, Grumbs & Thomas, Publishers, Inc., 142 West 72nd St., Suite 9, New York, NY 10023

Morninghouse, Sundaira (1992) *Habari Gani? What's the News? A Kwanzaa Story*, Open Hand Publishing, Inc., Seattle WA.

115

The Black Snowman

Written by Phil Mendez   *Illustrated by Carole Byard*

This is Mendez's first book, and he shows a feeling for the complex interactions of heritage and family with life events.

Byard's familiarity with both African and African-American life contributes to her emotional illustrations.

Summary:

Two brothers build a snowman from black snow. Through pride in their African heritage and caring for one another, both boys find hope through the magic of the snowman.

Scholastic, 1989

STORY TIME

Theme

Pride in African heritage, self-esteem, identifying feelings, family relationships.

Introduction

1. This book has many small stories written into one long story. Evaluate your children's needs and experiences to know how best to present the book.

2. An easy introduction would be to read only the short story about the kente. Be sure to wear a kente. Have one or more kentes for your classroom. Make the kente and *The Black Snowman* available for the children to use. Then your children will come to you asking that the story be read.

Reading

1. Review the kente story. You could wear the class kente. Your children could wear theirs.

2. Show your children the illustrations and read the first paragraph. Depending on the experience of your children, you may want to tell the rest of the text.

3. Each illustration can be read as well as told about. On re-readings of the book, more of the text can be read.

4. Starting with the family relationship theme and moving to include the snowman's magic, then the African heritage, will allow your children to grow as Jacob grew. This may take three separate readings. For the children to relate to the total message of the book, the time will be well spent.

Response

1. Give your children time to believe in the magic of the kente. Use it for story time when reading or telling other stories.

2. Encourage your children to talk about Jacob's angry feelings. Let them express their angry feelings and accept their feelings as valid. For a child to control and change feelings, they must first be identified by the child.

3. Help the children identify the pride the African warriors gave to Jacob.

4. Let the children tell you why Jacob changed his mind about looking for cans and bottles in the garbage.

EXTENSIONS

Make a Kente

Materials

One yard of white cloth for each child, bright-colored permanent magic markers, cardboard or some kind of backing (use this to protect your tabletop from the markers when they bleed through), book: *The Black Snowman*.

1. Let your children tell you about the kente and its magic powers. Ask if they would like to make one.

2. Show your children some illustrations of African designs. Tell them the kente is theirs and they can have any design they would like on it.

3. Be sure each child has plenty of work space. He should be able to spread the cloth out so he can see the whole piece.

4. Plenty of markers should be provided. Each

116

child should be able to have two markers at any time. Work in small groups.

5. Give your children many opportunities to tell stories wearing the kente.

6. Display the kente. Some children may want to sleep with them at naptime.

Another Thought

A kente could also be tie-dyed or drawn on with crayons (ironing the kente between blank news-print will set in the crayon, or you can use special easy-melting fabric crayons made for this pur-pose).

Cognitive Development

Positive self-image, Ashanti tribal customs, eye-hand coordination, visual perception, oral language.

Make A Snowman

Materials

Play dough, food coloring, yarn, colorful cloth strips, construction paper circles for eyes, nose and mouth, pieces of felt scraps for hat. Books: *Mudworks, The Black Snowman.*

1. Have the children help make the play dough or color some dough you already have.

2. Show your children the story again. Re-read the part when the children decide to make a snowman.

3. Give your children some play dough. Ask each child what color she would like her snowman to be. By respecting the child's right to choose a color, you are teaching her to respect that all colors are good choices.

4. Encourage the children to talk abut the magic of the Black Snowman. They will also want to say that their snowmen are magical.

5. Use your art scrap box, construction paper circles, and the kente to dress the snowman.

6. Let the snowman dry.

Another Thought

Each snowman's magical powers can be dictated on a 3" x 5" card and placed next to it. While the snowmen are drying out, encourage your children to have visiting adults read the cards.

NOTE: There is a construction paper snowman in *Children & Scissors.* Be sure to let your children choose what color they want their snowmen to be.

Cognitive Development

Representation, imagination, eye-hand coordi-nation, oral language.

I Hate Mural

Materials

Pictures, children's drawings or paintings, book: *The Black Snowman.*

1. Leaf through the book and help your children remember all the things Jacob was angry about.

2. Let the children talk about them. Give your children the opportunity to say, "I hate that, too."

3. Understand children's need to say, "I hate."

4. Ask the children if they would like to put up an I Hate mural.

5. Work in small groups. The children could draw or paint a picture, cut a picture out of a magazine, bring the wrapper or label from a hated food or cut a construction paper shape.

6. The more variety you have in the art media, the better the message that everyone hates different things will come across. It is important that every child's "hate" is given value. This will help the children empathize with each other.

7. Have the children add their "hates" to the mural and help the other children respect the hates. Then start talking about what you can do when you hate something. Help your children feel they have the power to change the hate. Jacob learned that black people can be strong. He saved his brother. A child who hates broccoli may negotiate with his mother to eat green beans. A child who hates himself can learn the good things about himself.

Another Thought

If the word "hate" is too strong for you, use "don't like" or "makes me angry."

Cognitive Development

Identifying and expressing feelings, learning how other people feel, figuring out how to change feel-ings.

Another Book

Hartman, Wendy, *All The Magic in the World,* (1993) Dutton Children's Books, New York

117

Tar Beach

Written and illustrated by Faith Ringgold

This is Ringgold's first book, taken from a quilt painting she completed in 1988 and augmented by her story and additional paintings in her colorful, primitive style.

Summary:
A young girl flies in her imagination as she lies on the rooftop she calls "Tar Beach," with Harlem and the George Washington Bridge as backdrop.

Crown Publishers Inc., 1991

STORY TIME

Theme

Making a child feel powerful, imagination, life in Harlem in 1939.

Introduction

1. Ask your children if they would like to be magic and make things happen, maybe even be able to fly!

2. Show the cover of the book. Tell your children someone in the picture was magic and could fly. Let them show you the magic person.

3. Read the title and encourage your children to tell you why they think the story is called *Tar Beach*.

Reading

1. On first reading, help your children relate to the magical powers of Cassie Louise Lightfoot.

2. Use Cassie flying to help your children feel powerful. You may want to talk about the illustrations and use only some of the text.

3. On re-reading, talk about Harlem, the George Washington Bridge, New York City, and what is a tar beach.

Response

1. Let your children tell you to where they would like to fly.

2. Help them remember what Cassie did so her father could own the union building.

3. Talk with your children about why the family was on Tar Beach and not inside watching TV.

EXTENSIONS

Tar Beach Picnic and Flyabout

Materials

A spot in your classroom or on the playground, food and drink, toys available in the 1930's (balls, jump ropes), pieces of cloth or towels to lie down on, book: *Tar Beach*.

1. Ask your children if they would like to go on a Tar Beach picnic. Decide with the children where the beach will be.

2. Plan a lunch or snack to take outside or eat in your room on a tar beach.

3. Talk with your children about the toys that are in your room. Choose some that you could take on a picnic and that children would have played with in 1939.

4. Have your picnic. Clean up the litter.

5. Each child should have a "beach towel" on which to lie down . Now it is flying time! Decide on some "do" rules on how to fly safely.

6. They may lie on their backs, close their eyes and make a picture in their minds about flying. Or they may get up and put their arms out and fly. Make sure they know the safety rules. Children will choose how and where they are flying.

Another Thought

Go to a real beach!

Cognitive Development

Imagination, relating to the past, oral language, planning for an event.

Quilt Picture

Materials

Drawing paper, markers/crayons, squares of cloth, glue, books: *Tar Beach, The Quilt, The Patchwork Quilt.*

1. Talk about the illustrations in *Tar Beach.*
2. Help the children recognize the patchwork borders. If you have read *The Quilt* and *The Patchwork Quilt,* show these to your children. Talk about how a quilt gets made.
3. Show your children Ringgold's picture in the back of the book and tell them about how she makes quilts and who she knows who made quilts.
4. Ask your children who would like to make a quilt picture.
5. Working in small groups in the art area, let the children draw any picture they like on the drawing paper. Then glue on a border of cloth squares.
6. Some children may want to put some of the cloth squares in their pictures.
7. The cloth squares could come from old clothes that belong to your children.

Another Thought

You could draw the picture on a piece of cloth. Then iron different bright squares of cloth to the borders of the picture, using iron-on hemming fabric (such as Stitch Witchery.)

Cognitive Development

Combining art media, visual discrimination, eye-hand coordination.

1939 Day

Materials

Photographs of your community in the 1930's and 1940's, including cars, toys, clothes, houses, movie stars, children's books.

1. Tell your children that you are going to have a 1939 Tar Beach Day. All day long you will be acting like Cassie Louise and Be Be.
2. Look at the illustrations in *Tar Beach* and talk about what the children wore and what they ate.
3. Get your parents involved by asking them for photographs and stories of people they know who lived then.
4. All of your girls can wear dresses and all your boys wear short pants for the day.
5. If you have two water fountains, mark one "white" and one "colored." Talk with your children about segregation. Read the page in *Tar Beach* where Cassie Louise says her father is colored or a half-breed Indian. Talk about what that means. Depending on your class makeup, your own feelings, and your relationships with your parents, enact the social rules of segregation in your classroom.
6. Have one of your children's parents or grandparents come and tell what segregation was like.
7. End the day by talking about how the laws of today give people more chances to be what they want to be.

Another Thought

In your talk about segregation, expand the concept of stereotyping by including the stereotypical roles men and women had.

Cognitive Development

Living social history, examining fairness in rules, expressing feelings, learning from the past, oral language.

NOTE: Read the extensions for Dr. Martin Luther King, Jr. for more ideas about presenting segregation.

Another Book:

Ringgold, F. (1993) *Dinner at Aunt Connie's House,* Hyperion Books.

119

Cornrows

Written by Camille Yarbrough

Yarbrough's poetic writing style evokes the royal origins of the hairstyle today called "cornrows." With her African experiences,

Illustrated by Carole Byard

Byard brings alive that continent to help children celebrate their blackness.

Summary:
Two children have their hair braided by their mother and great-grandmother and enjoy a loving experience while the women tell tales of Africa and African Americans.

Coretta Scott King Award

Coward-McCann Inc., 1979

STORY TIME

Theme

Self-worth, respecting heritage, learning from others.

Introduction

1. Talk about hair styles and the names for different hair styles. The children will know many of the current styles.

2. Compare cornrows to other braids and listen for the names the children may have for braiding and plaiting hair.

3. Ask children if anyone in their families tells stories to them.

4. Get girls to tell who braids their hair and what happens during that time. Get boys to tell about barber-shop talk.

5. Show the children the cover of the book and get their comments.

6. Tell them you are going to read a story about hair and hairstyling.

Reading

1. Read the story, showing the pictures, or just "read" the pictures.

2. Ask if the hairstyles are like those of people they know or people in the class.

Response

1. Ask the children, "How do you decide if something is pretty or you like the way it looks?"

2. Ask the children how people act if they think something is pretty or nice and they are proud of it. How do the children act when they are wearing a new shirt or a new hair style?

3. Ask what they do when someone tells them they look nice. Ask what they do when they are proud of something and someone else says it is ugly or no good.

EXTENSIONS

Braid Children's Hair

NOTE: Be sure your parents know and give permission for their children's hair to be braided.

Materials

Hair bows, child's comb/brush, colored rubber bands, beads, ribbons.

1. Invite adults into the class to help braid children's hair.

2. Encourage adults to tell stories while they are braiding hair.

3. Teach children to braid hair.

4. Encourage children to tell what happens when they get their hair braided.

Another Thought

Children with short hair can have a long, gentle hair-brushing to tell about.

Cognitive Development

Relating an everyday occurrence to family history, storytelling, manual dexterity, friendliness between generations.

120

Style Show

1. Write notes home so parents can braid their children's hair in a special way. Ask them to tell their children a family story or a folktale while braiding the children's hair.

2. Include in the note the fact that the children will be telling about what happened while their hair was being braided.

3. Have the children with braids show off their cornrows or plaits and tell what happened when they were sitting to have their hair braided.

4. Each child can make up a name for the braids.

Cognitive Development

Learning about family traditions, relating occurrences, oral language.

Class Book and Tape

Materials

Camera, film, tape recorder or camcorder and tape, drawing paper.

1. Take a picture of each child's hairdo and on the paper write the name the child calls the braids or style. Put the pictures on the paper with the child's name. If using a camcorder, have the child hold the paper with his name and the name of the braids and speak the names while being taped.

2. Make an audiotape or videotape of the children telling how their hair was done.

Another Thought

Be sensitive to your girls with short hair and your boys. Take their pictures and tape their tales also.

Cognitive Development

Oral expression, imagination, family tradition, keeping family and class records.

Learn How To Braid

Materials

Three different color strips of material (one yard x 2" wide), staple gun, cardboard, elastic bands.

1. Firmly staple lengths of cloth in three different colors to a piece of cardboard. Write child's name on the cardboard.

2. Show how braids are made. Place the child directly in front of you with his back to you. Ask another child to hold the cardboard firmly while you hold the fabric pieces and show the first child how to braid with the fabric. Then ask the child to move the pieces from one of your hands to the other. When the children learn the pattern, they will want to hold the cloth. Continue to watch the braiding until the child moves off by himself. Make the material available for many tries.

3. When the braids are complete, help the children to tie a bow or place a colorful elastic band or barrette at the end to hold it in place.

4. If you have parents' permission, the children can then practice their new skills on each other's hair.

Cognitive Development

Close concentration on a task, manual dexterity, using a newfound skill, following oral direction.

Another Thought

Children may twist or wrap instead of braiding. As long as they are pleased with the outcome, that is fine. Give help as the children request it.

Another Book

Johnson, A. (1989) *Tell Me a Story, Mama,* New York: Orchard.

121

Follow the Drinking Gourd

Written and illustrated by Jeannette Winter

Winter began writing and illustrating children's books in a natural progression ... she always liked telling stories with pictures. Children will love the old story and will want to study her fascinating paintings.

Summary:
Peg Leg Joe teaches a song slaves used to escape via the Underground Railroad.

Alfred A. Knopf Inc., 1988

STORY TIME

Theme

Choosing to stand up for your beliefs, changing the conditions you live in, solving social problems.

Introduction

1. Say the word "slave," and ask your children what it means. Accept as valid your children's meanings.

2. Focus on any information your children have about slaves in the United States of America.

3. Show both of the books, if they are available to you.

4. Tell your children that these are stories about how slaves escaped to freedom.

5. Focus on *Following the Drinking Gourd* and the Big Dipper. Ask if any of your children have ever seen the Big Dipper in the night sky.

Reading

1. These illustrations are interesting enough that your children can make up a story about the people and their journey.

2. On reading, they will want to know more about the people and why they were running away.

3. Talk about how Joe and his family felt along the way, and how they felt when they reached freedom.

Response

1. Turn to the page with the sign, "Negroes for Sale." Talk to your children about the things that they can buy at the store, and what people sell at the store.

2. Ask if they think people should be for sale. Would they like someone to sell somebody they knew?

3. Often, the evil of slavery is portrayed through the example of the mean and cruel master. This allows people to take the position that good and kind masters were only protecting their slaves and helping them to exist in the world.

4. ...This author suggests that the buying and selling of people is evil enough to teach young children. To concentrate on the one idea that nobody has the right to buy and sell other people is certainly a strong and clear message for young children to think about and to believe in.

5. Within your classroom, you are already in many ways helping your children to be kind to and respect one another. Teach the lesson of not being mean and cruel to children in relation to mutual respect and caring.

6. The physical cruelty many slaves suffered will be discussed as your children study history. Your message of not selling and buying people is a strong enough one for your children at this level.

7. The escape of the slaves is an exciting tale. Give your children the opportunity to show the pictures and tell the stories of their favorite parts.

122

EXTENSIONS

Make the Big Dipper

Materials

Glue-on or pre-cut stars, construction paper squares (4" x 4"), background paper, glue, scissors, book: *Follow the Drinking Gourd.*

1. Re-read the story. Be sure the children identify the Drinking Gourd in each illustration.
2. You may want to make chalk dots where the stars should be placed.
3. Make the stars of the Big Dipper all one color. The children can then choose other color stars to fill their night sky.
4. Encourage your children to take their Drinking Gourds home and tell their families about them.

Another Thought

If you have a dark place in your room or school, stick pinholes in the shape of the Big Dipper in a piece of black construction paper, tape it to the lens of a flashlight, and shine the image on the ceiling.

Cognitive Development

Visual discrimination, recall of information, eye-hand coordination, oral language.

Things Our Children Like To Do

Act Out The Story

Materials

Clothing from your housekeeping area, cardboard boxes, books: *Follow the Drinking Gourd, The Drinking Gourd.*

1. Re-read the story and ask your children if they would like to act out the story on the playground.
2. Look at the illustrations and identify what you have in your classroom that could be used to act out the story.
3. Gather your players and their props and move out onto your play area.
4. After you are re-settled on the playground, choose the children to play the parts. If you have enough children, combine the two stories.
5. Before starting the play, be sure to discuss the safety concerns of play on your particular playground.
6. Your play may get very involved and complex, or may only be brief. Follow the lead of the children.
7. After you re-group, again discuss why the slaves were escaping, the choice they made so that nobody could buy or sell them.
8. Also discuss the great internal strength it took to run away, to change their lives.

Another Thought

If your children become interested in the story, this is a play you could put on for other classes.

Cognitive Development

Role-playing, empathy, oral language, recalling a sequence, body language.

Another Book

Ringgold, Faith (1992) *Aunt Harriet's Underground Railroad in the Sky,* Crown Publishers, Inc. New York.

Book of Black Heroes, Vol. 2

Great Women in the Struggle

Editor, Toyomi Igus

Contributing writers: Toyomi Igus, Veronica Freeman Ellis, Diane Patrick, Valerie Wilson Wesley. For more information, please read in the Author/Illustrator section.

Summary:
Eighty-three biographies of contemporary black women.

Just Us Books, 1991

STORY TIME

Theme

Women who were and are dedicated to improving the life of their people.

Introduction

1. At the beginning of the year, when you know something about the women on the cover, show the book to a small group of children.

2. Ask them if they know any of the women in the picture. They may want to tell you their stories. Listen.

3. Tell them this book is about Black Women or African American women who used their own brains to do smart things.

4. Tell them your class will be using the book all year long to learn about these women.

Reading

1. Ask your children to tell you someone they have seen on TV and you'll look and see if they are in the book.

2. Whoever your children say, look up that person and talk about her.

3. Depending on the age of your children, you can read the bio, or just tell about the woman.

Response

1. Let your children look through the book and see who they know.

2. Do use this book as a reference throughout the year.

EXTENSIONS

Circle Time

Materials

The musical resources in your classroom.

1. Look in the section on performing artists.

2. Choose one at a time to dance and sing to the music she loves.

Another Thought

Choose a woman not listed and learn something about her. Explore her music with your children. Read *Charlie Parker Played be bop*.

Cognitive Development

Knowledge of women in history, moving to music, learning songs.

House/Block Area

Materials

Items your children use to play hospital.

1. On a day when your children are playing hospital or as a planned activity, take this book into the House/Block area.

2. Show your children the pictures of these women in medicine. Encourage your children to use their names as your children play. If your children do not, you take on one of these women's names and join in the play as that woman.

Another Thought

Find pictures of medical women in your community and give your children the opportunity to role play those women. Invite them to your classroom.

Cognitive Development

Role -play representation, oral language, body language.

Dramatic Play

Materials

Your dress up costumes.

Use the freedom fighters section and act out these people.

Another Thought

See *Rosa Parks*, *Martin Luther King, Jr.* and *Harriet Tubman* books for further activities.

Art Area

Materials

Your art materials, sand and water tables.

Artists and scientists can come to life through your children's activity in the art area. Introduce them to your children.

Another Thought

Use *George Washington Carver* and *Stop & Go* activities.

Cognitive Development

Creativity, changing materials by shapes and color consistency.

Book of Black Heroes
Volume Two
Great
WOMEN
In The Struggle

AN INTRODUCTION FOR YOUNG READERS
Toyomi Igus
Veronica Freeman Ellis   Diane Patrick   Valerie Wilson Wesley

Cover Copyright © 1991, Just Us Books, reproduced with permission from Just Us Books, Inc., Publisher.

125

Additional Activities In This Book

Charlie Parker Played be bop
A Weed Is A Flower
Picture Book of Martin Luther King, Jr.
Stop and Go
Life Doesn't Frighten Me

Outside Play

Materials

Your outside play equipment.

There is a section on athletes. Take that section of the book to the play ground with you and act out the athletes.

Another Thought

Encourage your chidren to role-play other athletes.

Cognitive Development

Physical coordination and development, eye-hand coordination, role play.

Another Book

Hudson, Wade and Wesley, Valerie Wilson, 1988 *Afro-Bits:Book of Black Heroes from A to Z.*, Just Us Books, Orange, NJ,

Rosa Parks

Written by Eloise Greenfield

This book received the Carter G. Woodson Award. Greenfield has received many awards for her biography and fiction for children.

Illustrated by Eric Marlow

Marlow's colorful illustrations complement the Greenfield text.

Summary:

An illustrated life for children of Rosa Parks, the heroine who refused to move to the back of the bus.

Thomas Y. Crowell, 1973

STORY TIME

Theme

Rosa Parks' refusal to move to the back of the bus, a positive self-concept, taking positive action to right a wrong, facing consequences.

NOTE: This is a talk-about book. The amount of reading depends on your children's listening skill level.

Introduction

1. Ask who has ridden the city bus. Encourage your children to tell about riding the bus.
2. Talk with the children about how they decide where to sit. Then show them the cover of the book and tell them about Rosa Parks, that she had to sit in the back of the bus because that was what the law (rules) said.

Reading

1. Show the illustrations and tell your children the story.
2. Select parts of Greenfield's text to read.
3. Help your children understand that Rosa Parks had thought about how she was being treated for a long time. She decided to stand up for what she thought was right.
4. Talk about the African Americans who wanted to change the rule about where to sit on the bus, how they decided to walk and go to the judge to have the rule changed so they could sit anywhere they wanted to on the bus.

Response

1. Encourage your children to talk about rules being fair to everyone.

2. Also talk about how you made up the rules in your classroom, and why you have the rules.
3. Ask your children if they would like a rule that lets only one child always be the line leader. Talk about fair rules.

EXTENSIONS

Look at Photos

Materials

Book: *Rosa Parks* by Kai Friese, Silver Burdett Press, 1990.

Use the photos of Rosa Parks and her experiences in this book to make her life more realistic to your children.

Act Out Rosa Parks

Materials

Furniture, clothes and props from your room, book: one of the Rosa Parks books.

1. Look at the book again and encourage your children to tell you about Rosa Parks.
2. Ask them if they would like to put on a play about Rosa Parks.
3. Talk through a sequence of events in Rosa Parks' life that the children remember and think are important.

4. Decide with your children who will play the roles.

5. Arrange your room for the scenes.

6. Everyone who wants to be in the play should be able to find a part.

Another Thought

Make your play part of your "We Shall Overcome March with Dr. Martin Luther King, Jr." (see Appendix).

Cognitive Development

Role-playing, recalling a sequence of events, positive self-image, problem-solving, oral language, body language.

Harriet Tubman

Written by Kathie Billingslea Smith *Illustrated by James Seward* *Cover by Joseph Forte*

Smith's easy-to-read text tells straightforwardly of the hardships and triumphs of Tubman's life.

The 19th Century and the Underground Railway are evoked in Seward's illustrations and Forte's cover portrait.

Summary:
An illustrated story for children of the life of the slavery abolitionist.

Julian Messner, 1988

127

STORY TIME

Theme

Changing your life, escape from slavery, helping others.

Introduction

1. Talk about what it meant to be a slave. Explain that people were bought and sold like property and that they could not say, "I do not want to go there." Even the children were owned if they are born into slavery.

2. Encourage your children to talk about being a slave and what they would do if they were slaves.

Reading

1. Use this book and the Harriet Tubman biography by Judith Bentley (Franklin Watts, 1990) to tell the story of how Harriet Tubman grew up.

2. Talk with your children abut how Tubman escaped from being a slave, and why she went back to help other slaves.

3. Talk about all the people who worked in the Underground Railway.

4. Tell about the things Harriet Tubman did for people when slavery ended.

Response

1. Hand the books to your children. Let them tell about the illustrations.

2. Encourage your children to talk about why Harriet Tubman would go back to the South to get more slaves.

3. If you are using the Kathie Billingslea Smith story of Harriet Tubman, be sure to help the children notice the strength in Joseph Forte's cover portrait of Tubman. The children will learn from this and other illustrations in both books.

Another Thought

Read Judith Bentley's book of Harriet Tubman as an additional resource.

EXTENSIONS

The Drinking Gourd and *Follow the Drinking Gourd* and their extensions will help your children understand Harriet Tubman's role in history.

Another Book

Ringgold, Faith (1992) *Aunt Harriet's Underground Railroad in the Sky*, Crown Publishers, Inc.

Uncle Jed's Barbershop

Written By Margarie King Mitchell

·Margarie has written this story based on her uncle's experiences

Illustrated by James Ransome

By painting his people, James gives us an insight into their emotions.

Summary:
Sara Jean's tale of her favorite uncle's life goal and the role his love for her played in his life.

Simon and Schuster, Books for Young Readers, 1993

STORY TIME

Theme
Having a goal and caring for others.

Introduction

128

1. Talk about barber shops and other places where people get their hair cut.

2. Explain this is a story that happened a long time ago.

Reading

1. Ransome's illustrations and your telling of the story will hold the attention of young children.

2. With older children, talk about this being a listening story. Listen to their comments. Then continue to read.

3. These words flow so easily your children will listen with little comment. They'll want to know what is going to happen next. Use it as a "read aloud" book.

Response

1. If there is time on the first reading, go back and encourage comment on the story and the illustrations.

2. With a small group, re-read -- allowing children to hold the book and examine the illustrations.

3. Use the peoples' clothing and transportation to help children realize this story happened a long time ago.

4. Give your children the opportunity to tell about good things people they know have done for them.

EXTENSIONS

I Want To Be

Materials
Magazines and catalogs, scissors, background paper, book: *Uncle Jed's Barbershop*.

1. Re-read the book. Emphasize Uncle Jed's decision of wanting to own his own shop.

2. Talk about how he had to be patient and save his money.

3. Listen to your children tell you what they would like to be when they grow up.

4. Be sure the magazines and catalogs you have available are racially, culturally and gender mixed.

5. At the same time reinforce the idea that this is the job I want to do, not that I want to look like this person.

6. Cut out the pictures. Give each child a choice of making his own poster, or make a class poster, display. Class displays often turn into a week's project.

Another Thought
Gather the career books in your school or local library. Allow your children to look through the books and talk about the jobs.

Cognitive Development
Future time - present time, delaying gratification, positive self-image.

I Wanted To Be

Materials

People from your community, photographs from them at work, any equipment they can bring to your classroom.

1. There are several ways to organize this as an activity in your classroom.

2. Invite one individual to come. Relate the job to something you are doing in your classroom. Remember the everyday things - - painting, cooking, books, etc.

3. Also remember the jobs of the people at your school. Uncle Jed had so many customers because he took pride in his work and did an excellent job. Help your children to realize it is important how you do the job as well as what job you have.

4. Another way to organize: have a career day. Invite several people to come to your school and tell about their jobs. We set up centers so that children moved about every 15 minutes, with 5 minutes traveling and settling down time.

5. Our children (3, 4 and 5 years old), stayed interested and on task for 2 hours. This gives you 6 time slots. In some settings we had more than one person; health care: nurse, doctor, etc.

6. Encourage the adults to talk about their jobs and have something the children can touch. Encourage your children to tell about experiences they may have had with each of these adults.

Another Thought

Field trips to the jobs are always appropriate and exciting!

Cognitive Development

Relating to an adult, classification, oral language, listening skills, positive self-esteem.

Additional Activities

Daddy and I
Things I Like About Grandma

Another Book

Feelings, Tom, 1991, *Tommy Traveler in the World of Black History*, Black Butterfly Children's Books, New York.

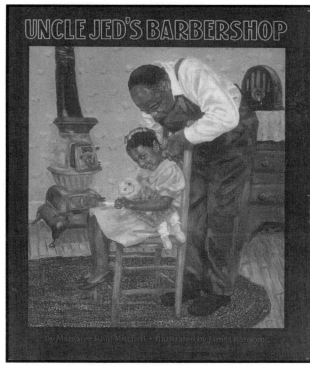

Jacket Illustration Copyright © 1993 by James Ransome with permission from Simon & Schuster, Publisher.

129

Our Barber

Materials

Your children's barber, a barber shop.

1. Invite your children's barber to the class.

2. Go to the barber shop.

3. Be sure that any child who has his hair cut also has parental permission.

Another Thought

Encourage your children to use items in House/Block to represent barber tools and play barber. Be sure to talk about who can actually cut a child's hair. See *Cornrows* for activities for girls.

Cognitive Development

Oral language, positive self-image, relating to adults.

A Weed Is A Flower: The Life of George Washington Carver

Written and illustrated by Aliki

Aliki visited a school where they cooked a whole meal made of peanuts, as George Washington Carver had done, and immediately wanted to write his story. Her remarkable paintings will delight children.

Summary:
Text and pictures present the life of the man, born a slave, who became a scientist and dedicated his life to improving the agriculture of the South.

Simon and Schuster Inc., 1988

STORY TIME

Theme
Life of George Washington Carver.

130 Introduction
1. Ask your children if they like peanut butter.
2. Tell them you are going to tell them a story about the man who invented peanut butter.

Reading
1. Use the pictures in *A Weed Is A Flower* and tell the story.
2. Each time you re-tell the story, you can add information. Encourage your children to tell what they already know about each illustration.

Response
1. Use the illustrations in *A Pocketful of Goobers* to tell about the peanut's African origin.
2. Each time you talk about something new, connect it to information your children are telling you about George Washington Carver.

EXTENSIONS

Make Peanut Butter

Materials
Blender, roasted peanuts in shells, oil, aprons, crackers or bread, spreading knife.

1. Working in a small group, tell the children they are going to be scientists like George Washington Carver.

2. Ask your children to tell you about Carver. When one tells about peanuts, ask if they would like to make peanut butter.

3. In your classroom, making peanut butter can really be an experiment. It is not necessary to follow an exact recipe.

4. Give each child some peanuts. Let the children tell you about the shell and which part you can eat and let them shell the peanuts. Be sure they cover their clothes.

5. Have the children put some peanuts in the blender. If they only chop and do not cream, have another child add a very little oil. The sooner you stop the blender, the crunchier it will be. For smooth peanut butter, let it run for a few minutes. Let the children decide which they want.

6. Take the peanut butter out of the blender and put it into a container. Let each child spread his own peanut butter. Small butter knives or large spreaders work best. Jelly or jam can be added.

Another Thought
Make peanut butter play dough with dry milk. Use the dry milk to absorb the oil in the peanut butter and work it like play dough. Raisins, honey, or coconut can be added when the children are ready to eat it. (See *Mudworks*.)

Cognitive Development
Visual discrimination, oral language, observing physical changes.

Making Decisions

Materials

Books: *A Weed Is A Flower, A Pocketful of Goobers.*

1. Ask your children to tell you what they remember about George Washington Carver.

2. Show the illustrations that represent what each child says.

3. As your children tell incidents in George Washington Carver's life, let the children talk about how Carver felt when the event occurred. Ask them what they would do if that happened to them.

4. Tell your children that some people think Carver should have gotten mad at the people who were mean to him. They think he should not have given them his ideas. Encourage them to talk about this idea.

5. Some people thought Carver did the right thing by not getting mad, that he should not have listened to the mean people and that he did right to learn new things and share his ideas with everyone. Ask what the children think.

6. Encourage your children to tell what they would do and why. Accept your children's feelings as valid. Try not to judge them.

7. George Washington Carver felt it was a waste of his time to be mad at anyone. He spent his time learning and helping people. Ask what the children think of his attitude.

Another Book

Mitchell. Barbara(1986), *A Pocketful of Goober's*, Carolrhoda Books, Minneapolis.

Jacket illustration by Aliki copyright ©, 1988, with permission from Simon and Schuster.

Draw A Plant

Materials

Any small plant, paper, pencils, markers/crayons, aprons.

1. Show your children an illustration of George Washington Carver painting. Ask if they would like to draw a plant the way Carver did.

2. Tell your children that Carver looked for real plants to draw and paint.

3. Go outside and let each child pull up a weed or break off a piece of a plant growing wild. Even the best-kept schoolyard has a few weeds.

4...You can paint or draw inside or outside. Talk to the children about the parts of the plant they have chosen.

5..Display the drawings and the children's descriptions of their plants at children's eye level.

Another Thought

If no plants are available to you, draw peanuts or sweet potatoes or anything the children think Carver would like.

Cognitive Development

Visual discrimination, eye-hand coordination creative expression.

Things Our Children Like To Do

131

Stop & Go

Garrett Morgan, Inventor

Written by Doris J. Sims

As a part of her doctoral program, Doris wrote a series of Black History stories.

Illustrated by Chuck Johnson

Your children will enjoy these pictures of days gone by.

Summary:

The story of how and why the stop light was invented.

Children's Cultu-Lit Book Company, 1980

STORY TIME

Theme

Solving problems, being an inventor.

Introduction

132

1. Show the cover of the book and ask your children to name the stop light and tell you what they know about it.

2. Talk about the word " inventor." Help your children to understand how people use their "own brains" to solve problems.

Reading

1. Encourage your children to talk about how the people are dressed and the style of the cars. Ask them if they have seen any like them.

2. Listen to any car accident stories your children may have.

3. Ask your children if they have ever seen a gas mask.

Response

1. Ask children how people got from one place to another a long time ago.

2. Discuss with your children why Mr. Morgan invented the stop light. Help them recall that he did all the thinking himself.

3. Talk about today's stop lights and what has been added (turn arrows, walk signs).

4. Tell your children that in some other places they call the stop light a robot.

5. Talk about the gas mask and why Mr. Morgan would invent it.

EXTENSIONS

Stop Light

Materials

School milk carton, small boxes or a piece of cardboard shaped like a stop light, paint, brushes, construction paper, scissors, glue, tongue depressor, book: *Stop & Go*.

1. Working with a small group, re-read *Stop & Go* then ask if anyone would like to make a stop light.

2. Depending on your resources, give each child a base for the stop light.

3. You may want to have the children paint the box. The milk carton will do better if you wrap black construction paper around it and glue it.

4. Given squares of construction paper, the children can cut their own circles.

5. Because this is a realistic representation, encourage the children to position the lights in a realistic way. You might provide your children with 2 bases; one to be realistic and one for the child to invent his own stop light or something else.

Another Thought

Talk with each child about his stop light. Write down what he can tell you. Be sure to include Garrett Morgan's name. Sent the written report home with the stop light to be read at home.

Cognitive Development

Representation, recalling information, oral language, eye-hand coordination, visual discrimination.

Recreate Horse & Car Accident and Solution

Materials

Plastic horses and cars in your room. Stop light your children made, blocks to designate streets, book: *Stop & Go*.

1. Re-read *Stop & Go* to a small group of children. Ask them if they would like to re-create the accident story.

2. Be sure you have enough cars and buses for several groups to work. One child moves the car, one the horse and one plays Garrett Morgan. Encourage the children to switch roles.

Another Thought

Develop safety rules for moving things and apply them to your tricycle path.

Cognitive Development

Role-playing, understanding consequences, visual discrimination, spatial relations, oral language, recall of events, traffic safety.

Changing the Color of Light

Materials

Several flashlights, colored cellophane, tissue paper or transparent plastic paddles, rubber bands, book: *Stop & Go*.

1. With a small group of children look at the pages of *Stop & Go* that show the stoplight. Talk about why the lights are different colors.

2. Have enough flashlights for the children to work in groups no larger than

3. Show the children how to put the paper on the flashlight with the rubber band.

4. Allow the children to experiment with the colored lights in the darkest place possible in your room. Encourage them to talk about what they are doing.

Another Thought

Make a "stained glass" picture. Use a clear plastic food tray and glue on pieces of colored tissue paper.

Cognitive Development

Visual discrimination, observing natural changes, eye-hand coordination, oral language, positive self-concept.

Make A Class Stop Light

Materials

Large cardboard box, paint, brushes, construction paper, book: *Stop & Go*.

1. This can be done with 2 small groups on different days. Use the book as a reference.

2. Day one, paint the box a solid color.

3. Day two, add the lights by painting the circles or gluing on construction paper circles.

4. Use the stop light with your wheeled vehicles. One child can be the light changer. Place a flap over the lights. The light changer can then lift up the flap to make the light red, green or yellow.

Cognitive Development

Representation, eye-hand coordination, recall of information, re-calling a sequence.

Invent Something

Materials

Scraps of wood, common nails, hammer, safety goggles or styrofoam pieces, glue, rubber bands or paper rolls, construction paper, your art scrap box, scissors, work aprons, book: *Stop & Go*.

1. Have a small group of your children tell you about Garrett Morgan and being an inventor.

2. Present the materials to the children and encourage them to put them together in a way that pleases them.

3. We have suggested 3 different groups of materials. All, some or one may be used, depending on your setting.

Another Thought

This is another opportunity for a child to describe what he has made and have his exact description written down.

Cognitive Development

Creative thinking, planning, eye-hand coordination, positive self-image.

Another Book

Towle, Wendy, *The Real McCoy*, (1993), Scholastic, New York.

133

A Picture Book of Dr. Martin Luther King, Jr.

Written by David A. Adler

Illustrated by Robert Casilla

Biographies of great Americans are Adler's specialty. This is the third in his Picture Book series.

With unusual angles and action paintings, Casilla brings life to another biography of a great African American.

Summary:

A brief, illustrated biography of the Baptist minister and civil rights leader whose philosophy and practice of nonviolent civil disobedience helped American blacks win many battles for equal rights.

Holiday House Inc., 1989

NOTE: Using this book, you will be able to teach your children about Dr. Martin Luther King, Jr. at their developmental level. Another book that could help is *Martin Luther King Jr.: Man of Peace* by Lillie Patterson, which won the 1970 Coretta Scott King Book Award.

134

STORY TIME

Theme

Life of Martin Luther King, Jr.

Introduction

1. Show a picture of Martin Luther King to your children. You may be in for a surprise: there may be some very young children who will recognize him.

2. Talk with your children about King. show them the book(s) and tell them you are going to find out more about him.

Reading (*A Picture Book ...*)

1. Each of the illustrations can be a story in itself. Depending on the age of your children, choose illustrations that would be meaningful to them.

2. Be a storyteller and tell the children what you know and like about Dr. Martin Luther King Jr.

3. Use the photographs in *A Man Who Changed Things* for a realistic picture of the illustrations in *A Picture Book.*

Response

1. Encourage your children to express their thinking.

2. Discuss what has to happen for people to respond to hate with love. Help the children identify things in their lives that they hate. Then help them decide how King would work to make it a positive.

3. Remind the children of *The Black Snowman* and *Tar Beach.*

EXTENSIONS

Martin Luther King Jr's Life

Materials

All the books you can find on Dr. Martin Luther King Jr.

1. Gather a small group of children and look, talk, and read the books.

2. Hand the books to the children. Talk about one page in one of the books. Ask the other children to find the same incident in their books. Compare the pictures and the information given.

3. Young children relate easily to Dr. King's feelings about all children playing together and being friends.

4. Make up a rap, poem, or song about Dr. King. (See Appendix, Songs), for one rap made up by my three-, four-, and five-year-olds.)

Cognitive Development

Gathering information, oral expression, sense of history.

What's Fair: Civil Rights Poster

Materials

Drawing paper, crayons/markers, magazine and newspaper pictures, books: *A Picture Book of Martin Luther King, Jr,* and *Martin Luther King, Jr: A Man Who Changed Things.*

1. Talk with your children about rules that let some people do something and other people not do the same thing.

2. Use classroom examples, such as: children who have on red shoes can be the line leader — nobody else. Children who have on red shoes can get a drink of water — nobody else. Children who have on red shoes can play the record player — nobody else.

3. Then go into the community with your examples: only children with one tooth missing can go to the zoo or a movie or the beach. Only children with one tooth missing can come to this school.

4. In a small group, talk to the children about things that they are glad they can do and "what's fair" about their having a choice to do them.

5. Have each child make a poster showing the things he is glad he can do. As the children are working, use the words "Civil Rights," "Bill of Rights," "Constitution," and "Emancipation Proclamation."

NOTE: Show your children copies of the Civil Rights Acts, the Bill of Rights, the Constitution, and the Emancipation Proclamation. Invite an elected official to come to your classroom. Talk abut voting for people and those people making rules for everyone to live by. Be sure to talk abut judges and what they do when people do not follow the rules.

Another Thought

T-shirts could be made instead of posters.

If there is a facility in your city named in honor of Dr. Martin Luther King, Jr., take the children there to see it on a class field trip. Make a photo of the class with the sign at this place and post it in your classroom.

Cognitive Development

Positive self-image, how rules are made, sense of fair play, visual perception.

Learn "We Shall Overcome"

Materials

Song (see Appendix, page 232)

1. Use your circle time for several days.

2. Talk with your children about when King and his friends sang this song.

3. Find someone who can sing the song in the spiritual tradition and invite him to come to your classroom.

4. Be sure to tape your children singing with this visitor.

Cognitive Development

Oral language, positive self-image, sense of history, listening to others perform.

Peace March

Materials

Tagboard, tempera paints, brushes, headbands (see *Children & Scissors)*, rhythm band instruments, What's Fair Posters.

1. Plan a march with your children. This can be as simple or as elaborate as your situation allows. Be sure to plan for several days.

2. Plan the time, place, length, who will be there, and what the children will wear or carry.

Cognitive Development

Planning for future events, oral expression, applying what has been learned.

Another Book

Green, Carol. (1989) *Martin Luther King,, Jr.: A Man who Changed Things,* Children's Press, Chicago.

Lillegard, Dee, (1987) *My First Martin Luther King Book,* Children's Press, Chicago.

Schlank. Carol Hilgartner (1990) *Martin Luther King, Jr.* Gryshon House, Mt. Rainer, MD.

135

Charlie Parker Played be bop

Written and Illustrated by Chris Raschka
Words and illustrations come alive as Chris applies humor to his talents.

Summary:
These wonderful sounds help children feel Charlie Parker's be bop. Children will want to play saxophone with their whole bodies.

Orchard Books, 1992

136

STORY TIME

Theme

Love of Jazz

Introduction

1. Show the jacket cover to your children. Ask your children to tell you about it.

2. If no one knows the name of the saxophone, you identify it for them.

3. Tell your children Parker played a special kind of music called jazz.

Reading

1. This is definitely a read-it-all-the-way-the-first-time book. Your children will love the sounds and the rhythm. Make them come alive. Read with your whole body.

2. The second time (or the first with very young children) read call and response. You read a line, the children chant the line.

Response

1. Give your children the opportunity to talk about the pictures.

2. Talk about saxophones.

EXTENSIONS

Make Instruments

Materials

Plastic bottles (dish detergent, milk jugs), tape: Charlie Parker "*Jazz 'Round Midnight*," Polygram Records, Inc. 1990.

1. Cut the bottom out of the bottle. You have an instant horn.

2. Experiment with cutting the bottles into different lengths.

3. Some of your children will be able to make a "horn sound." Others can hum or talk through the horns.

4. Play tape Charlie Parker "*Jazz 'Round Midnight*;" encourage children to play their instruments.

Another Thought

Use papier mache to cover the bottles and decorate them. Or simply use white glue to glue on colored paper.

Use the tape at naptime. It is relaxing.

Cognitive Development

Creativity, self-expression, eye-hand coordination, experimentation with sound, development of speech muscles, oral expression, imitation.

Perform

Materials

The instruments you made; clothes you and your children select (we used sun glasses [shades] and baseball caps), jazz tape, book: *Charlie Parker Played be bop.*

1. Send the words home with your children.

2. Practice a couple of times a day. We use walking in a line to lunch, or anywhere as practice time.

3. Find an audience, any audience. Could be one adult (how about in your principal's office), another class or, of course, an on-stage invite-everyone performance.

4. Use any jazz tape as background music. If your sound system is not high-quality, tape a performance in your room. Let the children practice with the tape of their voices. Use that tape and the live voices of your children for the performance.

Another Thought

Take it on the road. Find a senior citizens' group and perform for them. Do a video tape and give it to your public access station.

Cognitive Development

Positive self-esteem, practicing to accomplish a long term goal, sharing positive abilities with others, accepting praise.

Listen to a Musical Instrument

Materials

A person playing a musical instrument, jazz tape.

1. Survey the adults you work with. Find someone who can play an instrument. Invite them to your class.

2. Try to find a saxophone. Remember your high school band.

3. Follow the player's lead as to touching the instrument.

4. Talk in advance about what music to play. It would be nice if the player could play some of your children's favorite songs.

5. Depending on the player, give your children an opportunity to play the instruments they made along with the player.

Another Thought

Go to a live musical performance, or have a group come for your school. Play tapes by Charlie Parker, Louis Armstrong and/or your favorite jazz musicians.

Cognitive Development

Listening skills, self-control, attending to sound, recognizing familiar songs, respecting others' performances.

137

Things Our Children Like To Do

Another Book

Lincoln, James (1989) *Louis Armstrong*, Chelsea House.

The People Could Fly

Written by Virginia Hamilton   *Illustrated by Leo and Diane Dillon*

Hamilton is one of the most honored children's writers. She has won the Newberry, the National, the Boston Globe-Horn, the Coretta Scott King, and the Edgar Allen Poe awards. She and writer Arnold Adoff have two children and live in Ohio.

The Dillons are also much honored for their work. They won the Caldecott Award in two consecutive years for the books *Why Mosquitoes Buzz in People's Ears* in 1976 and *Ashanti to Zulu* in 1977, and have illustrated many beautiful books for children.

Summary:

Four themes of American black folktales are presented: animals; tales of the real, extravagant and fanciful; tales of the supernatural; and slave tales of freedom.

Dial Books for Young Readers, 1986

STORY TIME

Theme

The stories take us back to the hopes and defeats of an enslaved people.

138

Introduction

Read the stories and choose the one you think your children will like the best.

Reading

Telling is probably the best way for your children to hear these stories. You can maintain eye contact with them and you will see their reactions and be able to "act" the story a little.

Response

1. If your children are interested in the tales, use the commercial tape that is available.

2. Ask your children for their comments on the stories.

EXTENSIONS

Naptime

Materials

Your naptime paraphernalia, tape recorder, tape of stories.

1. The rich voices on the tape will capture your children's attention.

2. Listen to the tape before you play it for the children, so you can select the portions that you think are appropriate for your children

Another Thought

Record the stories as you tell them, selecting the ones your children like best. Make the tape available in your listening center.

Cognitive Development

Auditory discrimination, relaxation, sleep habits, rhythm of language.

The People Could Fly

Materials

Your children's imagination, your outdoor space, book: *The People Could Fly.*

1. After your children know the story, take them and the book outside.

2. Have your children tell you the story. Choose children to play the parts. Talk about safe ways and places to fly in your outdoor space.

3. Act out the story.

Another Thought

The children may come up with their own versions of the tale. They may even update it to where they live and a place they would like to fly to.

Cognitive Development

Recalling a sequence of events, role-playing, personalizing history.

Little Eight John

Materials

Book: The People Could Fly

1. First telling of the story can be for the pure wickedness of Little Eight John. Let the children discover the moral.

2. On another telling, ask your children if they would like Little Eight John to come to their classroom.

3. Working with a small group, ask your children to tell what they think Little Eight John would do if he came to their classroom.

4. With safety as a major concern, let your children tell or act out the bad things Little Eight John might do.

5. Encourage your children's comments and ideas about what will happen if Little Eight John does that bad thing. Example: run in class = fall down or bump into other children.

6. The same child then demonstrates positive behavior and the outcomes can be discussed.

Another Thought

By allowing your children to demonstrate Little Eight John's bad behaviors, you are allowing them to test the rules in a controlled environment. This allows the child who never breaks a rule to see how it feels and realize the control he has by following the rules. And it allows the rule-breaker to be in the position of showing the bad behavior and controlling it.

Both children then can tell the consequences of the behavior. This complete scenario helps the child identify unacceptable behavior, know he can control whether to behave that way, and understand the consequences of that behavior. You have helped empower the child to make decisions about his behavior that will bring about positive outcomes.

Things Our Children Like To Do

139

Dancing With The Indians

Written by Angela Shelf Medearis   *Illustrated by Samuel Byrd*

Using the legacy of her great-great-grandfather, Angela shares some of her family history with all children.

Samuel brings his experience as a painter, muralist and illustrator to bring this oral history story to life.

Summary:
A black family visits their Oklahoma Seminole Indian relatives and join in the celebration.

Holiday House Books, 1991

STORYTIME

Theme
Connecting with relatives and enjoying their customs.

Introduction
1. Give the children time to comment on the cover.
2. Be sure that the children know this story happened a long, long time ago. Even before their grandmothers were born.
3. By looking at the children's clothes, your children can recognize that these children lived a long time ago.
4. Establish this for the Seminoles as well as the African-Americans. Tell your children that today, most of the time most Seminoles wear clothes like your children wear.

Reading
1. Depending on the age of your children, you may want to "read" the illustrations first.
2. Reading with a small group your children can easily make up a story for each page.
3. These words lend themselves to listening. So with older children, you may want to read them as a poem. Encourage your children to make their own pictures in their mind. (Mental image is a developmental skill, so continue to talk about it. One day, your children will say "I can see it!".)
4. This is definitely a read it again book!

Response
1. Talk again about the time setting of the book. Use the characters clothes and the wagon to help children realize this is not a "today story."

2. It is important to help your children understand that the Seminole Indian children dress the way your children dress. Talk about the clothes your children wear for different occasions. Relate that to the Seminole children and adults wearing their traditional clothes for special occasions.
3. Talk about the word "Indian." Help your children understand that those people who came from other lands used the word Indian to describe the people that lived here. Tell them today many people use the words "Native Americans, Indigenous People, First Americans." My best understanding of the inhabitants of this land is that they referred to themselves as "People of the Mother of the Earth." The age and intellectually curiosity of your children will dictate how much time to spend on the "names" of groups of people.

EXTENSIONS

Making Things Like the Indians Did

Materials
Book: *Dancing With The Indians,* refer to materials with each activity
1. See the following books for instructions
    Necklace - *Jafta's Mother*
    Drum or Rattle - *Jafta's Father*
    Decorate T-shirts - *Moja Means One: Swahili Counting Book*
    Blowing Instrument - *Charlie Parker Played be bop*
    Papier Mache Mask - *Who's In Rabbits House?*
    Mask - *Ashanti to Zulu*

2. After you have made your costumes, encourage your children to make up a name for their group "People of the Mother of the Earth." Then everything your children make can be labeled with that name. Say your children called themselves the "Good Thinking People," then they would have made a "Good Thinking" necklace or drum.

Another Thought

Visit a display of Indian artifacts or at least have pictures available.

Cognitive Development

Classification, language development, creative thinking.

Dancing With The Indians

Materials

Tape - "Stomp Dances," Vol. 1 or 2; ribbon, paper, cloth streamers, rhythm band instruments, book: *Dancing With The Indians.*

Note: This is a tape of Seminole Indian music. See Source in the back of this book for ordering information.

Please don't just sing "Ten Little Indians" and think you have done an Indian dance. Ask your librarian, or, better yet, ask your local Indian people for music and dance.

1. Re-read about the ribbon dance. Encourage your children to describe how the dance was performed.

2. Talk about your space for dancing and how your children may use the space.

3. Establish who will dance, what kind of dancing movements are permitted, who will play instruments and how turns will be taken for each job.

4. Give your children an opportunity to describe their own dancing.

Another Thought

Sit and listen to Native American music, dancing only with your hands. Then let children describe how to use the rest of their bodies.

Cognitive Development

Moving body parts to a rhythm, creative expression development, oral language, description of body movements.

Black Seminoles

Note: Our purpose here is only a brief history. To get a complete history of African-Americans and/or Indians, please do further research.

Among and alongside the Seminoles in Florida in the 1800's lived many Africans.

These Africans lived in separate settlements and within the Seminole tribes. Some Africans lived as free men and some were slaves to the Seminoles. Where they lived did not seem to indicate whether they were free or slave.

The Africans farmed the land and raised animals. The crops and animals were either owned or paid for by the Seminoles. The Africans also were used by the Seminoles as interpreters when dealing with the Americans.

President Andrew Jackson's administration passed the Indian Removal Act on May 28, 1830. The Indian Wars began. Seminoles and Africans were transported to Oklahoma. Some Africans were sent back or sold into slavery. Some remained in Oklahoma with the Seminoles.

One group, known historically as Black Seminoles, escaped from the reservation in Oklahoma and went to the Mexican frontier (where they remained.)

United States government records state in 1869, Negroes lived as free men among the Seminoles. Eventually these Negroes were given allotments of land and citizenship in the United States.

Historical Information From:
Littlefield, Daniel F., Jr., *Africans and Seminoles* (1977) Greenwood Press, Westport, CT
Weisman, Brent Richard, *Like a Bead on a String,* (1989) University of Alabama Press, Tuscaloosa, AL.

Note: "Seminole" is a Muskogee word meaning "wild or runaway." Beginning in the 1770's, it was used by the settled Creek people to describe those among them who migrated to Florida.

Josephine's 'magination: a Tale of Haiti

Written and illustrated by Arnold Dobrin

Dobrin's knowledge and love for the "beautiful and friendly" Haitian people is evident in the brilliantly colored paintings and the sensitively told story.

Summary:
Josephine and her mother go to the market every Friday. Among the sights, sounds, smells, and people there, Josephine meets a man who tells her to use her 'magination.

Scholastic Inc., 1973

STORY TIME

Theme

Life in Haiti, family relationships, how your imagination works, positive self-image.

Introduction

1. Help your children remember times when they used their imaginations.

2. Show the cover of the book and ask your children how they think Josephine got her doll.

3. Talk about Haiti and explain that some of the people who live there have different things from what your children have.

4. Ask your children if they think Josephine will have "'magination."

Reading

1. If your children are just beginning to sit and listen, use the illustrations to tell the story.

2. Your children will be interested in talking about the house, the dress of the people, and how they carry things.

3. Talk about the marketplace. Compare it to a flea market.

Response

1. Encourage your children to tell you how Josephine discovers she has an imagination and how it made her feel.

2. Talk about Josephine saying she wanted to take two different things and make something new.

3. Talk about using your own brain figure things out. That concept can be used to help children decide to follow the rules as well as create throughout your classroom. It empowers the child to be an independent thinker.

4. Talk about he relationship between Josephine and her mother.

EXTENSIONS

Make A Doll

Materials

Yarn, cornhusks, straw or other natural material from your area, pieces of bright fabric, tongue depressor or small stick, scissors, raffia or string, play dough, tempera paints or latex paints, your art scrap box, books: *Josephine's 'magination,* Mudworks.

1. Talk about the story and re-read the pages where Josephine figures out how to make her doll.

2. Ask who would like to make a doll. Work in a small group. Show them the materials you have gathered. Talk with your children about how they can use the materials to make a doll similar to Josephine's. They may choose to make heads for the dolls from play dough, skirts from straw, bandannas and scarves from fabric, or go in another direction.

3. Remember the story is about "magination," so encourage your children to use the materials in a way that pleases them.

4. Animals and monsters could come from your children's "'maginations."

Another Thought

Construction paper, paper tubes, and markers could also be used for materials to imagine with.

Cognitive Development

Representation, eye-hand coordination, imagination, positive self-image.

Make Cornbread

Materials

Cornbread mix (see box for ingredients needed), mixing bowl, spoon, measuring cup and spoons, baking dish or muffin tins and paper muffin cups, oven.

1. Working in a small group, have the children wash their hands.

2. Ask if anyone knows how to make cornbread. Give the children a chance to talk.

3. Before you put out everything that is needed, ask the children what you will need to make cornbread.

4. As the children tell you, put out the item. Name the remaining items and put them out.

5. Choose attentive children to put the ingredients into the mixing bowl.

6. Pass the bowl around and give each child 10 stirs. If you can count in French, do it!

7. Muffins allow children another step in the preparation. Children can fill the muffin cups. Discourage the children from tasting the dough if you have added an egg. Explain that cooking will destroy the salmonella bacteria carried in eggs.

8. Groups can take turns on different days making only enough cornbread for that group. When children realize that they will have an opportunity to cook another day, they usually can wait.

9. Make sure you talk about texture, color, wet, dry, liquid, solid, and heat changing the size and state of the cornbread.

10. As the cornbread is cooking, recall the sequence of making it. Talk again about the observations made of the physical changes that took place.

Another Thought

Have pineapple jam and mango spread available to put on the cornbread as well as butter.

Cognitive Development

Observing physical changes in matter and describing them, oral language, visual discrimination, classification, sequential order.

NOTE: Other foods to prepare: Fruit salad (mango, pineapple, bananas), sunflower seeds, peanuts in the shell. See *A Weed Is A Flower* for peanut butter.

Market Day

Materials

Furniture in your room, toys, clothes, educational materials in your room, food (cornbread children made), baskets or small boxes, head scarves, straw hats, book: *Josephine's 'magination.*

1. Re-read the book. Talk with your children about having a marketplace in your classroom.

2. Help your children identify what they will need and what you have in the room that they can use.

3. Working with small groups of your children, decide where the shops will be in the room and what they will sell.

4. If two or more children want to sell the same thing, help them negotiate to sell together, take turns, or think of something else to sell.

5. This activity can be as elaborate as you like. Friends and relatives might come to your marketplace. Several kinds of snacks can be sold.

6. A complete lesson might be taught in barter and trade. Each child could be given tokens. Or the children may be comfortable with imaginary money.

Another Thought

Use pennies for trade. Depending upon the money experiences of your children, the number of pennies for an item may vary. Allow each child to set his own price. Be sure there are plenty of pennies so that nobody runs out before Market Day is over.

Cognitive Development

Role-playing, barter and trade, assessing physical needs for a marketplace, oral language.

Things Our Children Like To Do

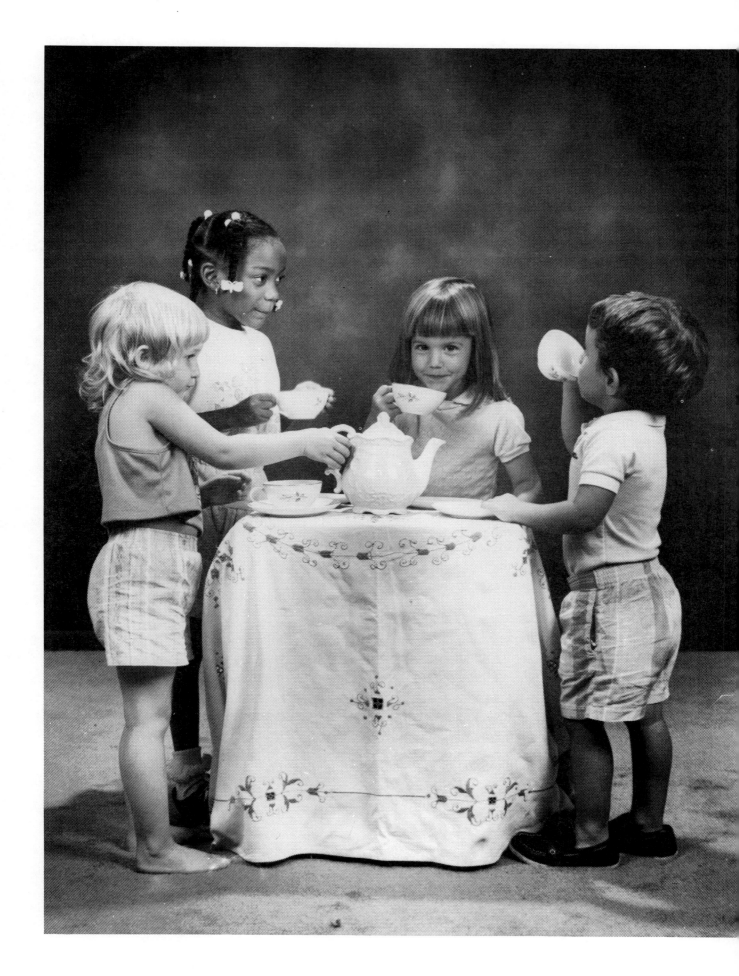

CHAPTER EIGHT

Friends

A Cat in Search of a Friend
A Letter to Amy
Stevie
Cherries and Cherry Pits
Me and Neesie
Chilly Stomach
You'll Be Me / I'll Be You
Straight Hair, Curly Hair
Your Skin and Mine
My Five Senses

A Cat In Search Of A Friend

Written and illustrated by Meshack Asare

Asare's story of an African cat was originally printed in Austria. The delightful illustrations show African scenes.

Summary:
A little yellow cat searches everywhere for a strong friend who will protect her.

Kane/Miller, 1986

STORY TIME

Theme

Assessing the attributes of others, self-reliance, faith in one's own abilities, choosing friends, accepting people's abilities, positive self-worth, assessing fears, need for friendship, purpose.

Introduction

1. Ask the children to tell about the things a cat can do.
2. Ask the children to tell about how a cat looks.
3. Ask the children to think about what a cat can do and how a cat looks, then to think about how strong a cat would feel.

Reading

1. Ask the children why the cat wanted a friend.
2. Encourage the children to guess what the cat thought each animal could do for her.
3. Encourage the children to tell why each new animal went away.
4. On re-reading, ask children what animal will come next in the sequence.

Response

1. Ask the children what the cat figured out about himself.
2. Ask the children what the cat figured out about choosing his friends.
3. Encourage each child to talk abut why he wants someone to be his friend. Does he want a friend who will do the work and take care of him? Or does he want a friend to have someone to play and talk and have fun with?

EXTENSIONS

On Being Friends

Materials

Book: *A Cat in Search of a Friend*

1. Sit in a small group of children (not more than eight) for the purpose of talking about being friends.
2. Use the book as an ice breaker and to move the discussion along.
3. Look at the pictures in the book and ask why the cat decided to be each animal's friend, and why the cat decided to move on to another friend.
4. Be more concerned with the children relating personal stories about choosing and un-choosing friends than the incidents in the book.
5. Listen to the children's thoughts and connect them to the cat figuring out that he did not need a strong friend. He could do his own work. He realized he had fun with all of his friends.

Cognitive Development

Understanding relationships, expressing feelings, oral language.

Cat Puppet Show

Materials

Animal puppets you have in your classroom, puppet stage. Book: *A Cat in Search of a Friend*.

1. Let children decide which animal puppets (stuffed toys, models) you will use for your class Cat Puppet Show.
2. Let children decide in what order the animals will appear in the story.
3. Let children perform their version of the story.

Cognitive Development

Representation, oral language, imagination.

146

Flannel Board Story

Materials

Flannel board characters, flannel board, tape recorder, tape, book: *A Cat in Search of a Friend.*

1. Tell the story using the flannel characters. Record on tape at the same time.

2. Allow the children to use the tape recorder and the flannel characters to act out the taped story.

3. Give the children the book and the flannel characters. Watch them "read" the story as they place the flannel characters on the flannel board.

Cognitive Development

Recalling a sequence, oral language, eye-hand coordination.

A Friend in Search of a Cat

Materials

Construction paper, paint, brushes, crayons, markers, magazine pictures.

1. Talk to the children about being a friend to a cat. Ask them what kind of things they would do for a cat to be its friend.

2. Have children tell what they would like their cats to look like and be like.

3. Have children draw, paint, find a picture, bring in a picture of the cat they have or would like to have. Some children may want to choose another animal for a friend.

4. Talk about the animal pictures and help children understand that the animals can look and act very differently, and that each child can still have fun with her own animals.

Cognitive Development

Choosing friends, expressing ideas, oral language, visual discrimination.

Categorizing Attributes of Animals and Friends

147

Materials

Miniature animals, pictures of animals, stuffed toys, book: *Mathematics Their Way*

1. Ask children to tell you something they like about a friend. Then ask the same child to tell you about an animal that could do the same thing. For example:

Betty makes me laugh.
A monkey makes me laugh.
I can ride Jason's bike.
I can ride a horse.

2. Give the children groups of animals and ask them to put them together in groups by how the children and the animals could be friends. Dogs and cats chase balls and birds, for example.

Cognitive Development

Classification and attributes of friends, visual discrimination, oral language.

Things Our Children Like To Do

A Letter To Amy

Written and illustrated by Ezra Jack Keats

Author of the Caldecott Medal book *The Snowy Day,* his books have appeared in 16 languages. Keats died in May of 1983. "I wanted to do *The Snowy Day* with a black child as the hero. I felt it was important for black children to have a book whose main character they could identify with. But a snowy day is also a universal experience, equally important to all children."

Summary:
Peter is having a birthday party. He hopes Amy will come. Because of a mishap, he is not sure she will.

HarperCollins, 1968

STORY TIME

Theme

Friendship, anticipation, celebrations, planning surprises.

Introduction

1. Show your children the cover of the book and ask them to tell you about it.

2. Ask your children if any of them have written a letter or received a letter.

Reading

1. Keats wrote this book for Augusta Baker, of the New York City Public Library. She was a storyteller, so read the book first as a listening story in her honor.

2. Re-read the story and talk abut the illustrations and Peter's feelings.

Response

1. If someone in your room is having a birthday party, let them tell how they let people know to come to the party.

2. Have the children tell how they think Peter felt throughout the story.

EXTENSIONS

Write and Mail Letters to Friends

Materials

Box painted like a mailbox, advertising stamps, writing paper, envelopes, ink pad, rubber stamp, pencils, pens, crayons, markers, letter carrier's old shirt and hat, makeshift mail carrier's bag.

1. Working in a small group of children, ask who would like to write a letter to a friend in the classroom.

2. Children draw, write, scribble, dictate a letter to a friend. Address the envelope and stamp it, using the advertising stamps. Children can use symbols to identify friends, children's names can be written on labels, or an adult can simply write the name on the envelope.

3. Mail the letters in the class mail box.

4. Postal clerk cancels the stamp and the letter carrier delivers the mail to each child.

5. Valentine's season is a good time to involve the children in this activity.

6. More study of the post office, including a field trip, could easily follow the children's interest.

Another Thought

Children enjoy mailing letters with stamps, with the letters either going to a friend or coming back to themselves. Try to find a mailbox that the children can reach, so they can put the mail in themselves.

Cognitive Development

Oral expression, written expression, sharing thoughts with someone else, process of mailing a letter.

Have a Birthday Party

Materials

Muffin tin, Duncan Hines yellow cake mix, cupcake papers, bowl, oil, measuring cups and spoons, candles, oven, party hats, party supplies provided by a parent, scraps of construction paper, scissors, glue, headband (see *Children & Scissors*).

1. The birthday party can be real or pretend. Your children may like to read *A Letter to Amy* as part of the routine when any class member has a birthday.
2. A parent may bring in all the birthday party or your children can make it.
3. Follow directions on the Duncan Hines box. It has never failed us. Let the birthday child be the chief cook and choose a group of friends to help make the cupcakes.
4. Have a party in the style to fit your class routine.

Another Thought

If you do the mailing at Valentine's Day, this could easily be a Valentine's Day party. Each child can give out her Valentine's. Be sure you have some extras so every child has something to deliver.

Cognitive Development

Distinguishing special days to celebrate, oral expression, positive self-image, expressing caring for other people.

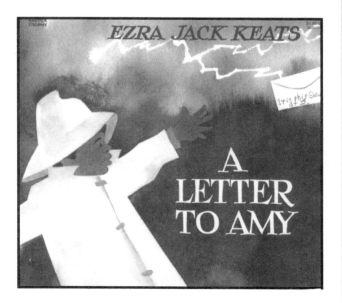

Children Receive an Invitation to an Event

Materials

Postcard-size card, postcard stamps, children's names and addresses.

1. Any copy store has 8-1/2" x 11" card stock you can use for postcard messages. Measure off standard postcards and cut to size.
2. If your children can have your letter carrier deliver their postcards to them, that would be special. If not, a child dressed up could deliver them. Or each child could deliver one card to someone else.
4. The event itself can be as simple or elaborate as you want.

Another Thought

It may even be your birthday party.

Cognitive Development

Written expression, self-esteem.

149

Wind Experiments

Materials

Different set of sizes of rectangles similar to a letter (4" x 5", 9" x 4", 8-1/2" x 11"), mailbox, book: *A Letter to Amy*.

1. Choose a windy day on the playground. Re-read *A Letter to Amy*.
2. Tell the children they are going to pretend to be Peter and Amy going to the mailbox. Have them tell you what happened.
3. Encourage the children to predict which size letter will fly the fastest, the highest, or the longest.
4. Let the children choose a friend to act out the play with. Could be two girls or two boys or a boy and a girl.
5. Talk about safety rules for the wind experiment so that the children do not bump into each other, as they chase their letters.
6. As you watch the children, encourage them to talk about what is happening to the letters
7. Come back to a small group and have the children tell about the flight of their letters.

Another Thought

Picking up the "mail" from the ground could become a lesson about litter.

Cognitive Development

Scientific observation, oral expression, noticing and caring for the natural environment.

Stevie

Written and illustrated by John Steptoe

This is John Steptoe's first book, written and illustrated when he was just 18 years old. His paintings already have that luminous glow.

Summary:

Stevie comes to stay with Robert and his mother while his own mother works. He annoys Robert but Robert misses him when he is gone.

Harper & Row, 1969

STORY TIME

Theme

Identifying feelings, accepting others.

150   Introduction

These illustrations are unusual and your children will want to be able to see them. Read the story to a small group so everyone can see them.

Reading

1. Encourage your children to talk about the illustrations and how Robert feels.

2. The text is very true to how the child is feeling. Some of your children will be able to tell about times they felt the same way.

Response

1. Encourage your children to talk about how Robert felt about Steve at the end of the story and why he called him Little Stevie.

2. Re-read your children's favorite parts of the story. They will love hearing Robert's complaints about Stevie.

3. Be sure to end with Robert's realization that he did like having Little Stevie around.

EXTENSIONS

Tape for the Listening Center

Materials

Tape, tape recorder, book: *Stevie*

1. Ask a few children to join you in the listening center.

2. Decide what you will do for a signal to turn the pages.

3. As you read, allow your children to put their two-cents' worth in about what is happening in the story. Because the language is "kid talk," their comments will fit right in.

4. Conclude with okay comments about Stevie from your children.

Another Thought

Make the book and the tape available in your listening center. Put small dollhouse figures and toys with the book so your children can act out the story.

Cognitive Development

Identifying with characters in a story, visual discrimination, oral language, listening skills.

Steptoe Art

Materials

Permanent markers, crayons, watercolors, drawing paper, book: *Stevie*

1. In the art area with a small group of children, look at Steptoe's illustrations. Ask your children to tell you what they think he used to draw the pictures.

2. Be sure each child has a supply of permanent markers, crayons, and watercolors.

3. Use a practice piece of drawing paper. Make a shape with the marker. Color some of the inside of the shape with crayon. Paint over the whole shape with watercolor. Do this process with your children.

4. Tell your children that this is the way Steptoe drew his pictures.

5. Give everyone a new piece of paper and let them use the art materials in their own way.

6. Some will repeat the process and will want to be reminded of the steps. Others will move on to their own processes.

Another Thought

Remind your children of this technique when they are looking for an art project.

Cognitive Development

Visual discrimination, understanding how a process works, working in a sequential order, recalling a sequence, combining art materials.

Identifying Feelings:

Two Sides to a Coin

Materials

Book: *Stevie*

1. Sit with a few children and ask them to show you the parts of the book they like best.

2. Encourage your children to talk about Robert's feeling about Stevie. Did he like him or did he think he was an old stupid?

3. Personalize the conversation if the children do not. Get them to talk about people they like sometimes and do not like at other times.

4. Talk about how they think Stevie felt when Robert talked tough to him. Do they think Stevie knew Robert liked him?

Another Thought

Do some role-playing with your children and give them positive language and actions to interact with younger children, like keeping toys out of reach, not calling names, taking shoes off when you get on a bed, playing with their own toys, playing together. Review the positive things Robert had to say about Stevie.

Cognitive Development

Identifying feelings, expressing feelings, oral language.

Another Book

Cummings, Pat (1985), *Jimmy Lee Did It,* Lothrop, Lee & Sheperd, New York.

Walter, M.P., (1990), *Two And Too Much,* Bradbury, New York.

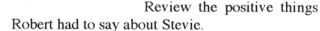

HARPER TROPHY

$4.95 US
$6.95 CDN

STEVIE

JOHN STEPTOE

Illustrations copyright©, 1969 by John Steptoe from Stevie, HarperCollins.
Reproduced with the approval of the Estate of John Steptoe

151

Cherries and Cherry Pits

Written by Vera B. Williams

Vera Williams wrote the Caldecott Honor book for 1985, *A Chair for My Mother*. Williams has held many kinds of jobs. She is a worker for world peace.

Summary:
Bidemmi loves to draw pictures and tell stories. Because of her generous nature, she draws enough cherry trees for everyone to eat cherries.

Greenwillow, 1986

STORY TIME

Theme

Self-expression, positive self-concept, planning for the future, being kind to friends and relatives, imagination, controlling events, having enough food for everyone, how things grow.
NOTE: This story can be read in several short sessions, one for each of Bidemmi's stories.

Introduction

1. Show the children the cover of the book. Tell them this little girl's name is Bidemmi. Ask them to tell you what she is holding. And ask them to tell you what they think made all the colors.

2. Read the title and ask if they think Bidemmi likes cherries.

3. Give every child a cherry to eat right now. Talk about the pits. Collect all of the pits.

Reading

1. If you are only going to read one story at a sitting, you may want to take the time to get your children involved by asking "why" or "how" questions.

2. Ask the children how Bidemmi knew what to draw and what to say about her drawings.

3. Be sure the children remember that, in each story, someone is eating cherries and spitting out pits.

4. Ask the children to guess what Bidemmi will do with her cherries.

5. Let the children predict why Bidemmi is saving her cherry pits.

6. Give the children the opportunity to read Bidemmi's pictures of the growing cherry tree.

7. Ask your children how Bidemmi felt about having all of those cherry trees.

Response

1. Talk to the children about why Bidemmi just kept on drawing and telling the story. She did not stop to answer questions.

2. Get the children to talk about sometimes when they just want people to listen. And get them to talk about how important it is to be a good listener for your friends.

3. Get the children to talk about why Bidemmi wants all of those cherry trees.

EXTENSIONS

Draw a Story

Materials

Variety of colors of construction paper, colored markers.

1. Remind your children how Bidemmi drew and made up stories. Tell the children you would like them to draw whatever pleases them.

2. Encourage but do not require the children to tell you the story of what they are drawing.

3. Some children may want their stories written down. Others will be satisfied with just telling their story. And some may do their own writing. Accept the writing as valid, at whatever level the child is writing.

Cognitive Development

Artistic expression, oral expression, eye-hand coordination, visual perception, positive self-image.

Grow a Seed

Materials

One-pint milk carton, potting soil, vermiculite, seed (Ask which seeds do well in your locality. Grapefruit seeds grow well. Winter rye grass grows quickly and so easily demonstrates going from seed to plant.)

1. Each child has a container with her name on it, potting soil, and seed.

2. Children put the soil into the container, then plant the seeds according to directions. Put more than one seed in a container to assure one grows, like Bidemmi did.

3. Talk about what Bidemmi had to do to make the plants grow.

4. Observe the natural changes that take place in the seeds.

Cognitive Development

Observation of natural changes, passing of time, possession, oral language.

Make a Seed Book

Materials

Cut 8-1/2" x 11" sheet into four equal rectangles, stack four or five pages together, place inside a construction paper cover, and staple. Markers, crayons.

1. Show your children the pictures Bidemmi drew about the cherry pits.

2. Let each child illustrate the cover of his book. Then the children can draw the seeds in the containers.

3. As the seeds grow, the children can add drawings to their books.

4. Children may want to dictate words for you to write down about their seeds.

5. If you let the children keep their books in their cubbies, don't be surprised if their drawings are unrelated to the seed. That's okay.

6. You may want to make these little books available for your children to make up stories about anything they please.

7. Be sure you measure the value of the amount of drawing on each page by the child's standards and values, not yours.

Cognitive Development

Observing and recording natural changes, visual representation.

Giant Feast

Materials

Popcorn popper, popcorn, salt, juice, milk, fruit drink, water, bowls or napkins.

NOTE: This is a good outside activity. The birds will clean up the mess, providing another activity for the children to discuss

Jacket illustration copyright © 1986 by Vera B. Williams, used with permission from Greenwillow Books, Publisher.

1. Popcorn is suggested. Choose a food your children will like. And choose a food you will let your children stuff themselves with.

2. Re-read the pages about how Bidemmi protected the cherries so they finally got ripe, and then all the people came to eat cherries. Ask your children how Bidemmi felt when everyone came to eat her cherries.

3. Ask the children if they would like to pop as much popcorn as Bidemmi had cherries.

4. Be sure to pop more corn than your children can eat. The lesson is that there can be abundance.

Another Thought

By repeating this lesson in abundance, children come to know there will be enough for them. Then they can begin to make sure other people have some. At that point, they will know the pleasure Bidemmi had when she grew enough cherries so that everyone could eat as many as they wanted to eat.

Cognitive Development

There can be more available to eat than I can eat, monitoring eating habits, providing enough food, positive self-concept, being sure everyone has enough to eat.

Another Book

Medearis, Angela S. (1994) *Annie's Gifts*, Just Us Books, Orange, N.J.

153

Me and Neesie

Written by Eloise Greenfield

Illustrated by Moneta Barnett

Writing with sensitivity about the black child is Greenfield's specialty.

Barnett's pencil drawings with warm, rosy overlay carry out the story's theme.

Summary:
A little girl learns to leave her imaginary friend at home when she goes to school.

Thomas Y. Crowell Company, 1975

STORY TIME

Theme

Imaginary friends, positive self-image, friendship, expressing feelings, power and control of one's environment.

Introduction

1. After showing your children the cover, talk with them about imaginary friends.
2. Encourage children to be positive and accepting of a made-up friend.

Reading

1. Talk with your children about why nobody could see Neesie but Janell.
2. Ask your children to predict if Janell will get into trouble because of the way Neesie is acting.
3. Let the children tell you why Janell's mother thinks Neesie would make Aunt Bea nervous.
4. Have your children predict when (if) Neesie will go to school with Janell.
5. Ask your children if Neesie made Aunt Bea nervous and what made the girls laugh in the bedroom.
6. Let the children tell you what will happen to Janell at school.

Response

1. Ask, "What happened to Neesie?"
2. Help the children talk about Janell having no friends, then going to school and making friends. Then see if they can relate that to Neesie's disappearance.
3. Ask for and accept your children's logic about why the grownups did not like Janell having a friend that grownups could not see.

EXTENSIONS

My Best Friend

Materials

Stand-Up Child (*Children & Scissors*), scissors, glue, pre-cut construction paper pieces, markers, scraps from your art area, paper for writing child's dictation.

NOTE: Because most young children in a group change friends often, who they name as friend may change even during the making of the friend. The child should certainly have the right to change the name as often as she wishes.

1. Working in small groups, talk to the children about having a friend. Encourage them to talk about Janell and Neesie.
2. Ask the children if they would like to make a best friend. Allow that friends can be other than people.
3. Using the construction paper and scraps from your art box, children can create their own best friends.
4. While the children are working, sit with each child individually and have her tell you about her friend. Write down the child's exact words as she tells you.
5. A table-top display or an eye-level bulletin board would be good ways for the children to show off their best friends.
6. The children may just want to play paper dolls and tell each other about their friends. Certainly a child could choose to make more than one model. One might even be himself.

Cognitive Development

Identifying positive behaviors in others, oral expression, expression, expressing feelings, eye-hand coordination.

Imaginary Friend Day

Materials

Book: *Me and Neesie*

1. Re-read *Me and Neesie*. Talk to the children about why Neesie did not want to come to school.

2. Ask the children if they would like to bring a friend that nobody but they can see to school tomorrow. Talk about the difference between friends you can see and imaginary friends. (Our children would say play-play friends.)

3. Encourage your children to use their own brains (imagination, thinking caps) to make up their friends.

4. Obviously you will need some communication with your parents and caregivers about how all of this relates to their children's education. We have a suggested note home in the Appendix.

5. Your Imaginary Friend Day will be as unique as your classroom and children. You could follow your usual routine or plan some special activities.

6. Of course, since your class will double in size, plan your activities for extra bodies. **Remember** that each child will need two of everything!

Another Thought

Some of the imaginary friends will stay around for a few days. Those children will have found a new kind of power and control. Accept these children's needs and find ways to empower them in your classroom.

Cognitive Development

Imagination, oral expression, responsibility, identifying behavior both negative and positive, distinguishing reality and fantasy, power and control of one's environment.

155

Things Our Children Like To Do

Chilly Stomach

Written by Jeanette Caines　　　　　　　　　*Illustrated by Pat Cummings*

Touching children's heartfelt feelings, is a talent of Caines. In this story, she empowers Jill to help her friend trust her "Chilly Stomach."

In each illustration, Pat has given children visual clues to begin conversations about this very important topic. Adults listen to what the children are saying and believe them.

Summary:
Sandy gets a chilly stomach when her Uncle Jim comes near her. She tells her best friend Jill. Jill tells Sandy to tell her parents.

HarperCollins, 1986

STORY TIME

Note: This book relies on your openness as a teacher and your respect for children and their right to say no to adults. Hopefully, you will have settled these ideas in your own mind before reading this book to your children.

156

Theme

Teaching children to trust their instincts and ask for help.

Introduction

1. Before you introduce this book to your children, check your own feelings, so that you do not give your children mixed messages.

2. Read the title. Ask your children to tell you about a chilly stomach and what makes their stomachs chilly.

Reading

1. Begin with the illustration on the title page. Encourage your children to talk about Sandy and her chilly stomach. Accept as valid your children's responses.

2. Continue to use the illustrations as well as the words to read the story.

3. Be sensitive to your children's comments. Reinforce their feeling of wanting to choose who touches them.

Response

1. Follow your children's lead. This is not a "teach to say no" book.

2. Rather, use it to encourage your children to talk about their chilly stomachs and how to trust their own feelings about adults they come in contact with.

EXTENSIONS

Sexual Abuse

1. Call on your guidance counselor, your local shelter for abused women and children to give you activities or bring a program to your school.

2. Because of the complexity of sexual abuse, rely on the counsel of trained people you trust for further activities with your children.

Self-Esteem

1. Look in the index for Expressing Feelings/ Growth.

2. Use *Life Doesn't Frighten Me.*

Stuffed Paper Bag Puppet

Materials

For each child, small paper bag, newsprint, tape, toilet paper rolls, pre-cut construction paper pieces; book: *Children & Scissors.*

1. Stuff the bag with newsprint and tape it on the toilet paper roll. Older children can stuff the bag.

2. Let each child paste the paper pieces on his puppet in a way that pleases him.

3. Be sure to put each child's name on his puppet.

4. After the puppets are dry, encourage the children to perform with them.

5. As the children perform, have them tell what their puppets are doing.

6. Re-read *Chilly Stomach* after the children have had an opportunity to play with their puppets.

7. During the reading let your children's puppets play the parts. This should be the child's choice.

8. Some of your children may take this opportunity to tell about their "chilly stomachs."

9. Listen to the child. Make the appropriate response for your school setting.

Another Thought

When your children are using the puppet or stuffed animals in your room, encourage them to talk about what the puppets or animals are doing. Make the book available for their shows.

Cognitive Development

Oral language, eye-hand coordination, amusing others, classification, representation, expressing feelings.

Another Book

Koplow, Lesley (1991), CSW, *Tanya and the Tobo Man,* Magination Press, Brunner/Mazel, Inc., 19 Union Square West, New York, New York 10003

Things Our Children Like to Do

157

You be me, I'll be you

Written and Illustrated by Pili Mandelbaum

Mixing paints and words, Mandelbaum gives an opening to children's questions about being bi-racial.

Summary:
A bi-racial child questions her appearance. Her daddy helps her feel happy with herself.

Kane//Miller Book Publishers, 1990

STORY TIME

Theme

Appreciation of self and one's appearance, bi-racial family.

Introduction

Note: A child's concern regarding her appearance is very real. Reading one book or doing one activity certainly won't resolve the concern for the child. This book may allow a child to voice her concern. Accept the concern as valid from the child's point of view. Your response needs to start with where the child's feelings are at the present time. Talk with the child to understand how her feelings have been developed (perhaps comments from peers or adults). Deal with the source of the child's concerns. Just telling her how you feel about her is not enough.

If you have a child in your classroom who is feeling uncertain about her appearance, you may want to read this book to that child alone. Then ask her about reading it to the class. She may want to keep it as her book for awhile. Respect those feelings.

1. Talk about the cover and what the relationship of the man and the little girl might be.

2. Accept comments from your children. You may spend your time with personal experiences from your children. Listen and read the book another day.

Reading

1. These illustrations tell their own story. Use the words as suited to your children. Your children may want to supply the words

2. Talk about the father saying how silly. Help your children understand the father was wanting to make his little girl feel better. Ask your chidren what else the father could have said to help his litttle girl tell him about how she feels. Perhaps "You are sad about how you look?" " What do you think we can do about it?" Help your children identify Anna's feelings, rather than disregarding them and putting down her wanting to be like him. Validate her feelings of wanting to look like her father. Then go on to help your children find ways Anna can believe she is beautiful just the way she is.

3. When you have established Anna's feelings and that her father wants to help, continue reading the book with the question. "How will the father help his little girl feel happy? What will he do?"

4. Anna's feelings about her father's hair should also be validated. The father saying he doesn't like his hair is a common response to children. It does not deal with Anna's feelings.

Help your children understand that saying that something is bad does not make something else good; and that saying something is good, does not make something else bad. Two things that are very different can both be good. The father could have said it made him feel good that Anna liked his hair. Then told Anna the things he liked about his hair and her hair.

Let your children tell you about their hair. Accept their comments as valid. You tell them or let other children tell what they like about each other's hair and their own hair.

Response

1. Ask your children how Anna felt at the end of the story.

2. Help them identify what happened to make Anna happy: her father playing with her, her mother's reaction, Anna knowing her mom and dad loved her.

EXTENSIONS

To help answer questions by your children about how people look and why they look the same or different use this book and *My Five Senses*, *My Skin and Yours* and *Straight Hair, Curly Hair* to answer those questions.

Additional activities in this book:

Bright Eyes, Brown Skin
Daddy and I
Amazing Grace
Something on My Mind

159

Another Book

Adoff, Arnold, *Black is Brown is Tan*, (1973), Harper Collins.

A lively, happy poem describing the author's bi-racial family experiences. A must in your classroom, especially if you are going to use *You be me, I'll be you.*

Straight Hair, Curly Hair

Written by Augusta Goldin

Emberley's simple drawings will amuse children and help carry the theme of the book.

Illustrated by Ed Emberley

Why some hair is curly and some straight will be clear to children after they hear Goldin's story.

Summary:

Experiments, measurements, and explanations show how hair grows.

Thomas Y. Crowell Company, 1966

STORY TIME

Theme

Facts about hair, positive self-image.

Introduction

1. Ask the children to look at one another's hair and describe it. Give them positive language for this exercise so they don't use "bushy" or "limp" or pejorative-sounding terms. Try suggesting: "has a lot of body," "smooth and silky," "curly," "straight."

2. Show *Straight Hair, Curly Hair*. Tell your children this is a science book. It will tell us facts about our hair.

Reading

1. Encourage your children to make comments about their hair or the hair of someone they know when you read each section.

2. Help them take the information and apply it to their hair. Everyone can make his hair crackle.

Response

1. Talk about how people make their hair straight or curly and why they decide to do that.

2. Your children will want to touch each other's hair. Be sure the child gives permission before anyone touches his hair. Respect the child's right to say "No."

3. A child will also tell about someone he knows who changes the color of her hair.

4. Your children will ask to do the experiments.

EXTENSIONS

Book Experiments

Materials

Hair, cellophane tape, hair brushes and combs, small piece of paper, something to hang from the strands of hair, large glass jars, lids, keys or washers, book: *Straight Hair, Curly Hair*.

1. Divide your children into three groups. Because these experiments take time, you may want to do one experiment a day with each group. Then you will need fewer jars and space to display them.

2. Follow the directions in the book.

3. The third experiment is hair and static electricity. If you are having a cold, dry day, let your children comb or brush their hair to produce static electricity. If you can darken your room, the children will be delighted to see the sparks in each other's hair or in a mirror.

4. Show the picture in the book of the hair scales. The friction between the hair scales and the comb or brush creates the static electricity. The children can easily feel the difference between sliding their fingers up their hair (against the scales), and down their hair (with the scales).

5. After combing the hair, the comb will pick up a small piece of paper or a little confetti.

6. If the weather conditions are not right to produce static electricity, have the children draw pictures of their hair.

7. Remind them of static electricity they may have noticed when their clothes first come out of the dryer or when they brush past a TV set. You can demonstrate it if you have a dryer or TV.

8. Some children might want to draw the hair follicle shapes.

Cognitive Development

Conducting experiments, making observations, waiting for an outcome, oral language, following directions, visual discrimination.

Your Skin and Mine

Written by Paul Showers

Showers explains the skin, how it protects, what happens when it's cut, how melanin affects color.

Illustrated by Paul Galdone

In amusing and informative illustrations, Galdone completes the story of skin, including fingerprints.

Summary:
The workings of the body's covering and differences in color are explained.

Thomas Y. Crowell Company, 1965

STORY TIME

Theme
Facts about skin, positive self-image.

Introduction
1. Ask your children to look at their skin and the skin of children around them.
2. Encourage the children to talk about the likenesses and differences of their skin.
3. Show *Your Skin and Mine* and give your children time to settle down and listen.

Reading
1. Depending on your children, you may want to read the book in sections. Then do the experiment that goes with that section.
2. Children who can sit and listen for a longer period of time will like to hear the whole book. You can involve them by asking questions related to each section.

Response
Your children will want to do the experiments.

Things Our Children Like To Do

EXTENSIONS

Book Experiments

Materials
Magnifying glasses, ink pads in several colors, blindfold, piece of paper, balloon, paintbrush, feather, markers/crayons, drawing paper, book: *Your Skin and Mine*.

1. Organize the children into three small groups. Each group will take turns doing all the experiments.
2. Expand the fingerprint experiment into an art activity. Let children add arms and legs to their fingerprints to make people, animals, bugs, monsters. By using different colored ink pads, you are teaching respect for individual choices of color.
3. Encourage the children to expand the touch experiment by finding things in the classroom to touch with their fingers.

Another Thought
Put the book in the library corner and let the children do the experiments individually.

Cognitive Development
Scientific discovery, observation, creativity, oral language, following directions, visual discrimination.

NOTE: Activities that include information from *Your Skin and Mine; Straight Hair, Curly Hair*; and *My Five Senses* are all listed under *My Five Senses*.

161

My Five Senses

Written and illustrated by Aliki

Aliki got the idea for this book while she was illustrating another author's book. It is the first book she both wrote and illustrated. She has since done 40 more.

Summary:
A child discovers sight, hearing, smell, taste, and touch with simple words accompanied by delightful paintings.

Thomas Y. Crowell, 1989

STORY TIME

Theme
Identifying the five senses

Introduction
1. Tell your children they are going to study about their senses.
2. Ask if anyone knows what a sense is. Clear up any confusion with cents.
3. Show the cover of the book and identify the five senses.

Reading
1. You read the action and let your children finish with the body part. When the book child says she can see, let your children say what they see with: "My eyes!"
2. Let the children tell a personal experience with a sense.

Response
1. Re-read and talk about the illustrations.
2. Ask your children to name their five senses.

EXTENSION

My Five Senses' Centers

Materials
Real-life objects for each sense easily available to you.

1. Divide your children into five groups. Each group does one sense. You may want to do one sense a day with one group so that by the end of the week every child has done every sense. Or the children could go through all five senses in one day.

2. The time you want to spend on a sense will determine how much material you want for each sense.

3. Eyes: Magnifying glasses, kaleidoscope, paper tubes to look through, sorting colors, shapes and so forth, talking about what you can see in the classroom. Game: I Spy.

4. Ears: Noisemakers of all kinds, matching sound boxes, identifying sounds from a recording or actual object, listening to loud/soft, high/low sounds.

5. Nose: Identifying, by smell, common foods for your children, scratch-and-sniff stickers, identifying pleasant and unpleasant smells.

6. Taste: Use sweet/sour, recognize favorite snack foods or drinks with eyes closed, talk about food your children like to eat.

7. Touch: Give the children the opportunity to identify rough/smooth, soft/hard. Use a feeling box and identify objects by feel.

Another Thought

Ask the children to turn off their senses one by one, covering their eyes or ears, holding their noses, rinsing their mouths with water and putting no food in. They will soon realize that they can mute all but the sense of touch, even if it's just the feeling of their seats on the chairs or their feet on the floor.

Cognitive Development

Positive self-image, things my body can do.

NOTE: Your children now know more about their bodies. The following activities will help them to understand further the likenesses and differences in their bodies.

162

My Body

Materials

One piece of paper for each child to lie down on, paint, markers, crayons, cloth scraps, yarn, books: *My Skin and Yours; Straight Hair, Curly Hair.*

1. Each child in your class will make a life-size cutout of himself. This project can take as long as a week. Let each child lie on his large sheet of paper while you draw an outline of his body.

2. Begin by identifying the color of the child's skin. Mix tempera paints or use skin-tone crayons. Color the parts that will not be covered by clothes. We mixed the skin-toned paints and put a dot of paint on the child's skin to be sure it matched each child's skin tone. The paint color will be lighter when it dries.

NOTE: Skin-color crayons can be obtained from Afro-Am Educational Materials, 819 South Wabash, Chicago, IL 60605, Phone (312) 922-1147.

3. Talk about skin. Have the children tell you what they know. Discuss how you get to have a certain skin color. Involve your parents in helping each child identify which of his relatives has the same color of skin he has.

4. Now put hair on the cutout. Use yarn, paint, curled ribbon, torn or cut paper.

5. Again let the children give you the scientific information they have learned about hair, and help the child identify which relative has the same hair type as he has.

6. Facial features can be painted or drawn or made with glued-on construction paper parts. Parents or relatives can help identify who the child looks like.

7. Your children can tell the information they have about taste, smell and vision.

8. Children can choose to paint on clothes, make construction paper clothes, or glue on scraps of cloth.

9. When the cutouts are finished, your children should have a better sense of who they are.

10. The three science books on skin, senses, and hair will give them the knowledge of how we are all alike, and how we are individuals.

11. With their cutouts and conversation about relatives, your children can gain a sense of uniqueness as well as a sense of family, how they come from the past, and inherited characteristics of their bodies from relatives.

12. Take a photograph of each child with his cutout.

NOTE: Too much light directed on a dark skinned face will make it lose definition. Reflect the light from a white paper or light-colored ceiling onto the face of a child with dark skin.

Another Thought

Children who do not have contact with any blood relatives can make up imaginary relatives or pretend to be related to a public figure who resembles them, or they can connect to adopted relatives they resemble.

Cognitive Development

These materials are included in the *Friends* section of this book to help build an understanding and pride of body image. When children can accept their own bodies, they are more likely to accept other people's physical features. They can then go on to learn and respect what people alike or different from themselves do or think.

NOTE: At this printing, we are unaware of an appropriate book that gives factual information about physical differences and deals with the emotional aspect, too. Please let us know if you find one.

163

CHAPTER NINE

African Folktales
& Customs

I Am Eyes - Ni Macho

Jafta

Jafta's Mother

Jafta's Father

Mcheshi Goes to Market

Mcheshi Goes to the Game Park

Anansi the Spider: A Tale from the Ashanti

Why Mosquitoes Buzz in People's Ears

Moja Means One: Swahili Counting Book

Who's In Rabbit's House? A Masai Tale

Jambo Means Hello: Swahili Alphabet Book

Bringing the Rain to Kapiti Plain

Ashanti to Zulu: African Traditions

I Am Eyes—Ni Macho

Written by Leila Ward

Ward reveals that in Kenya one wakes up and says in Swahili, "Ni macho" (I am eyes), a poetic expression for "I am awake." She has lived in Kenya.

Illustrated by Nonny Hogrogian

The colorful and convincing illustrations by Hogrogian show the sights of Kenya from snowy Kilimanjaro to grassy plains and warm rivers.

Summary:

A child awakens and steps through a day of Kenyan sights.

Scholastic Inc., 1978

STORY TIME

Theme

Beautiful sights of Africa

166

Introduction

1. Tell your children this story is about what a little girl sees in Africa.

2. Read the Swahili words and explain that is how the little girl says she is looking at something.

Reading

1. Encourage your children to tell you what they see in the illustrations, and to relate their own experiences to them.

2. If you are working on the alphabet, this text easily reinforces letter sounds.

Response

1. Give your children the opportunity to "read" their favorite pages.

2. Your children will learn the sequence on re-reading and will be able to tell you what the girl sees next. Encourage them to say, "Ni macho, I see" the next illustration.

EXTENSIONS

Large African Animal

Materials

Tagboard, tempera paints, paintbrushes, construction paper, your art scrap box, scissors, glue, book: *I Am Eyes - Ni Macho*.

1. Re-read the book and ask the children what animal they would like to make.

2. Pre-cut a tagboard silhouette of the animal the child would like to make. Make it at least a foot tall. Use an overhead projector to blow up a shape, draw it, and cut it out.

3. Children can paint the animals any color they like and decorate them from your scrap box. Older children may want to cut construction paper pieces to add to their animals.

4. Encourage your children to tell you about the animals they have created, which may be very different from the silhouette you cut out for them.

Another Thought

Put on a play. Let each hold his animal. First have each child say, "Ni macho, I see (the name of this animal)." Then have one child say, "Ni macho, I see (any of the animal names)." All of the children with that animal stand and move around the room imitating that animal's movements.

Cognitive Development

Representation, visual discrimination, eye-hand coordination, oral language.

Finding Animals

Materials

All the animals in your room, book: *I Am Eyes - Ni Macho*.

1. Re-read *I Am Eyes* to a small group of children. Ask your children who would like to be the child and find the animals in your room.

2. First, put the animals in plain view and let the children find them.

3. Give a few children the opportunity to place the animals around the room. Then let another group of children find the animals.

4. The game can be made suitable for toddlers. Let the child put her animal down. The adult says, "Ni Macho," and the same child finds her animal. These toddlers will change the game to hiding the animal when they are ready. Be patient.

Another Thought

Take your animals and the book out to your play area for this activity.

Cognitive Development

Visual discrimination, figure-ground, oral language, recalling information, body language, representation, following through on a task.

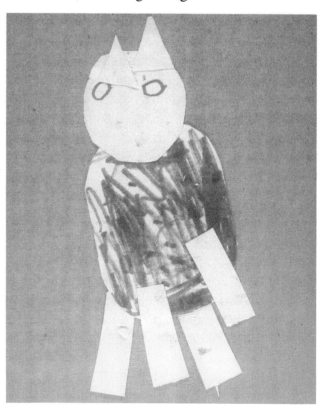

Visit a Zoo

Materials

Parent information, letter, permission slips, camera, film, snack, bag lunch, permissible food for the animals.

1. While studying about Africa, a trip to the zoo would certainly be appropriate. Consider going at the beginning of your study. Your children then have a real experience to relate to African animals. This will give them something in their memory banks to attach all of the new information to, and will make learning the names, sounds, and habits of the animals more meaningful.

2. Plan the trip with your children. How they will get there, how to act on the bus, what they will pass on the way, what they will see when they first get to the zoo, what kinds of animals they will see, where the bathrooms are, when they will eat. Having a map of the zoo would be helpful. Make some rules for the zoo. Practice acting out the positive ways that they will behave at the zoo.

3. On your way to the zoo; praise your children's good behavior, point out things you said they would see along the way, and ask them to recall from your class discussions what they will see next.

4. Follow your plan while at the zoo. Be sure to praise your children for their good behavior throughout your visit.

Another Thought

Use the animal activities in this book to follow up your zoo trip and extend your study of African animals.

Cognitive Development

Learning with all senses and emotions, recalling a plan, positive self-image.

167

Another Book

Ellis, Veronica Freeman, (1993) *Land of the Four Winds,* Just Us Books, Orange, NJ.

Jafta

Written by Hugh Lewin   *Illustrated by Lisa Kopper*

Lewin writes with great simplicity and love about a little boy in South Africa who could live anywhere.

Gold and brown drawings by Kopper warm up the page as Jafta and the animals play together.

Summary:
A little boy feels like various African animals.

Carolrhoda Books Inc., 1981

STORY TIME

Theme

Feeling good about oneself, understanding one's feelings, visual representation of feelings.

Introduction

1. Jafta introduces himself very well. This is another cover your children will talk about easily.

2. Encourage your children to talk about the feelings in the illustrations and feelings in general.

3. Tell your children that Jafta lives in South Africa. He watches the animals and he thinks that he can feel like they do.

Reading

1. Even very young children will enjoy Kopper's illustrations and naming the animals. Also identify the feelings Jafta is having on each page.

2. Older children will enjoy predicting what Jafta will do. Read the words. Ask your children what Jafta will look like in the illustrations. Then show the illustrations, and your children will be delighted that they were right.

Response

1. Talk again about where Jafta lives. Help your children understand that they can feel the same way that someone who lives far away feels.

2. Each child can show his favorite picture and act like Jafta.

3. On re-readings, you could show pictures of Nelson Mandela and Bishop Tutu and tell your children that they have lived in South Africa, too. Then wait for your children's comments.

EXTENSIONS

Book of Animals and Feelings

Materials

Paper (8-1/2" x 11") for book pages, magazine pictures, construction paper, markers/crayons, scissors, glue, your art scrap box, books: *Jafta, Children & Scissors*.

1. Re-read Jafta and ask your children if they think they can feel like Jafta's animals. Would they like to make a book about themselves and Jafta's animals?

2. Children should choose which animals they want in their books. Animals could be drawn, magazine cut-outs, cut-and-paste construction paper, or pre-cut shapes that children add to.

3. When the animal is complete, encourage the child to dictate the feelings he associates with the animal.

4. The book may take the form of a class book, which is laminated and put in the library corner.

5. Each child could make his own book. Give each child a manila envelope to store her pages in until the book is completed. This could easily be a week's project.

Another Thought

If you make a class book, try these other projects: put it on audiotape or videotape, make a class bulletin board with each child creating an animal, present the animals in a play with each child acting like that animal feels.

Cognitive Development

Identifying and describing feelings through pictures and words, visual discrimination, eye-hand coordination, expression of feelings.

168

Observation of Familiar Animals

Materials

Animals in your school and the children's environment, book: *Jafta.*

1. Re-read *Jafta* and talk again about all the feelings expressed.

2. Tell your children that you would like them to be scientists, like Jafta, and observe how the animals they know feel and act.

3. Ask your children if they have animals at home. Encourage them to talk about how they know their animals feel.

4. With a small group of children and during the course of your day, watch the animals around you and talk about how they feel.

Cognitive Development

Identifying and describing feelings, making observations, visual discrimination, oral language. Appreciating animals' feelings.

Things Our Children Like To Do

Jacket illustration copyright © 1981, by Lisa Kopper, used with permission from Carolrhoda Books, Publisher.

Identifying African Animals

Materials

All the plastic, stuffed and puppet animals you have in your room, books: *Jafta* and any books you have about animals.

1. Talk again about Jafta living in South Africa and his animals being African animals.

2. Working in a small group, give each child some of the animals and a book.

3. Have the child find the animals in his book.

4. Your classification of animals will depend upon the books you have.

5. You may want to limit it to two categories at first: animals who live wild in Africa, and those who do not. Of course, all animals live in Africa today, just as all animals live in the Americas, Europe, Asia, and Australia. African animals live in zoos everywhere, so explain to the children that the African animals mean those that originated there and which still live in the wild.

6. While cows live in Africa, most of them are a different kind from American farm cows.

7. Also explain that big-eared elephants are African and small-eared elephants are Indian.

8. Encourage your children to sort the animals during their worktime.

Another Thought

Also begin to classify by the animals' characteristics, that is, all kinds of cats, monkeys, what animals like to eat, etc.

Cognitive Development

Classification using one characteristic, visual discrimination, logical thinking, eye-hand coordination, oral language.

NOTE: Any of the activities in this section could be used with Jafta. Also look at the Animals section for ideas.

Another Book

Isadora, Rachel (1992) *Over the Green Hills*, Greenwillow Books, NY.

169

Jafta's Mother

Written by Hugh Lewin

Illustrated by Lisa Kopper

Kopper catches the expressions of a little boy's feelings about his mother. Jafta could be from anywhere.

Lewin's feelings for his people in South Africa are evident in his simple prose in the *Jafta* series.

Summary:
A young South African boy tells about his mother, her work, and her feelings.

Carolrhoda Books Inc., 1981

STORY TIME

Theme
Expressing pride in someone special, identifying caring roles other people play for us.

Introduction
1. If you have read *Jafta*, ask your children to identify the people on the cover of the book.
2. Let your children tell you it is Jafta's mother, then read the title of the book.
3. Ask your children if they remember who wrote the story and who drew the pictures. Also talk a little about Jafta, the animals, and South Africa.
4. Talk about the way Jafta told us his feelings about the animals. Now, he will tell us about how his mother "feels" to him.

Reading
1. Lisa Kopper's illustrations tell a story even to very young children. Your initial "reading" can be just talking with the children about the pictures.
2. Throughout the book, encourage your children to talk about their own mothers, grandmothers, or whoever cares for their daily needs.
3. Encourage your children to tell why Jafta thinks his mother is like each thing she does for the family.
4. Then say, "Tell us what your mother is like." Give examples: "My mother is like a bird flying around 'cause she likes to go places."
5. Help your children relate to the metaphors and similes of *Jafta's Mother* by telling what their own mothers are like.
6. Be sensitive to those children with missing mothers. Help them substitute the names of their primary caregivers for mother.

Response
1. Let each child choose a page to tell about Jafta and his mother. Each child can re-tell the page in his own way, and may want to say how it is like his own mother.
2. Talk about the jobs Jafta's mother has to do. Ask your children to identify which of the jobs are similar to the jobs their mothers do. Also talk about the pots, food, bed clothes, and how they are similar or different.

EXTENSIONS

Dramatize *Jafta's Mother*

Materials
Cloth for head wrap, blouse, shirt, clothes to wash, pot for cooking, cover for sleeping children, other things you have in your classroom that would follow the story line, book: *Jafta's Mother*.

1. Re-read the book and ask the children if they would like to act out the story.
2. Talk about the story and what props you will need and what you have in your room to use.
3. Choose children to play the parts of mother and child.
4. A child with the book, as director, could keep the book in sequence, which may or may not be important. Encourage the children to make up new scenes and add to the play by using their own mother-child experience.

170

Another Thought

Take the book and props outside and perform the play. Your children may come up with other ideas. The uninterested children can come and go as an audience. Some of the children may just move into the group and play cooperatively, with Jafta as their theme.

Cognitive Development

Things Our Children Like To Do

Jacket Illustration copyright © 1981 by Lisa Kopper, used with permission from Carolrhoda Books, Publisher.

Necklace for Mother

Materials

Plastic straws, magazine pages cut into triangles, string, glue.

1. Work with a small group of children.
2. Cut plastic straws into 1" pieces. Cut triangle base 1", height 2".
3. Put a small amount of glue on the paper triangle.
4. Place the plastic straw piece on the base of the triangle. Roll the triangle around the straw piece to make a bead.
5. String the bead onto the string.
6. This is a fun, simple necklace. Allow your children to make as many as they would like to make.

171

Another Thought

Other kinds of beads can be combined with these. Or you may already have a necklace you like to make. Be sure to make a card to go with the present. Some fathers may wear this necklace, too.

Cognitive Development

Positive feelings of making something to give to others, positive self-esteem, eye-hand coordination.

NOTE: Other activities about mothers, grandmothers, fathers, grandfathers, and special friends are found in the Family section of this book.

Another Book

Hartman, Wendy (1993) *All the Magic in the World*, Dutton Children's Books, New York.

Jafta's Father

Written by Hugh Lewin   *Illustrated by Lisa Kopper*

A happy father-son relationship is evident in Lewin's prose description of their relationship.

Kopper shows us more about Jafta with new expressions in her lively pictures.

Summary:
While his father works in the city over the winter, a young boy thinks of some good times they've shared and looks forward to his father's return to their South African home in the spring.

Carolrhoda Books Inc., 1981

STORY TIME

Theme

Closeness to someone special, missing someone special.

172

Introduction

1. Your children will know that it is Jafta's father when they see the book and will be eager to talk about the books.

2. Ask again where Jafta lives and give your children time to tell what they remember about Jafta.

Reading

1. As with Jafta and Jafta's Mother, your children can easily tell a tale by looking at the illustrations.

2. Some of your children will be able to relate to their father's being somewhere else. Ask them, "How does it feel when your father is gone? How do you think Jafta feels? And how does it feel to remember the good times?"

3. Again, give your children time to tell about their experiences with their fathers, grandfathers, uncles, brothers, or some special adult.

Response

1. Your children can share the page they like best and relate it to their own fathers.

2. Be sure to adjust the word "father" to apply to any adult who cares for the child, so that children with missing fathers can have a positive experience with the book.

EXTENSIONS

Make a Hideout

Materials

Blocks from your block area or dryer box (an appliance store will give you the box and it will fold down and go in the back of a station wagon), latex paint (many paint stores will give or sell very cheaply odd-color paints), two-inch paintbrushes, paint clothes, book: *Jafta's Father.*

1. Read about Jafta's hideout. Talk to your children about making a hideout and how you could do it safely.

2. Your block area could easily be used by a small group of children.

3. For a more permanent, moveable structure, use a dryer box. This can be a project of several days.

4. Permanent marker and crayons could be used to decorate the hideout. The children could also glue on materials from your art scrap box.

5. Two children can work together to paint one side. After that dries, another group can paint on the designs. Markers can also be used to decorate. Tempera paints, with a little liquid dish soap added, will stick to the sides, and not peel off.

6. After the box has been painted, cut out windows and doors. Save the pieces. Children love to fit them back into the holes.

7. About four children can fit into one box. Make as many as your room or play area can hold.

Another Thought

Look around your play area for a safe, visible place for a hideout. It may be that some of your large playground equipment can become a hideout.

Cognitive Development

Representation, eye-hand coordination, visual discrimination, spatial relationships.

Make a Drum or Rattle

Materials

Oatmeal box, juice cans or larger cans, plastic bottle, newsprint, water, basin, wheat paste, book: *Jafta's Father*.

1. Show the picture of the drums to your children. Also talk about rattles and shakers. Let the children decide what they would like to make.

2. Have the children bring a box, can, or bottle from home to make this instrument. Have a few extras at school for those children who do not bring anything.

3. The shape of the box, can or bottle can be changed by using papier mache. Wrap it with newspaper strips. As you wrap, put small or large crumpled balls of newspaper on the sides. Then wrap the strips over the balls to create odd shapes on the object. An adult may have to make a final inspection to be sure the pieces are well secured. Boxes and cans make the best drums.

4. To make a rattle from a plastic bottle, put some small items inside the bottle as noisemakers. Then wrap the bottle with papier mache as you did with the drums.

5. Dry for at least a day in the sun or a very dry place.

6. Paint with tempera paints (add some liquid dish soap to prevent flaking) or with latex paint.

7. Small decorative items can then be glued to the drum or rattle.

Another Thought

The making of instruments can be as simple or as complex as you wish. Drawing on a can with permanent marker will certainly turn it into a drum in a child's imagination.

Cognitive Development

Eye-hand coordination, visual discrimination, oral language, recycling discards, auditory discrimination, positive self-image.

Additional Activities In This Book

Josephine's 'magination
My Daddy and I
Daddy Is a Monster...Sometimes
When I'm Old with You

Present for Father

This could be a painting, a necklace, a card, a key chain, or see *Moja Means One* to make a T-shirt.

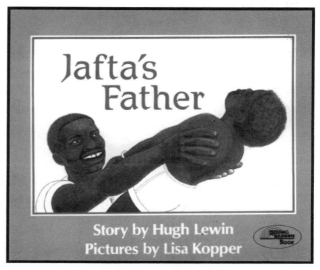

Jacket illustration copyright © 1981 by Lisa Kopper, used with permission from Carolrhoda Books, Publisher

173

Things Our Children Like To Do

Mcheshi Goes To The Market

Written and Illustrated by an editorial team in Nairobi, Kenya.

Nicholas Sironka Averdung, Judy Wanjiku Mathenge, James Okello, Martin Otieno, conceptualized and developed Mcheshi. In Kiswahili, Mcheshi is a jovial, playful character.

Summary:
It is market day and Mcheshi goes with her mother. They go from stall to stall buying what they need.

Jacaranda Designs 1991.

STORY TIME

Theme
Market day and all of its excitement.

Introduction
1. Ask your children if they have ever gone to a flea market. Encourage them to describe it.
2. Show the cover of the book. Wait for response.
3. Tell your children that Mcheshi lives far away in Nairobi, Kenya.

Reading
1. The market is shown on the inside cover page. Ask your children to predict what Mcheshi and her mother will buy.
2. Each page invites your children's comments. Listen and give them information.
3. Be sure to talk about the peoples' clothes. There is a wonderful mix of people and their clothes.

Response
1. Remind your children of their flea market experiences. Ask them to compare Mcheshi's market and their flea market.
2. Read using the voices of Mcheshi and her mother.

EXTENSIONS

Make Hard Boiled Eggs

Materials

Raw eggs, tempered glass pot, pepper & salt, paper towel, book: *Mcheshi Goes To The Market*.

1. Re-read the book. Talk about the egg man. Encourage your children to talk about the eggs. Are they cooked? How?

2. In a small group, show the raw eggs and talk about them. Use the terms raw and cooked.
3. Listen for the words your children have for cooked eggs. Tell them the words you know they did not use.
4. Show the pot and explain the process of hard boiling. Let the child tell you also.
5. Let children carefully put the eggs into the pot, and add water. Add a shake or 2 of salt. This will make the eggs easier to peel.
6. With a see-through pot your children can watch the boiling process.
7. Use an egg timer or the clock to determine the length of time to boil the eggs.
8. Talk about how the eggs will feel when they come out of the water and what you could do to change the temperature of the eggs.
9. Pour cold water over the eggs.
10. When the eggs are cool, let your children peel and eat them.

Another Thought

Sit in your house area, and ask a child who is cooking to make you an egg like Mcheshi got at the market.

Cognitive Development

Time, observing and describing how change occurs in matter.

174

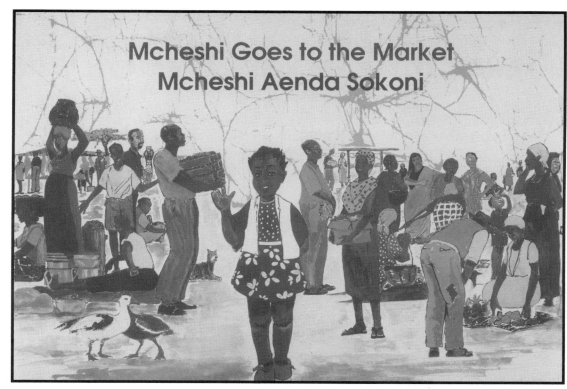

Mcheshi Goes to the Market
Mcheshi Aenda Sokoni

175

Jacket illustration copyright © 1991, by Jacaranda Designs, used with permission from Jacaranda Designs Publisher.

Market Day

1. See *Josephine's 'magination* for details.

2. Involve your parents and make a fund-raiser out of the market day.

3. Use items from your dramatic play area to allow children to dress in costume if they wish. Look at the pictures again to get ideas. Help your children realize some people are dressed very much like your children.

4. Look at all the activities in this chapter for ideas.

Another Thought

Market day may envolve in your classroom from your children's experiences. Use that as a cue to read *Mcheski Goes To Market* at story time.

Cognitive

Development

Classification, social interaction, imagnition.

Another Book

Feelings, Muriel, (1990) *Zamani Goes to Market,* Africia World Press, New Jersey.

Alexander, Lloyd, (1992) *The Fortune Tellers,* Dutton Children's Books, New York.

Visit Market Or Store

1. See *We Keep A Store*

2. Ask your parents to take their child to a flea market in your area.

3. Using the book *Mcheshi Goes To The Market*, talk about your children's trip to their flea market.

Another Thought

A trip to any store can become a tale. Use your children's experiences to relate to Mcheshi. Some of your children may go to a neighborhood store by themselves.

Cognitive Development

Relating one's own experience to a storybook, recallingpersonal events, planning an activity with an adult.

Mcheshi Goes To The Game Park

Written and illustrated in Nairobi, Kenya, by an editorial team who created Mcheshi and her stories. See our chapter on authors and illustrators for more information.

Summary:
Mcheshi lives in Kenya today. In this story she visits animals in a game preserve. The text is bi-lingual Kiswahili and English.

Jacaranda Designs, Nairobi, Kenya, 1992

STORY TIME

Theme

176

Protecting the endangered animals in Kenya.

Introduction

1. Your children will easily talk about this book cover. Let them relate their own experiences to it.

2. When reading the book title, explain about a game park and Mcheshi who lives in Kenya.

Reading

1. This book will be read many ways, and many times in your classroom.

2. Young children will love the illustrations and have much to tell you about them.

3. The written information on each page is the starter for conversations with your children about the animals.

Response

1. Re-read the book and, as suggested on page 2, change your voice for the characters.

2. Let groups of children play a role. You read, they repeat in an appropriate voice.

EXTENSIONS

Land Rover Trip

Materials

Classroom chairs, blocks, props from your classroom, book: *Mcheshi Goes To The Game Park*.

1. Gather a small group of children and ask if they would like to ride in a land rover.

2. Look at the pictures of the land rover in the book. Let the children gather the materials.

3. When every one is settled in the land rover, decide how to use the book. You read, one child reads, children take turns finding their favorite page and read.

4. Follow your children's lead to finishing the activity. (Clean up time may be the ending.)

Another Thought

See the book *Truck* and make a land rover out of a cardboard box.

Cognitive Development

Representation, oral language, cooperative learning.

Make A Pair of Binoculars

Materials

Empty toilet paper rolls (paper towel or anything of similar shape with no sharp edges), glue, markers, 4 1/2" x 6" piece of construction paper to cover each roll. String, hole punch, stapler, book: *Mcheshi Goes To The Game Park*.

1. Re-read the book. If your children do not talk about the binoculars, you point them out and label them.

2. Ask who would like to make some binoculars. Gather these children and your craft materials.

3. Children choose 2 pieces of construction paper to cover the rolls. Draw a design on the construction paper.

4. Help your child put a strip of glue down each side on the back of the construction paper and on each end.

5. Lay the construction paper on the table. Start at one end and roll the construction paper onto the roll. The child will need to hold the covered tube for a minute or two for the glue to dry.

6. Staple the two tubes together. Punch a hole in each tube. Put a string through the holes for a strap.

Another Thought

Make a telescope or just use your hands to look through. Talk about the difference between a telescope and binoculars.

Cognitive Development

Language-labeling, eye-hand coordination, making your own design, self expression.

Learn Animal Names in Kiswahili

Materials

Flash card with a picture of the animal and its name in both languages.

Chui	Leopard
Kuro	Waterbuck
Ndovu	Elephants
Kiboko	Hippo
Mamba	Crocodile
Nyati	Buffalo
Twiga	Giraffe
Simba	Lion
Kifaru	Rhino
Wanyama	Animals

Mcheshi
Goes to the Game Park
Mcheshi Aenda Hifadhi Ya Wanyama

Jacket illustration Copyright © 1991, by Jacaranda Designs, Ltd. used with permission from Jacaranda Designs, Publisher.

Kiswahili is a Moroccan trading language spoken in Kenya. It is a form of Swahili.

Another Thought

If you have bi-lingual children in your classroom, learn the names of these animals in those children's native languages.

Cognitive Development

Oral language, pre-reading, classification, labeling, appreciation of other languages.

Another Book

Stock, Catherine (1993), *Where Are You Going Manyoni*, Morrow Junior Books, New York.

177

Anansi the Spider: a Tale from the Ashanti

Adapted and illustrated by Gerald McDermott

McDermott's primary vocation of film-making can be seen in the active nature of the illustrations. The film version won the 1970 Blue Ribbon at the American Film Festival.

Summary:

Anansi the Spider, folk hero of West Africa, is saved by his six sons. He cannot decide which will get the prize, the moon, and it is set in the sky instead.

Caldecott Honor Book   Holt, Rinehart & Winston, 1972

STORY TIME

Theme

Folklore, coming to someone's rescue, rewarding helpers.

Introduction

1. Identify Anansi as a folk hero. Talk about stories that people tell each other for generations.

2. Talk about how people make up stories to explain how and why things happen.

3. Encourage your children to tell you about spiders.

4. Give your children time to talk about how Anansi looks and how living spiders look.

Reading

1. Ask for comments from your children on the abilities of each son.

2. Use the illustrations, the text, and your children's comments, and Anansi will entertain your children.

Response

1. Talk about which son should get the moon and why.

2. Someone will say that the sons could share the great globe of light. Encourage this thought.

EXTENSIONS

Draw A Spider Book

Materials

Drawing paper, some preprinted pages, crayons/markers, book: *Anansi the Spider*.

1. Re-read *Anansi*. Ask your children if they would like to make their own books.

2. One of the forms most young children draw is a mandala. It is very much like a spider, particularly if the adult viewer is not concerned about the number of legs the child's spider has.

3. Pages with a teacher-drawn fish and falcon can allow the child to experiment further with his mandala spiders. These pre-drawn photocopied pages can aid the child in his drawing of the story. Of course, any child who wants to draw his own fish and falcon should be encouraged to do so.

4. Additionally, any child who chooses to create his own story line should be encouraged to do so.

5. Gather the pages together, make a cover, and add a back. Use staples or brads to hold the book together.

Another Thought

This could be a class book, with individual children contributing single pages. Be sure to laminate it.

Cognitive Development

Representation, recall of a sequence of events, eye-hand coordination, positive self-image

178

Study Spiders

Materials

Big jars, books: *Anansi the Spider*, and spider books from your library.

1. Discuss with your children the differences that they know between living spiders and Anansi.

2. Talk about eating, sleeping, magical powers, living through words and words that make things happen.

3. Use the books to give your children scientific information about spiders.

4. Identify safety concerns about handling spiders. Know the poisonous spiders for your location.

Another Thought

Keep a non-poisonous spider in a jar for a few days. Talk about its need for food. Help your children empathize with a spider that is kept in a jar. Tell how spiders help us by eating insects.

Cognitive Development

Scientific observation, distinguishing between live and folktale animals.

Cut-and-Paste Spiders

Materials

Scissors, glue, paper towels, crayons/markers, string, construction paper, your art scrap box, books: *Children & Scissors, Anansi the Spider*.

1. Re-read *Anansi the Spider*. Ask your children if they would like to make Anansi.

2. Working in small groups in the art area, talk about how a spider looks, how many legs and eyes it has.

3. Talk about whether Anansi is a living or a pretend spider.

4. Be sure your children understand that their spiders can look any way they want them to look.

5. Bodies and legs may be pre-cut, torn, or cut by the children and glued together.

Another Thought

Listen while the children re-tell this Anansi story and make up their own Anansi stories.

Cognitive Development

Representation, oral language, recalling information, eye-hand coordination.

Tape Story

Materials

Tape, tape recorder, book: *Anansi the Spider*.

1. With a small group of children, re-read the story and tape it.

Draw a Spider Book

Mandala
4 year-old child.

2. Decide ahead of time what signal to give to turn the page.

3. How much, if any, conversation about the story will take place while taping needs to be decided with the children before you start taping. If your children know the story well, they may want to take turns speaking or "reading" parts.

4. The tape and book can be made available in your library corner.

Another Thought

This would make an excellent flannel board story.

Cognitive Development

Auditory discrimination, anticipation of an event.

179

Another Book

Bryan, A. (1977) *The Dancing Granny*, Atheneum, Hartford.

Why Mosquitoes Buzz In People's Ears

Written by Verna Aardema
Because her hiding place as a child was in a swamp behind her small-town Michigan home, Aardema knew mosquitoes. She wrote her first stories in that swamp.

Illustrated by Leo and Diane Dillon
The Dillons wanted the antelope's mother to be proud of him, so they made him big and beautiful. The little red bird listens with the children to the story.

Summary:
African tale about the misbehavior of a mosquito and its effects on the other animals.

Caldecott Medal and 3 other awards   Dial Books for Young Readers, 1975

STORY TIME

Theme
Fear, looking at the facts, problem-solving.

Introduction
1. Encourage your children to talk about the cover of the book. Ask if anyone has ever had a mosquito buzz in her ear.
2. Tell your children that this is a story told in Africa. The story explains why mosquitoes buzz in people's ears.
3. Help them remember other folktales you have read.

Reading
1. Our first reading of the story was just from the pictures. The children made up a delightful story. Your children could, too!
2. Ask the children why the iguana did not want to listen to the mosquito.
3. Get the children to predict what each new animal will do.
4. Develop the children's short-term memory by having them recall the animal before the animal is called to talk to the lion.

Response
1. Explore with your children how one little mosquito could cause so much trouble in the jungle.
2. Lead your children to the conclusion that, if one of the animals had stood up and said, "What's going on?" there might not have been so much trouble.
3. Let the children tell you their favorite animals in the story and what they would have done if they were that animal.

EXTENSIONS

Flannel Board Story on Tape
Materials
Flannel board pieces, flannel board, tape recorder, tape, book: *Why Mosquitoes Buzz in People's Ears*.
1. You pre-tape the story or tape it while reading it as a listening story to your children. Use some signal for page-turning.
2. Instruct your children in the use of the tape recorder.
3. Give the children the pieces, book, and tape recorder. Let them manipulate the pieces and tell the story.
4. Place the materials in the library corner for independent use.

Cognitive Development
Sequencing of events, re-telling a story, oral expression, eye-hand coordination, motor sequencing.

Dramatize the Story
Materials
The animals your children made, headbands with pictures of animals on them, puppets from your room, clothes from your dress-up box, model animals.
1. Talk with your children about how they want to show the animals (headbands/puppets/costumes/ models).
2. Choose children who are good listeners to be the animals. The acting out is important. Only a few children may want to sit and be part of an audience. A small listening audience is better than a big inattentive audience.

180

3. Allow the children to repeat the play as long as they are interested. Encourage them to add their own ideas to the play.

4. Talk about taking turns being an animal and changing parts. The children may also want to add parts.

Another Thought

Put on the play in your room for those older children who helped teach about the mosquito.

Models of Animals in the Story

Materials

Basic pre-cut animal shapes, pre-cut squares and rectangles (1" x 1" to 2" x 6"), background paper, markers/crayons, scissors, glue, your art scrap box, book: *Children & Scissors*.

1. Look through the story again with the children, looking at the animals. Talk with the children about how they were illustrated and how the Dillons make the animals.

2. Working in a small group, show the children the basic pre-cut shapes. Let the children tell you what animals they want to make.

3. Give the children access to the scrap box and the pre-cut squares and triangles.

4. Encourage the children to cut their own shapes out of the pre-cut paper as well as the materials in your scrap box.

5. Some children may want to create from the beginning, cutting or drawing their own animal shapes. Some may find a suitable (to them) base for an animal in the scrap box.

Another Thought

The Dillon illustrations inspire creative animals. Let your children follow the Dillons' lead. Then find an unusual way to display the animals in your room, a place where adults will ask and the children can explain about their animals.

Cognitive Development

Representation, visual discrimination, eye-hand coordination.

From *Why Mosquitoes Buzz in Peoples' Ears* by Verna Aardema, illustrations by Leo and Diane Dillon, Copyright © 1975 by Leo and Diane Dillon, illustrations. Used by permission of Dial Books for Young Readers, a division of Penguin Books USA, Inc.

Learn About Mosquitoes

Materials

Printed materials about mosquitoes and mosquito control (call your local health department and ask for them), plastic straws (cut end to sharp point), plastic wrap, clear drinking glasses, red Kool-Aid or other punch, your playground.

1. Let your children tell you about their experiences with mosquitoes.

2. Share the materials you have from the health department with your children.

3. Tell your children they are going to do an experiment. Talk about how the mosquito draws up blood from their bodies.

4. Give each child a glass half-full of red punch (the top of the glass covered snugly with a piece of plastic wrap) and a straw with a pointed end.

5. Let each child be a mosquito. With the straw, pierce the plastic wrap, which represents the skin. Then suck up the blood (red punch).

6. Now explore your playground for mosquito larvae. If you find and kill some mosquitoes, ask the children where the blood came from and why some mosquitoes have no blood. Explain that the blood from other people is what can give them diseases, that the blood is simply carried by mosquitoes. Ask your children to explain the importance of secure screens at open doors and windows in the mosquito season.

Another Thought

Some of the older children in the school may have information about mosquitoes in their science books. Have these children come and interact with your children using the mosquito information.

Cognitive Development

Observation, experimentation, classification, environmental awareness.

Another Book

Grifalconi, Ann, *Darkness and the Butterfly.*

181

Moja Means One:
Swahili Counting Book

Written by Muriel Feelings   *Illustrated by Tom Feelings*

Muriel Feelings, the writer, and her husband Tom Feelings, the artist, collaborated on children's books. After they lived in Africa, Muriel taught school, introducing African crafts and Swahili. The experience culminated in *Moja Means One*.

Summary:

Counting for children in the Swahili language, illustrating African country lifestyles.

A Caldecott Honor Book   Dial Books for Young Readers, 1971

STORY TIME

Theme

Common language of eastern part of Africa, language helps people understand one another better.

Introduction

1. Show the cover of the book and ask your children to tell you about it.

2. Have the children count in unison the balls the boy has. Talk about language and how people all over the world use different words to count. If you have bilingual children in your room, encourage them to count in their primary language.

3. Tell your children this boy is counting in Swahili, and read the title of the book.

Reading

1. Each page has something that corresponds with the numeral of that page. On first reading, count the items in English, then say the Swahili name for the final numeral.

2. Encourage your children to talk about the illustrations.

3. Re-read the book, saying the Swahili counting words.

Response

Take turns letting your children show pages in the book. Have them tell about the illustrations and say the Swahili word.

EXTENSIONS

Learn Ella Jenkins Song

Materials

Record player, record: *Ella Jenkins' Jambo and Other Call and Response Songs and Chants*, book: *Moja Means One*.

Use your music time to learn this song.

Another Thought

As you sing the song, show some of the illustrations in the book. Use tape by TAIFA Productions; see "Sources" for ordering information.

Cognitive Development

Pronunciation of Swahili, musical rhythms and sounds, auditory discrimination, oral language.

Make a Mankala

Materials

Egg carton, permanent markers, papier mache (newspaper, water, basin, wheat paste), paint and paintbrushes, small stones, plastic bottle caps or seeds.

1. Decorate the egg carton simply by drawing on it with the permanent markers, or cover the outside of the egg carton with papier mache, let dry, and paint.

2. Encourage your children to use the mankala for counting, sorting, and making up their own games.

Cognitive Development

Representation, eye-hand coordination, creativity, oral language, one-to-one correspondence.

Tie-Dye Something To Wear

Materials

T-shirt, piece of cloth for headgear or to wrap as a dress or baby carrier, cloth dye, hot water, assorted buckets or other containers, rubber bands, masking tape.

1. Decide what kind of clothing you will make, then talk with your children about what they will be making. Let them choose the colors of dye.

2. This can easily be a two-day project.

3. When you use rubber bands, take a handful of cloth, push it through a rubber band, then wrap and rewrap the rubber band around the cloth until very snug. This will make circles on the cloth when it is dyed. The more cloth pulled through the rubber band, the larger the circle. Most children can pull the cloth through the rubber band, although some need help in pulling and wrapping the rubber band tightly enough. The children may make as many or as few circles as they feel like.

4. Another way to mark off the cloth is to use masking tape. Roll the shirt or cloth into the shape of a long stick. Wrap the masking tape around the shirt at the places where you want no color. Again, be sure the tape is very tight.

5. Now you are ready to dye. Follow the directions on the dye package. Each color needs an individual container.

6. If you use a washing machine, a cup of vinegar in the water will help set the color. If you use a dryer, your next load will pick up the color of your dye.

Another Thought

Cloth can be decorated by small children with spray paints, by sponge-painting with latex paints, permanent markers, crayons, hot-wax crayons. Use crayon melter.

Cognitive Development

Eye-hand coordination, oral language, visual discrimination, positive self-image.

Another Book

Haskins, J (1989) *Count Your Way Through Africa,* Carolrhoda, Minneapolis.

Lester, J. (1989) *How Many Spots Does a Leopard Have? And Other Tales,* Scholastic, New York.

Make a Counting Tape

Materials

Tape, tape recorder, book: *Moja Means One.*

1. After singing with Ella Jenkins, you will know the Swahili words.

2. For each numeral, say that numeral. Then begin with Moja and count the illustrations on the page.

3. Make the tape available in your listening center.

Another Thought

Encourage your children to bring small items to the listening center to count with the tape. Also suggest that they bring other counting books to the center and count those pages in Swahili.

Cognitive Development

Auditory discrimination, one-to-one correspondence, visual discrimination, oral language, recalling a sequence of words.

183

From *Moja Mieans One: Swahili Counting Book* by Muriel Feelings, pictures by Tom Feelings, Copyright © 1971, Tom Feelings, pictures. Used by permission of Dial Books for Young Readers, a division of Penguin Books, USA, Inc.

Who's in Rabbit's House?
A Masai Tale

Written by Verna Aardema

Aardema's small daughter did not like to eat, so her mother told her African stories. She sent one to an editor and it was published.

Summary:

In a re-told Masai tale, the Rabbit's house is occupied by a strange creature until Frog scares it away.

Four Best Book Awards and List

Illustrated by Leo and Diane Dillon

The Dillons, who work as a team, have created the lions as a curious audience, trying to understand what the Masai are doing now.

Dial Books for Young Readers, 1977

STORY TIME

Theme

Humorous Masai folktale, problem-solving.

184

Introduction

1. The cover illustrations dramatically introduce this story. Ask why, who, and what questions.

2. Your children will be brimming with curiosity to hear this story.

Reading

1. Use the gathering of the audience again to help your children relate to the likenesses in people everywhere. Everybody likes a good story.

2. Also point out that the characters in this story will be Masai wearing masks.

3. Learn the story and judge the listening skill level of your children. You may want to tell the essential parts with your children being able to view the pictures at all times.

4. Be sure to encourage your children to chant, "Who's in Rabbit's House?"

5. Encourage them to chant the bad voice's response at the appropriate time. Chanting the bad voice gives children an appropriate outlet for negative energy.

Response

1. Talk about why the caterpillar was able to trick all of the animals.

2. Ask how the rabbit solved his own problem.

3. On re-reading, talk more about the Masai people in the audience.

4. If none of your children have noticed the lions, point them out.

EXTENSIONS

NOTE: Activities for *Why Mosquitoes Buzz in People's Ears* can be adapted easily for *Who's In Rabbit's House?*

Jewelry of the Masai

Materials

Small hammers, small metal file, piece of flat steel, copper telephone wire or copper electric wire (or string or fishing line), beads or pieces of plastic straw or macaroni or styrofoam packing pieces.

1. Find a source for scrap telephone and electrical wire (building going on around you, repair people in your community).

2. Use the telephone wire to string the beads. Braid or twist the wire together for another style.

3. Of course, fishing line can be used to string any of the things your children use for beads.

4. Take the plastic coating off the electric wire. Cut the wire in a length long enough to go loosely around the child's arm at least twice.

5. Be sure you file the end of the wire smooth, so there are no rough edges. Use a metal file.

6. Each child can hammer her bracelet to mark it or to change the shape. Flatten the end of the wire by hammering it into a flat circle. Again, file it with a metal file to smooth it off. The metal file can also be used to make designs on the bracelet.

Another Thought

Look at the pictures of the Masai people to see how many different kinds of bead jewelry they made.

Cognitive Development

Inventing patterned designs, eye-hand coordination, visual discrimination, positive self-image.

Papier Mache Mask

Materials

Plastic tub, strips of newspaper (2' x 3"), wheat paste (flour), large balloon, paint, paintbrushes, construction paper, your art scrap box, scissors, glue, hot glue gun, books: *Mudworks, Who's In Rabbit's House?*

1. By using a large balloon (10" to 12" diameter), you can make a mask that will fit over your children's heads.

2. Use permanent markers to draw 3" eyes and mouth on the blown-up balloon. Then draw a circle on the bottom of the balloon. Make the circle big enough for the child's head to go through.

3. Mix the wheat paste with enough water to make it the consistency of pudding. Pull the newspaper strip through the mix to cover the strip entirely.

4. Help each child wrap his balloon around and around, as if he were bandaging it. Every strip will not have to be dampened.

5. Do not put newspaper over the drawn eyes, mouth, or head entry. Leave those spaces open so there will be holes in the mask.

6. The newspaper strips should go on the balloon in several layers, so the mask will hold its shape.

7. Put in the sun or a very dry place to dry.

8. Paint with tempera paints or latex paints. Add ears, horns, and other decorations that please the child.

Another Thought

Encourage your children to work in small groups. They can think about the animal masks in their groups. Then make up a story patterned after *Who's In Rabbit's House?* This can be performed for themselves or an audience.

Cognitive Development

Representation, visual discrimination, completing a sequence for a final product, delayed gratification, oral language.

Another Book

Walter, M (1985), *Brother to the Wind*, Lothrop, Lee & Shepard, New York.

Animal Sounds

Materials

Your rhythm band instruments, record (or CD or tape) of any animal sound recording you may have, book: *Who's In Rabbit's House?*

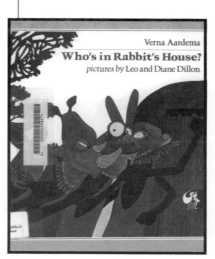

From *Who's In Rabbit's House* by Verna Aardema, pictures by Leo and Diane Dillon, copyright © 1977 by Leo and Diane Dillon, pictures. Used by permission of Dial Books for Young Readers, a division of Penguin Books USA, Inc.

1. Talk with a small group of your children about Swahili and how it sounds different from the language your children speak. Say some of the words.

2. Ask your children if they think the sounds animals make seem the same to the Masai as they do to your children. Some of your children may remember that the animal sounds in the story were different.

3. Tell your children that the French people say that cats meow "mieux, mieux" instead of our "meow, meow," and that the Japanese say that roosters crow "kiri-kiru" instead of our "cock-a-doodle-doo."

4. Read those parts of the story describing the sounds of the animals leaving.

5. Make the sounds with your children. Talk about how they think it sounds when the animal leaves.

6. Encourage your children to describe the sounds in terms of loud/soft, high/low, long/short, and so forth.

7. Also help your children consider whether a big animal can make a little sound, a long animal can make a short sound, and so on.

8. Have your children choose rhythm band instruments or other noisemakers to show how the animals sound when they move.

9. Be sure your children include how their animals are feeling when they are making this noise by moving.

Cognitive Development

Auditory discrimination, logical thinking, oral language, recall of information.

185

Jambo Means Hello: Swahili Alphabet Book

Written by Muriel Feelings *Illustrated by Tom Feelings*

The experiences of Muriel and Tom Feelings in Africa are reflected in their books. Children all over the world will be delighted to learn Swahili words.

Summary:

The alphabet in Swahili, daily life of country people in Africa.

Caldecott Honor Book Dial Books for Young Readers, 1974

STORY TIME

Theme

Language as a means of gaining new ideas and understanding of people.

Introduction

1. Ask your children if they know anyone who can talk in a language other than English.

2. Let your children tell you their experiences with language. Perhaps their families have special words or expressions. Talk about baby talk and how they learned to talk.

3. Tell your children about some of the languages spoken in the United States. Help them understand that people use different words for the same thing.

4. Relate to *Moja Means One* if you have read that for your children.

Reading

1. Tom Feelings' illustrations will draw your children into conversation about them.

2. Let those who can identify the letter say it each time.

Response

1. Your children can choose the letters they like best and tell the class about the illustrations.

2. Have each child say "Jambo" when he tells about his letter.

EXTENSIONS

Paint in the Feelings Style

Materials

White drawing paper, black markers, white tempera paint, tissue paper, linseed oil, books: *Jambo Means Hello, Moja Means One*.

1. The last page in the book describes how Tom Feelings creates his illustrations. Read it, then talk to your children about the illustrations.

2. A simpler version would be: The child draws any picture that pleases her. Place wet tissue paper over the drawings. Then the child adds white tempera paint to the picture as she likes. The linseed oil may or may not be used.

3. Find some of the Swahili words to describe the paintings, especially "Uzuri."

4. Because this is another experience with art materials, it is worth a try. Remember, your children need some time to experiment with this new way to use their materials. So make plenty of materials available.

Another Thought

Paint with only black and white tempera or use different color markers for the bottom picture. Lay down the tissue and use different color tempera for the top picture.

Cognitive Development

Using familiar materials in a new way, visual discrimination, eye-hand coordination.

186

African Animal ABC Book

Materials

Drawing paper, construction paper, magazine pictures, markers/crayons, scissors, glue, staples, stapler, books: *Jambo Means Hello, Children & Scissors.*

1. Show your children the animal pictures in the book. Ask if they would like to make an alphabet book of African animals.

2. Work in small groups. The book could be as simple as using just the letters in the child's name, or the child's favorite African animals.

3. The entire alphabet could be a week or two-week project.

4. Children may choose to draw, cut-and-paste, or paint their animal pictures.

5. An adult may write the letter on the page. Children may then want to add their own writing to the page.

6. Make front and back covers and staple together.

Another Thought

Make a partial alphabet book, using those Swahili words that you use in your classroom. See *Children & Scissors.*

Cognitive Development

Visual discrimination, eye-hand coordination, completing a long-term project.

Clay Jar

Materials

Salt, dough, clay, paints, books: *Jambo Means Hello, Mudworks.*

1. Show your children the Gudulia picture and ask if they would like to make a clay jar.

2. See *Mudworks* for various dough recipes.

3. Ask your art supply person about available clays.

Another Book

Onyefulu, Ifeona, *A is for Africa.*

Steptoe, John (1987), *Mufaro's Beautiful Daughters: an African Tale*, Lothrop, Lee & Shepard, New York.

From *Jambo Means Hello* by Muriel Feelings, Illustrated by Tom Feelings. Copyright © 1974, by Tom Feelings, illustrations. Used by permission of Dial Books for Young Readers, a division of Penguin Books USA, Inc.

Things Our Children Like To Do

187

Bringing the Rain to Kapiti Plain

Written by Verna Aardema   *Illustrations by Beatriz Vidal*

For about 10 years, Aardema thought about how to re-tell this folktale. One night she lay awake until 4 a.m. when the first stanza came to her.

Vidal grew up in a small town in Argentina, and her colorful paintings in this, her first children's book, reveal a childlike delight in nature.

Summary:
The plain is dry, the animals thirsty, and the hero brings the rain as rhythmic verses repeat on each page.

Dial Books for Young Readers, 1981

STORY TIME

Theme
Life cycle on the African plain, folklore.

Introduction
1. Show your children the cover of the book and let them tell you about it.
2. Talk about rain, and what happens when it does not rains for a long time.
3. Tell your children about folktales and how they last for years.

Reading
1. Your children can easily tell this story to you by looking at the illustrations.
2. As their listening skills increase, you will want them to read the tale with you.
3. If you give the new line, they will — with practice — be able to complete the rest of the tale from its beginning.

Response
1. Talk about people being able to make it rain, and whether that is real or make-believe.
2. Remember, sometimes airplanes are flown into clouds to "seed" them. Iodine salt is one of the chemicals that are seeded into the clouds. Often, it does rain after the clouds are seeded.
3. Ask if anyone can stand like Ki-pat, and if anyone knows an animal that stands like Ki-pat. (Many water birds stand on one leg. Identify your local water birds which stand on one leg.)

EXTENSIONS

African Plain Mural

Materials
Craft paper (3' x 10'), your art scrap box, paint, paintbrushes, construction paper, magazine pictures, markers/crayons, dry grass, black tissue paper, glue, scissors, books: *Bringing the Rain to Kapiti Plain, Children & Scissors.*

NOTE: This is at least a three-day project, or perhaps up to 2 weeks.

1. Re-read the book to your children. Ask if they would like to make a big picture about the story. Tell them that, when a picture is as big as the one they are going to make, you call it a mural.
2. Paint the full length of the mural as a sky with a small group of children. The next day, paint the full length of the mural as the ground.
3. Now you are ready to put the characters on the mural. The children can paint, draw, or cut-and-paste the characters. These can be added by small groups from day to day. Dry grass can also be glued to the mural.
4. The big black cloud could be made from black tissue paper, crumpled up, and glued onto the mural.
5. Add Ki-pat and family to the mural and display at eye level for the children.

Another Thought
Each child could make her own picture of the story.

Cognitive Development
Representation, planning a display, oral language, visual discrimination, eye-hand coordination.

Flannel Board Story and Tape

Materials

Construction paper, markers/crayons, glue, scissors, flannel strips, tape, tape recorder, books: *Bringing The Rain to Kapiti Plain, Children & Scissors.*

1. Re-read the book. Ask your children if they would like to make the characters for a flannel board story.

2. Work in a small group to make the animals and Ki-pat's family for the story. Remember the big black cloud. Laminate the characters, then hot-glue a strip of flannel on the backs.

From *Bringing the Rain to Kapiti Plain* by Verna Aardema, illustrated by Beatriz Vidal. Copyright © 1981 by Beatriz Vidal, illustrations. Used by permission of Dial Books for Young Readers a division of Penguin Books USA, Inc.

3. On another day, re-read the book using the flannel board. Be sure the children repeat the story as you go. Tape this presentation.

4. Make the book, flannel board characters, and tape available in the listening center.

Another Thought

Your children may want to make up their own stories using their own characters. A metal tray will serve as a story-telling board. Use magnetic tape on the backs of the characters instead of the flannel strip.

Cognitive Development

Recalling a sequence of events, oral language, representation, visual discrimination, eye-hand development.

Another Book

Anderson/Sankofa, David A. *The Origin of Life on Earth*, Sights Productions, Mt. Airy, MD.

Bryan, A. (1994), *The Story of Lightning and Thunder*, Atheneum.

Cause-and-Effect Relationship

Materials

Marbles, pan of water, Dr. Drew blocks, unit blocks, dominoes, rain gauge, playground balls or small balls.

1. Let a small group of children take turns dropping a marble into the pan of water. Talk about what happens.

2. Set up the blocks in a row. Ask your children to predict what will happen if you push down the first block. Have one child give the block a gentle push. Be sure you have enough blocks for each child to have a set of blocks to experiment with. Do the same thing with dominoes.

3. Place the balls in a row. Ask the children what will happen if you roll a ball into the first ball. Roll the ball. Be sure to have enough balls for each child to have several. (Look for a busy tennis club as a source for old "dead" tennis balls.)

4. Put a rain gauge outside your room and watch it fill with rain throughout the year.

5. Talk about how the events on Kapiti Plain show cause and effect. One thing happened, then another, then another.

6. The next time there is hitting in your room, help your children understand that hitting can keep on going. One child hits another child, the other child hits back, and back and forth. Relate it to good things also. One child does something nice, so another child does something nice, and so on.

Another Thought

Make these materials available to your children. Encourage them to find other materials that will show cause and effect relationships. Planting rye grass seed can be a good experiment, because it comes up fast enough for your children to see the relationship between seed and ground, water and grass.

Cognitive Development

Cause and effect relationships.

189

Ashanti to Zulu: African Traditions

Written by Margaret Musgrove

Musgrove has studied African traditions first hand, living there for two years and then returning four times.

Illustrated by Leo and Diane Dillon

Most of the Dillons' illustrations show an artifact, a local animal, and a family with its living quarters to represent that tribe. Compare them.

Summary:
Each letter of the alphabet is represented by a different African tribe.

The 1977 Caldecott Medal Winner and 12 other honors   Dial Books for Young Readers, 1976

STORY TIME

Theme
An array of customs and cultures of the peoples of Africa.

Introduction
1. Be sure to read for yourself the note from the author and the text on the page that precedes it before you "read" this book to your children.
2. The illustrations are so intriguing that you will want to read this book with a small group of children so they can see.

Reading
1. Children will have many comments and questions about the Dillons' pictures. Tell or read from the text to let the children know more about the customs and traditions in the pictures.
2. This is a book you will want to refer to often. Use it when you talk about Africa or when your children have questions about Africa.

Response
1. Continue talking with your children about each letter.
2. If your children are learning the alphabet, be sure to point out that this is an alphabet book.

EXTENSIONS

Book of Community People
Materials
Newspaper pictures, local magazine pictures, markers/crayons, scissors, glue, paper for book pages, book cover.

1. Help your children understand that this book will show the many ways people live by finding examples of the way different people live in your community (ethnic groups, homeless, group homes for exceptional persons, homes of farmers, apartment dwellers, project housing, condominiums).
2. These groups should be shown in their most positive light with the good things they do for your community. For example, many homeless people help keep the streets clean by recycling our litter (cans, paper, bottles).
3. Our purpose is to make the people in the book real by showing in your own community the different kinds of people who live there.
4. Help your children understand some of the harmonious ways that people who are different from one another can live together.

Another Thought
Have a family supper and ask each family to bring its favorite food.

Cognitive Development
Social consciousness, oral language, visual discrimination.

Kye Kye Kula
Materials
Your rhythm band instruments and everything your children have made: masks, drums, rattles, clothes, headbands, jewelry.

1. Look in the Appendix for the Kye Kye Kula words.
2. This is a call-and-response song your children will enjoy. They can make up the dance steps.

190

3. Initially, you make the call and let the children respond. Then let individual children (or a small group of children) make the call.

Another Thought
Your children will love performing this for anyone.

Cognitive Development
Integration of brain functioning, hands, feet, body, voice ears, all working together to perform the song and dance, positive self-image, respect for African tradition and culture.

Living In Africa Day
Materials
All of the items you have made in this section, flat baskets, black jelly beans, cold cream, tempera paints, brushes, sand table.

1. By using everything your children have worked on, you can produce an African atmosphere in your classroom. Your worktime will become an African village.

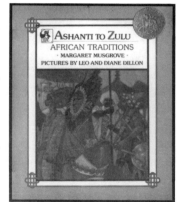

2. Encourage your children to carry soft materials in baskets on their heads, like the Vai people.

From *Ashanti to Zulu: African Traditions* by Margaret Musgrove. Copyright © 1976 by Margaret Musgrove. Used by permission of Dial Books for Young Readers, a division of Penguin Books USA, Inc.

3. Everyone will want black teeth like the Uge. Explain that the Uge's teeth take years to become black.

4. Put cold cream (or hand lotion) on your children's cheeks and chins. Paint their faces with tempera paints. Be sure to keep the paint and cold cream away from your children's eyes.

5. Make the River Nile or the Congo River in the sand box. Use your small plastic people and animals to tell stories with your children about life on these rivers.

6. Generally encourage your children to draw from all their activities about Africa to role-play.

Another Thought
You may want to invite visitors for this special day. Encourage your children to continue their role-playing beyond this day.

Masks
Materials
Paper plates, paper bags, heavy tagboard, paint, paintbrushes, glitter, markers/crayons, construction paper, your art scrap box, scissors, glue, any headband, book: *Children & Scissors*.

1. Masks can be made simply or take several days to complete. Relate the making of the mask to some experience your children have already had with masks.

2. A paper plate can be used as a base. The plate can first be colored or painted. Then add decorations from your art scrap box. If you are unsure how to start, use one of the activities in *Children & Scissors*.

3. The trick to a mask is keeping it on. One solution is to use a headband as a base. String, ribbon, and elastic bands can also be used.

4. With any of the masks your children make, be sure the eyes are large — at least 3 inches in diameter. Cut out the eyes before the child starts to work so she can plan her mask around the eyes.

5. Paper bag masks can be used. Eyes and mouths should be precut. If a large bag is used, shoulder cuts can be made from the side. This will allow the bag to slip over the child's body. Our experience is that paper bags tear up easily, so get some wide clear tape to reinforce them.

6. Your children will love making and wearing their masks. Encourage them to look at all the pictures you have of masks and then create their own designs.

7. Listen to your children as they plan and make their masks. Some may want to dictate some information about their masks. Write it down for them.

Another Thought
See *Who's In Rabbit's House?* for how to make a papier mache mask.

Cognitive Development
Appreciation of other cultural traditions, representation, visual discrimination, spatial relations, eye-hand coordination, oral language.

191

CHAPTER TEN

Authors and Illustrators

The artists and authors whose work is represented in *Children & Books I* have created an interesting range of children's literature. As you prepare yourself to read a new story to your children, look here for those who created the book so you can tell your children about the people whose work they will hear and see.

The names are presented here in alphabetical order for ease of access. Listed after the name of each author are books that are reviewed in *Children & Books I* and a few other favorites that your children will enjoy.

Your children will particularly like knowing such details as nicknames, favorite things to do, games played, pets and such details from the days of childhood for authors and illustrators. When we have been able to contact the books' creators, we have included such information.

The children will also be interested in knowing that authors make up stories and that illustrators paint and draw, just like children do. Make the point that a story is talk, written down, and that the illustrations are paintings, much like theirs. Let them know that these are vocations that grown-ups follow.

You will notice that some of the biographies presented here are much longer than others. You've already guessed it, but the reason, for the record, is that these are very busy people. We were unable to reach some of the authors and illustrators and had to rely on printed material for our biographies. African American and African authors are identified by a * next to their name, when known.

We are deeply appreciative to those authors and illustrators who took time out of their busy schedules to respond to our questions and help make this book a more complete reference for teachers who want their children to develop an understanding of the writing and illustrating processes. Some of them have been allowed us to print an address so that your children can write to them. You can always send letters to the book publisher, who will send them to the author or illustrator.

Verna Aardema

Who's In Rabbit's House
Bringing the Rain to Kapiti Plain
Why Mosquitoes Buzz in People's Ears

The little town of New Era, Michigan, population 200, became 201 on June 6, 1911, when Verna Aardema was born. She was third in a family that would eventually grow to six girls and three boys.

Like most people in the United States today, she had a mixed background. Her father, Alfred Norberg, was born in Sweden, and both parents of her mother, Dora Norberg, were born in The Netherlands.

When she was a little girl, Verna's family and friends called her Ernie. Little Ernie was a bookworm from the minute she learned to read, which didn't make her popular with her family. With so many children, her mother valued help with the housework. To get Ernie to do anything, she first had to get her away from her book.

When Ernie's next younger sister came along, she was a "Mother's-little-helper-with-a-bow-in-her-hair." She helped Mother all the time. Well, it wasn't all work and no play. There was a white rabbit named Fluffy for the children to play with. Little Ernie liked to play card games, go skating and go swimming, but mostly she liked to read. Their mother read to them, too. There were no picture books in the family that she remembers, but Little Ernie loved *The Little Mermaid* by Hans Christian Andersen.

Still, her hard working little sister made little Ernie look bad, until one day in the sixth grade.

On that day, Ernie's teacher had the class write poems at school. Ernie got an "A" on hers. When Mother read it, she said: "Why Verna, you're going to be a writer -- just like my grandfather." Ernie had been noticed a lot for failing to help around the house, but this was the first time she had been noticed for something good. She made up her mind then and there to make a career of being like her mother's grandfather.

At last, lazy Ernie was going to be good for something. From then on, her mother was more interested in helping her become a writer than in trying to get her to help around the house.

Ernie's mother knew that writers need a quiet place to think. But, with nine children, there wasn't a quiet corner in the house. Every corner had kids in it. Out behind the house was a swamp, and Ernie soon discovered a "secret room" in the swamp, surrounded by fallen logs, that could be her thinking place.

Even after a meal, when there were piles of dishes to be washed, Ernie could get away by taking a couple of dishes from the dining room table out to the kitchen -- and then flying out the back door. She would hear her mother say, "Let her go. She's going to the swamp." Her mother thought the swamp was a good place for a bookworm to hatch into a writer.

It was in that swamp that Verna Aardema made up her first stories. She would sit on one of the logs that formed the boundary of her secret room, dig her heels into the spongy black earth, and think and think. She would think until she thought that surely her sisters had finished washing dishes.

Verna's father had once owned a store. A leftover grey ledger became her manuscript book. In it, she wrote the little stories she thought up in the swamp. And she asked God to help her become as good a writer as Gene Stratton-Porter.

When she was in high school, Verna wrote news from school for the Oceana Herald and learned about news writing from a real editor. At Michigan State College, she took every writing course in the catalogs. Verna placed first in three writing contests in her senior year.

After graduation, she started teaching school. Within a couple of years, she married Albert Aardema and forgot about writing for a while. They had a son and a daughter, and Verna concentrated on reading when she wasn't teaching school or taking care of her own children.

At one time, almost all of her reading was about Africa. As it happened, Verna's baby daughter did not like to eat. To help distract her little girl, Verna began making up stories. Because she was reading books about Africa, the "feeding stories" were usually set in that exotic land.

One of her African stories turned out so well that Verna sold it to a magazine and sent it to a book publisher, Coward-McCann, Inc. The editor there asked her to use the story as chapter one of a juvenile novel. Verna answered quickly, by return mail. She told the editor she couldn't think of a chapter two, and suggested that she could do a collection of African folktales for children that had not yet been written for Americans. The editor liked the idea and told her to go ahead.

That is how Verna Aardema happened to become a writer of African tales. She has published 22 books, four of which are collections of tales. And she has several more books forthcoming.

Aardema retired from teaching in 1973 and works full-time on her stories and correspondence.

194

She and her husband, Dr. Joel Vugteveen, live in Florida. Her favorite children's stories today are *Roll of Thunder* and *Hear My Cry*.

She works hard on re-telling African tales. Aardema wondered for almost ten years about how to re-tell the wonderful story about *Bringing the Rain to Kapiti Plain*. "One night, I lay awake until four a.m., thinking. Then the first stanza came to me. The next day, I finished it," Aardema said.

Another of Verna Aardema's books, *Why Mosquitoes Buzz in People's Ears,* was a Caldecott Medal Book in 1976.

David Adler

A Picture Book of Martin Luther King, Jr.

David Adler specializes in biographies of great Americans. *A Picture Book of Martin Luther King, Jr.* was his third Picture Book biography, after he wrote about George Washington and Abraham Lincoln. After *A Picture Book of Martin Luther King, Jr.* he planned to write books about Thomas Jefferson, Benjamin Franklin, Thomas Alva Edison and others.

Earlier, he wrote A First Biography series for ages 7-11, which was launched in 1986 with *Martin Luther King, Jr.: Free at Last.* Both his King biographies were illustrated by Robert Casilla.

He lives in New York with his wife and children.

Arnold Adoff

MA nDA LA
Black is Brown is Tan

Arnold Adoff is a poet, married to author Virginia Hamilton. They and their two children, Leigh and James, live in Yellow Springs, Ohio, near a big extended family of many aunts, uncles and cousins. After spending many years in the public schools of Harlem and the Upper West Side of Manhattan, he travels and lectures extensively.

He is author of more than a dozen poetry books for children, including *Flamboyan* (Harcourt, Brace, Jovanovich, 1988) a Parents' Choice Award winner. He is also the editor of seven volumes of poetry, and won the 1988 NCTE Award for Excellence in Poetry for Children. Adoff is an advocate of using literature in the classroom. He has edited several anthologies of poetry and prose, including *The Poetry of Black America: Anthology of the 20th Century.* He is the author of *MA nDA LA* and *Black Is Brown Is Tan,* both picture books illustrated by Emily McCully and *In For Winter Out for Spring,* illustrated by Jerry Pinkney.

Aliki

(Aliki Brandenberg)

A Weed Is A Flower
My Five Senses

Aliki studied first to be an artist. While working on illustrations for *The Listening Walk* by Paul Showers published by Thomas Y. Crowell, Aliki developed the idea for *My Five Senses*. This book brought on more ideas. She has written and illustrated more than 100 books. She has also written a number of nonfiction books, including *Mummies Made in Egypt, A Medieval Feast* and *How a Book is Made.* Aliki has also written several dinosaur books.

She was nicknamed Ali in her childhood in a Greek-American family in Philadelphia. There were few books in her childhood, but this, she said was because of her verbal, story-telling family. Little Ali drew pictures before kindergarten and was not only artistic but musical, also playing the piano.

In her childhood, Ali had many favorite stories, including "The Little Match Girl" and Treasure Island." Her favorite picture book was the charmingly illustrated *Peter Rabbit.*

Her family included her parents, two sisters and a brother. Teachers and librarians read to her.

What about pets in her childhood? "There was always a dog around, sometimes a cat," says Aliki. And she liked to play jacks, jump rope, play baseball, dress up, skate and play the piano. The family went to the seashore every summer and later to the mountains, which she loved.

Now that Aliki has grown up, she lives with her husband, Franz Brandenberg, who is also a children's book author. Longtime residents of New York City, they and their two children, Jason and Alexa, moved to London in 1977, where she has developed a passion for gardening. She also loves reading, the theater, films, traveling, "and my hand could not move without music." Best, she loves her work. "Work is my life."

Aliki's children are now grown. She has a huge family besides her husband and children, including brother, sisters, nieces, nephews, aunts, uncles and so forth. Asked for her favorite children's book today, she says, "That's too hard" because there are so "many good ones, among them *Good Night Moon,* E. B. White's , on and on."

About George Washington Carver, Aliki says that she "was impressed with him immediately,

195

and also that he could do that much with peanuts." I wrote non-fiction before people (and I) knew the word -- so it was natural to write about him, a wonderful personality.

Ideas came naturally to *A Weed is a Flower*, she said. "I visited a school where they cooked a whole peanut meal. But every time you pull out a weed or plant something, you can think of George Washington Carver."

Maya Angelou *

Life Doesn't Frighten Me

To know Maya, you must read her. We encourage you to go to the library and select from her many works.

Born in St. Louis, MO. in 1928, her parents moved to California. Later they divorced and sent Maya and her brother Bailey to Stamps, Arkansas, where they lived with their father's mother. Read *I Know Why The Caged Bird Sings* for your enjoyment and information.

President Bill Clinton commissioned Ms. Angelou to write a poem for his swearing- in ceremony for the 1993 inauguration.

"Life Doesn't Frighten Me" is from the collection *And Still I Rise*, copyright 1978.

She encourages every one to read as much as they can. Select from diversity, and especially read Shakespeare.

Meshack Asare

A Cat in Search of a Friend

Meshack Asare is author and illustrator of *A Cat in Search of a Friend* (Kane/Miller Book Publishers, 1986), translation of *Die Katze sucht sich einen Freund*, (Verlag Jungbrunnen, Vienna, 1984.)

Nicholas Sironka Averdung *

Mcheshi Goes to the Market
Mcheshi Goes to the Game Park

Manager of Art and Illustrations at Jacaranda Designs, Nicholas Sironka Averdung composes the illustrations and designs for the Mcheshi series.

Sironka lives with his wife and three children in Nairobi, Kenya.

Augusta Baker *

Storytelling, Art and Technique

Augusta Baker is well known for her storytelling ability. She is co-author (with Ellin Greene) of *Storytelling, Art and Technique*, Bowker, 1977 , and has inspired many teachers to tell stories to their children.

After receiving her AB and BS in Library Science at State University of New York in Albany, her first position in a library was in 1937 in the New York Public Library. She began as children's librarian at the 135th Street Branch. There she began the James Weldon Johnson Memorial Collection of Children's Books About Negro Life. The bibliography she wrote for that collection became ,in 1971, *The Black Experience in Children's Books*.

While she continued her New York Public Library career until retirement 37 years later as Coordinator of Children's Services, Baker was also busy traveling, lecturing and storytelling. She was an adjunct faculty member at Columbia University, Rutgers University and the University of Southern Nevada, and was a library consultant in Trinidad, inspiring the organization of libraries there.

When she retired, Baker became storyteller-in-residence at the University of South Carolina in Columbia. She is the widow of James Baker and has a son, James Baker III. She is married to Gordon Alexander.

She has won many awards. A few are the American Library Association's Grolier Award for her outstanding achievement in guiding and stimulating children's reading, the Women's National Book Association's Constance Lindsay Skinner Award, the Parents Magazine Medal, the Clarence Day Award and the Regina Medal from the Catholic Library Association. St. John's University awarded her an honorary doctorate.

Among her books are *The Talking Tree* (Lippincott, 1955) and *The Golden Lynx* (Lippincott, 1960), both out of print but still available in some libraries. Baker also edited *The Young Years: Anthology of Children's Literature* (Parents, 1950).

196

Ray Barber

I Am Freedom's Child

With the help of Ray Barber's clear and easy-to-read large lettering, many children will be able to follow by themselves the story of *I Am Freedom's Child*.

Monita Barnett

Me and Neesie

Working in Brooklyn where she was born, Monita Barnett illustrates children's books.

Joyce Durham Barrett

Willie's Not the Hugging Kind

Willie is the first children's book Joyce Durham Barrett wrote. She lives in Georgia where she teaches elementary school.

Jean-Michel Basquiat *

Life Doesn't Frighten Me

Drawing was a major part of Jean-Michel's life from the time he was four years old. He was raised in middle-class Brooklyn by his parents. Family visits to Manhattan introduced him to art, music and theatre. His mother is a graphic artist.

Writing was another love, as well as music. He played several instruments and listened to a wide range of music. His works are exhibited throughout the world. He passed away in 1988.

This collection of his paintings was brought together by editor Sara Jane Boyers in hopes of introducing children and adults to poetry and contemporary art.

Judith Bentley

Harriet Tubman

Judith Bentley is the writer of *Harriet Tubman* (Franklin Watts).

Barbara Higgins Bond *

When I Was Little

Cheryl Hudson of Just Us Books started Higgins on her first picture book. As a free lance illustrator she had drawn and painted for a wide range of assignments, including collector's plates.

Her work has been exhibited in museums, including the DuSable Museum of African-American History, in Chicago, 1977.

Born in Arkansas, Barbara Higgins lived with her partents, one brother , two sisters and two very close cousins. She received the Medal of Honor from the Arkansas Sesquicentennial Committee, honoring distinguished Arkansans, in 1986.

As a child, her nickname was Bobbie. She drew pictures and liked science fiction. Her favorite movie was "The Day the Earth Stood Still."

Her mom read to her. The favorite book was *The Water Babies*. She always had a dog or a cat. Her newest collector's plate collection will be of kittens. Drawing and painting and collecting stamps led her to becoming the illustrator of the Jan Malezeliger and W.E.B. DuBois 29 cent commemorative stamps for the U. S. Postal Service.

197

Carole Byard *

The Black Snowman
Cornrows
Africa Dream

Carole Byard was born in Atlantic City, New Jersey and studied at the Fleischer Art Memorial in Philadelphia and at the New York Phoenix School of Design.

She is a brilliant young painter who has amassed an impressive list of fellowships and awards. Her pictures have appeared in many exhibitions in the United States, Africa, Germany and Venezuela. She has lectured and conducted workshops for the Baltimore School of the Arts and the National Conference of Artists at Pratt University.

Byard first went to Africa on a grant from the Ford Foundation. She went to Nigeria on a second trip as a delegate to an international black artists' conference. She has lectured at the University of Ibadan in Nigeria. Her exciting pictures for *Africa Dream*, *The Black Snowman* and *Cornrows* reflect her loving study of African life and culture. Byard is active in art education programs in the New York City area. She has twice won the Coretta Scott King Award.

Samuel Byrd *

Dancing with the Indians

Philadelphia is home to Samuel, his wife and daughter Talauren, one of his six children.

He paints and creates murals, as well as illustrating books.

Jeanette Franklin Caines *

Chilly Stomach

Author of many picture books about children and their relationships with their families, Jeanette recieved the National Black Child Development Institute's Certificate of Merit and Appreciatioin. Her book *Just Us Women* was selected as a Reading Rainbow Book.

Ms. Caines now lives in Freeport, Long Island. She grew up in Harlem.

Northern J. Calloway

I Been There

Northern J. Calloway grew up in Harlem and graduated from new York City's High School of Performing Arts.

A talented and energetic performer, he is well known to children and their parents for his role as David on "Sesame Street." He conceived the idea for the book, *I Been There.*

His list of dramatic credits is impressive, including the Leading Player role in Pippin. In his free time, he enjoys basketball and puts on musical and storytelling concerts for handicapped and retarded children.

Robert Casilla *

A Picture Book of Martin Luther King, Jr.

Robert Casilla's lively action paintings in *A Picture Book of Martin Luther King, Jr.* by David A. Adler will delight children.

He angles some of his pictures from overhead, some from beside or below, and he enjoys putting action in the illustrations. Because most depictions of King show him looking either severe or sad, children will take pleasure in the smiling picture on the cover.

Casilla received a BFA from the School of Visual Arts in New York City. He also illustrated Adler's earlier biographies of King and Jackie Robinson. He lives with his wife and son in Yonkers, New York.

His work has appeared in Black Enterprise magazine, The New York Times and other publications.

Deborah M. Newton Chocolate *

Kwanzaa

She lives in Chicago with her husband and two sons.

Wil Clay *

The Real McCoy

Illustrator, storyteller, graphic designer, painter and sculptor, Wil received the 1993 Coretta Scott King Honor Award for his illustrations in *Little Eight John.*

In downtown Toledo stands Clay's six foot sculpture "Radiance" that honors the late Dr. Martin Luther King, Jr.

During a three month independent study in Cameroon, Africa he worked primarily with the Bamileke people in the South and the Fulani people in the North. As he painted and drew, he studied woodcarvings, metalsmithing, beadwork, painting and tribal festivals and dances.

Lucille Clifton *

Everett Anderson's 1-2-3
Everett Anderson's Nine-Month Long
Everett Anderson's Good-bye
All Us Come Cross the Water

As the writer of *All Us Come Cross the Water,* Lucille Clifton shows herself to be a master of the black child's words and thoughts. Her characters are so true to life that many children will identify strongly with them. Her picture books of poetry have been received with great enthusiasm.

Her grandma (her mama's mama) called her "genius." Clifton was the first in her family to go to college; no one else had even graduated from high school. Her name came from her father's grandmother. He saw baby Lucille and knew she was a Dahomey woman (a region of West Africa) and was he proud.

Clifton was born in Depew, New York in 1936 and attended Howard University and Fredonia State Teachers College, where her friends were a small group of blacks interested in theater. Ishmael Reed, whom she met at Fredonia, showed some of her poems to Langston Hughes, who included some in his anthology, *Poetry of the Negro.*

One of the group was the man who would become her husband, Fred Clifton, who became a writer, artist and philosophy teacher at the University of Buffalo. They married in 1958 and had six children.

198

Clifton has received numerous awards for her poetry, including the Discovery Award from the YW-YMHA Poetry Center in New York. She has received grants from the National Endowment for the Arts and was Poet-in-Residence at Coppin State College in Baltimore and a visiting writer at Columbia University School of the Arts. She was Poet Laureate of Maryland from 1969 through 1972. After her husband's death, she moved to California.

She feels that her husband, her six children and being a black woman have had the greatest influence on her writing.

Donald Crews *

Bigmama's
Truck - A Caldecott Honor Book, 1981
Freight Train
Flying
School Bus
Short Cut

Memories of summers as a child in Cottondale, Florida resulted in three of Crews' books - *Bigmama's, Shsort Cut* and *Freight Train*. Born in Newark, NJ in 1938, he and his family spent summers on his grandparents' farm.

Crews' mother was born on the farm. The train journey from Newark was three days and two nights. Crews and his family were the summer labor corps.

His mother was an accomplished craftswoman. She encouraged all of her children to draw and sketch.

All children love to scribble on paper. Crews says to encourage these markings. Provide a variety of media and form (paint, sculpture, collage) for children to express themselves.

Crews' is married to Ann Jonas (*The Quilt*). They have two daughters, Nina Melissa and Amy Marshanna.

Pat Cummings *

Chilly Stomach
Willie's Not the Hugging Kind
My Mama Needs Me

Pat Cummings, who was known as Patty in her childhood, loved the Narnia series by C. S. Lewis, and fairytales in general. Her mother often read to her and she drew pictures, too, as a child.

"My earliest memories are of stories that my mother must have read to us from a book called *Tales of the Rhine*. We lived in Germany then, and I remember the scenes of the stories she read about dragons and princesses and heroes who turned into stars in the end. I don't think the book was heavily illustrated, but I still remember the scenes as they appeared in my mind while she read."

Patty was in a military family (her father was in the U. S. Army) and lived with her parents, two sisters and a brother, in Virginia, Okinawa, Germany and Kansas. Growing up she had dogs for pets, and she liked to go to the movies, to the pool and out with friends. Her favorite activity was swimming games.

"When I was in fifth grade, I was doing a healthy business selling drawings of ballerinas during recess. The all had pinpoint waists and huge flowered tutus and their legs tapered down to tiny needlelike toe shoes... I was very lucky that my parents encouraged my interest in art," she said.

She graduated from Pratt Institute with a portfolio filled with story ideas and class projects, and a dream of illustrating children's books. Cummings became an illustrator by showing her work to publishers. She also illustrates for magazines, newspapers and ads. She likes to put surprises in her pictures, such as "patterns on fabrics, ladybugs, butterflies -- objects that draw children into the story and, hopefully, personalize it for them."

Cummings does not recall having picture books with black characters when she was a child. She feels that Martin Luther King was pivotal in "awakening an entire country to the realities of a mixed audience that must be addressed." The first picture book she completed was *Good News* by Eloise Greenfield, which she completed with the generous guidance of artist Tom Feelings. He gave her pointers and explained procedures "in such a way that I've always felt obligated to do the same for other artists if I can."

Her husband Chuku Lee and their cat Cash live in Brooklyn. She often uses family and friends as models. Her cat Cash is on the cover of *Storm in the Night* by Mary Stolz. Usually Cummings illustrates other authors' work but she also written several books that she illustrated:*C.L.O.U.D.S., Clean Your Room Harvey Moon!* and *Jimmy Lee Did It.* Her books have been widely honored.

My Mama Needs Me by Mildred Pitts Waller, illustrated by Pat Cummings, was a Notable Children's Trade Book in the Field of Social Studies, won the Coretta Scott King Award for Illustration and was a Reading Rainbow Review Book *C.L.O.U.D.S.* was an honor book in the Coretta Scott King Awards. *Springtime Bears* by Cathy Warren, illustrated by Cummings, was a Children's Book of the Year of the Child Study Association.

Leo * and Diane Dillon

Who's in Rabbit's House
Why Mosquitoes Buzz in People's Ears
Ashanti to Zulu: African Traditions
The People Could Fly

Leo and Diane Dillon are a husband-and-wife team who also team up to illustrate children's books.

The Dillons were known as Lee and Di when they were kids. Lee's favorite stories were the Arabian Nights, and Di loved all fairytales. Their mothers read to both of them.

Both made up stories and drew pictures as children, Lee in New York and Di in California. Lee's hobbies were cats and drawing. Di's were her collie, cats and sewing. Both loved bicycle riding. Lee liked to play kick-the-can at night and Di liked to play hide-and-seek at dusk.

They met while attending Parsons School of Design and married soon after graduation. They have a son Lee and live in Brooklyn.

The Dillons are full-time artists. They started doing children's books when an editor saw a cover they illustrated and asked if they wanted to do a picture book.

Ashanti to Zulu: African Traditions, by Margaret Musgrove, illustrated by Leo and Diane Dillon, was the Caldecott Medal Book for 1977. *Why Mosquitoes Buzz in People's Ears* was also a Caldecott winner.

Arnold Dobrin

Josephine's 'magination: A Tale of Haiti

Dobrin first wrote a children's story at thirty six. He was born in Omaha, Nebraska in 1928.

When his third grade teacher showed his paintings to the class, he began to think of himself as an artist. Many of his books have come from his travels throughout the world. Arnold Dobrin is both writer and illustrator of *Josephine's 'magination: A Tale of Haiti.* He dedicates this book "to the beautiful and friendly people of Haiti."

Ladan Doorandish-Vance *

Mcheshi Goes to the Game Park

Jacaranda Designs Ltd's manager for training in art and design, Ladan Doorandish-Vance supervises their books designs.

Her Graphic Design BA degree is from Boston University. At Harvard, she earned a masters in Educational Children's Television Production. She has worked all over the world as a graphic designer.

She has two children.

Crescent Dragonwagon

Half a Moon and One Whole Star

Crescent Dragonwagon gave herself this new name when she was married. She lives in Eureka Springs, Arkansas, where she runs the award-winning country inn Dairy Hollow House.

Children's titles are among the twenty-five books she has to her credit.

Veronica Freeman Ellis *

Book of Black Heroes Vol. 2:
Great Women In The Struggle

Children's literature is Ellis' focus. She has written several books for children and has books on Liberia, her country, in the works.

She teaches children's literature at Wheelock College, Boston and writing at Boston University. At the Davis Educational Foundation's Children's Literature In-Service Program, she is a consultant/instructor.

Ed Emberley

Straight Hair, Curly Hair

Emberley was born in 1931 in Malden, Mass. When he is not writing or illustrating books, Emberley pursues interesting and unusual hobbies. He experiments with toymaking, studies early Americana and prints limited editions of children's books on his own hand press.

As a children's book illustrator, he has a few ideas of his own about children's art. Though he understands and appreciates Viktor Lowenfield and others' opinions about children's creativity, Ed Emberley submits there is a place for copying. He says Van Gogh, the Eskimo sculptures and Egyptians did it...why not children of today.

Learning the "vocabulary" of drawing allows the child to then go on to experiment with, modify, embellish and improve his own creation.

Emberley received a bachelor of fine arts degree in illustration from the Massachusetts School of Art in Boston. He lives in Ipswich, Massachusetts.

Drummer Hoff by Barbara Emberley, illustrated by Ed Emberley, was the Caldecott Medal Book for 1968.

Muriel Grey Feelings *

Jambo Means Hello: Swahili Alphabet Book
Moja Means One: Swahili Counting Book
Zamani Goes to Market

She was born in 1938 in Philadelphia, Pennsylvania. She is an artist, a teacher and an author.

She studied at the Philadelphia Museum School of Art and received her BA at Los Angeles State College in 1963.

Feelings taught Art and Spanish in secondary and elementary schools in both New York and Philadelphia. She worked as a teacher in New York, meeting people from Africa, and was recruited by the Uganda Mission to the United Nations to work as an Art teacher in a Kampala high school.

Tom Feelings wrote to her while she was teaching at Kampala. They met and were married. Their children Zamani and Kamili were born during their six year marriage.

While teaching in Brooklyn, Muriel Feelings introduced African crafts and Swahili. In Kampala, the Ministry of Education considered her students' work when decisions were made on publishing literature. The Feelings and their son Zamani lived in Ghana in 1971-74. Her first story, *Zamani Goes to Market*, features her son as the hero of the book. The market represents places visited around East Africa, but particularly one in a Kenyan village.

Life in rural Africa was a rewarding experience for Muriel. The culture was intact, with warmth and hospitality built-in.

Tom Feelings *

Jambo Means Hello: Swahili Alphabet Book
Moja Means One: Swahili Counting Book

Feelings was born in 1933 in Brooklyn, NY. He served in the U. S. Air Force as an illustrator in the Graphics Division in London, England. He then attended the School of Visual Arts.

While working as an illustrator for the African Review in Ghana, he wrote to Muriel Grey. They met and were married for about six years. They had two children, Zamani and Kamili.

While in Ghana, he worked for the government. He was a consultant for children's books and taught illustration.

His main interest is black people of the world. This interest has taken him to East and West Africa, as well as South America.

His comic strip, "Tommy Traveler in the World of Negro History", was published in Harlem's, the New York Age. Black Butterfly Children's Books has printed this comic strip in a book.

Tom Feelings makes a drawing and transfers it onto a rough board in pencil, then in pen and water-soluble ink and white tempera. Then he lays a sheet of wet tissue paper over it, which causes the black ink and white tempera to run together. While the tissue is wet, he paints ink washes and more white tempera, re-wets and continues. Then linseed oil is used for accent.

The Feelings' books, *Moja Means One: Swahili Counting Book* and *Jambo Means Hello: Swahili Alphabet Book* were both selected as Caldecott Honor Books.

Valerie Flourney *

The Patchwork Quilt

Beginning as an editor, Flourney now writes children's books. She has a twin sister , Vanessa.

Bernette G. Ford *

Bright Eyes, Brown Skin

A children's book editor, Bernette has worked for many major publishers. She heads Cartwheel Books as Executive Editor and Director of Special Projects at Scholastic, Inc.

Using a pseudonym, she has written several books for young readers. She helped launch the Soft and Furry books and the Fast Rolling board books.

Her husband, George, used their daughter Olivia to illustrate Bernette's poem. They live in Brooklyn.

George Ford *

Bright Eyes, Brown Skin
Good Night Baby

With inspiration from his daughter Olivia's beauty and his wife Bernette's words, George illustrated *Bright Eyes, Brown Skin*.

He has used his talents as an artist to illustrate more than two dozen books for young readers. He was the President of the Council on Interracial Books for Children, 1972.

Barbados in the West Indies was a part-time home for George. His grandmother would draw people's faces on his school slate with ordinary chalk. George loved her drawings and tried to imitate her. She priased his drawings, taught him social concerns, helping him to portray human character and expressing feelings in his drawings. Most of his growing up years were spent in Brownsville and Bedford Stuyvesant sections of Brooklyn. The Ford family lives in Brooklyn.

He won a Coretta Scott King Award for his illustrations of *Ray Charles*, 1974.

Joseph Forte

Harriet Tubman

The strong, beautiful face of Harriet Tubman is shown in the cover portrait of *Harriet Tubman* (Julian Messner) by Joseph Forte.

John Galdone

Your Skin and Mine

The illustrations in *Your Skin and Mine* were drawn by John Galdone and they clearly show the importance of this often-forgotten major body organ.

His amusing and informative illustrations complete the story of skin, which goes from the hair on your head right down to your own exclusive fingerprints.

Jan Spivey Gilchrist *

Nathaniel Talking
The Baby
Sweet Baby Coming
Daddy & I
I Make Music
Big Friend, Little Friend

Jan illustrated Eloise Greenfield's wonderful words to help young children relate to the words' meanings.

Augusta Goldin

Straight Hair, Curly Hair

Goldin was born in 1906 in New York City and grew up on a farm in the Catskill Mountains near Ellenville, New York. Her father told her girls were people, so she proceeded to become a tomboy and do all the things boys do on the farm.

When she was ten and it snowed for a week, she wrote her first poem... about snow. Her mother read it and told her to go to the barn with a shovel. She did not write again until she was an adult.

After attending a children's literature conference in1955, she wrote her first juvenile book. *My Toys* was written after watching her young daughter play with her toy. That was her instant success. Then she wrote for nine years before selling her stories regularly.

She has worked on the staffs of education publications and is principal of a school on Staten Island, New York. She has written several other science books for children.

Carole Greene

Martin Luther King, Jr.: A Man who Changed Things

With degrees in English literature and musicology, Carole Greene has worked in international exchange programs, as an editor and as a teacher. She lives in St. Louis, Missouri, and is a full-time writer.

She has written many biographies for children besides her book on the life of Martin Luther King, Jr. Among them is the biography of Bishop Desmond Tutu.

Eloise Greenfield *

Me and Neesie
Africa Dream
Nathaniel Talking
Daddy and I
I Make Music
Big Friend, Little Friend

Seeing the need for a body of literature in which black children can see themselves, their lives and history, Greenfield has set out to help develop that literature. We are certainly pleased she continues to add to her collection.

When she was an infant her family moved from her birth place, Parmele, NC in 1929. Her father found work in Washington ,DC. There was little money but the memories of family, neighbors and friends are

202

enjoyable.

She grew up with a love for words. First she read them. Until there was a library iwthin walking distance, Greenfield's father took the whole family to the nearest libreary in the car. When a branch opened in her neighborhood, she became a regular patron, even working there part-time while she was in college.

Humorous rhymes were her first writings. She was a young wife and mother and also worked outside her home as a clerk-typist. She practiced writing skills to improve her writing talent.

Writing enriches her life. she hopes to give children "word-madness" so that they will live in the book and take a part of it with them.

Ann Grifalconi

Everett Anderson's Nine-Month Long
Everett Anderson's Good-bye
Everett Anderson's Year

A native of New York City, Ann Grifalconi studied art at Cooper Union and New York University. She has written and illustrated several books, including *The Toy Trumpet and City Rhythms*, and has collaborated as illustrator with many writers on more than 30 books, including the Everett Anderson stories.

A former art teacher, Grifalconi devotes full time to writing, illustrating and photography for filmstrips. She is President of Media Plus, Inc.

Nikki Grimes *

Something on My Mind

Nikki Grimes was born in 1950 and moved around new York City with her mother, an older sister and at other times, foster parents. She was an avid reader, going trhough about five bookds a week. *The Ugly Duckling* was her favorite.

Her hobbies were reading, reading, reading, and her favorite place to go when she was a child was to the library. "I was the kind of kid who took a flashlight to bed so that I could continue reading after lights out!" she said. Nikki also played softball, hardball and basketball and enjoyed word games.

At Livingston College and Rutgers University, Grimes majored in English and studied African languages. with a Ford Foundation grant in 1974, she was able to live in Tanzania for a year collecting folktales and poetry.

As an adult, Grimes started reading children's books before she started writing them. she began reviewing juvenile books for a number of children'sbook review

services. "In the process, I was reminded of the dearth of quality literature for black children and began to write books of my own. I remembered as a child wishing that there were books that related to my life, my reality, that spoke to my needs, about my problems. I wanted and still want, to create the kinds of books that I longed for those many years ago."

Today, her favorite childrens books ar *M. C. Higgins the Great* by Virginia Hamilton, *The Garden of Abdul Gasazi* by Chris van Allsburg and *The Chronicles of Narnia* by C. S. Lewis.

Grimes is author of the sensitive poetry book, *Something on My Mind*. she wrote it after studying Tom Feelings' drawings for weeks, and getting to know the children who are seen there. This is one of the cases where the pictures came first, then the words.

As she puts it: "For one thing, the book was created in reverse. That is to say, while most children's books are written and then illustrated, in this case the artist invited me to select a body of already existing art and, as it were, to illustrate the art with poetry. As such, I very much approached the project as an actor approaches a script."

"I studies the face in each drawing and tried to imagine what that boy/girl had been thinking of at the moment his/her image was captured. That done, I tried to become that character, to climb into that character's skin, to feel what he felt, think what he thought. I drew quite a bit from memories of my own childhood, of course."

"As much as possible, I tried to use language that seemed natural for that particular character. I talked each poem out loud, as I always do. (I can always tell when a poem or piece of prose, is not right because it doesn't ring true when read aloud.)"

"As for visual memories in connection with writing this book: I lived in a studio in New York at the time. I had a loft bed and I taped photocopies of the drawings all along the wooden posts of the bed, and spread the rest out on the floor in two rows and I studied each face in each drawing until I knew every line, every curve, the attitude in every expression by heart."

"At the end of six weeks, the children in those drawings were like family to me. That's how long it took me to write that book."

Besides writing, Grimes also has a small business making and designing hand knitted garments. She lives alone in San Pedro, California and also has a mother, sister and grandmother in her family. She is also interested in journalism and photography.

Carol Hall

I Been There

Carol Hall is a song writer who grew up in Abilene, Texas. She is a graduate of Sarah Lawrence College and lives in New York City. She has recorded two albums of her own songs and her lyrics and music have been sung on "Sesame Street," "Captain Kanga-roo" and the Emmy Award winning "*Free to Be... You and Me,*" which was also a record and a book.

Hall has two children, Susannah and Daniel and is author of the authentically expressed *I Been There*. It is illustrated by Sammis McLean.

Virginia Hamilton *

The People Could Fly: American Black Folktales

Virginia Hamilton is a noted author and is married to writer/poet Arnold Adoff. They have been writers-in-residence at Queens College of the City University of New York. The Adoffs live in Yellow Springs, Ohio, near many aunts, uncles and cousins. The have two children Leigh and Jaime.

Virginia Hamilton was born in 1933 in Ohio, where her mother's ancestors went after the Civil War. She centers her books around her family heritage and the black heritage in general.

Hamilton has been recognized many times for her books. She has won the Newbery Medal, the National Book Award, the Boston Globe-Horn Book Award, the Coretta Scott King Award and Certificates of Honor from the International Board of Books for Young People.

Peter Hanson

A Pocketful of Goobers

Peter Hanson is the illustrator for Carolrhoda's George Washington Carver life story, *A Pocketful of Goobers,* written by Barbara Mitchell.

Francine Haskins *

I Remember 121
Things I Like About Grandma

As a storyteller living in Washington DC, Francine tells of a granddaughter/grandmother relationship in her African-American community.

Being a dollmaker and a teacher are other ways she contributes to her community. She believes traditioins, histories and the art of story telling must be preserved. She wants her childrens' books to reflect her culture and plain old human nature.

Nonny Hogrogian

I Am Eyes - Ni Macho

Nonny Hogrogian has been honored three times in the Caldecott Medal awards. One of Nonny Hogrogian's books, *One Fine Day,* was the Caldecott Medal Book for 1972. Another, *Always Room For One More,* written by Sorche Nic Leodhas, illustrated by Nonny Hogrogian, was the Caldecott Medal Book for 1966.

Another of her books, *The Contest,* was named a Caldecott Honor Book in 1977.

Hogrogian made the fine illustrations for Leila Ward's tale, *I Am Eyes - Ni Macho,* featured in this book. She is illustrator of more than 50 children's books. She and her husband, the poet David Kherdian, live in Oregon.

Varnett P. Honeywood *

Shake It To The One That You Love The Best

Born in Los Angeles, California, Varnette P. Honeywood has become well-known for her original style as a visual artist.

Cheryl Willis Hudson *

Bright Eyes, Brown Skin
Good Night Baby

Recognizing the need for self-affirming literature for African-American children, Cheryl and her husband Wade founded Just Us Books.

Their books are distributed throughout the USA and the world by their $2 million dollar company operation. Her desire "to offer an alternative to the all- white world of children's books" is certainly blooming.

As a child, Cheryl made up stories and drew cartoons on a "rags to riches, justice, equality and the American way"Themes. Her early visions certainly continue to pay off, as Just Us Books continues to grow.

Her mom, dad and Sunday school teacher read to her as a child. Childhood was also filled with climbing trees, day dreaming and being outside. Reading was her hobby and she loved to listen to her relatives talk about "the good old days".

A nuclear family is a part of her experience. In childhood, she lived with mom, dad, three brothers and a grandmother in Portsmouth, VA. Now, husband Wade, two children and her mother-in-law live with her in Orange, NJ.

You may write to her at Just Us Books.

Wade Hudson *

Good Night Baby

A corporate President that can have dinner on the table when his wife gets home. No wonder Just Us Books is a successful publisher of African-American children's books.

Wade and wife Cheryl had successful separate careers. After having children, they realized the need for books for their children. They combined their professional talents and $7,000 from their savings account to build a $2 million business, and their business is still growing!

Wade is a magazine writer, playwright and public relations specialist.

Paul Hunt

Dave and the Tooth Fairy

An illustrator who lives in England, his works bring magic to this up-to-date tooth fairy.

Toyomi Igus *

Book of Black Heroes Vol 2.: Great Women in the Struggle
When I Was Little

Coming from a storytelling family, her parents' stories were a part of her life. When she saw the effect of these family stories on her own children, she decided to write *When I Was Little*.

"As a child my favorite picture book was Danny Kaye's *Stories from Around the World*. I'm not sure if that is the correct name, but I loved the book. Because my mother is Japanese (from Japan) and my father is African-American, I was and am very curious about other countries and other cultures. This book had folk stories from many other countries, including Africa and Asia, along with pictures that depicted these different cultures."

"I wrote a lot as a child because I went to very demanding private schools. I did not do a lot of making up of stories then, I did do a lot of reading, however. When I got older, I enjoyed Nancy Drew Mysteries in particular."

"Although I am not an artist now, I did study art for many years in junior high school and then in college. My first profession was as a magazine editor. I am now a book editor and also am a consultant communications and design firm. As an editor, I get to work with both words and pictures, which is a process I enjoy very much."

"My parents read to me when I was very small. There were always many, many books in our home. We had a library that was filled floor to ceiling with books and magazines. Once I learned to read by myself, however, my parents stopped reading to me because I read all the time!"

"I was born in Iowa City, Iowa, lived with my parents and grandmother in Cedar Rapids, Iowa until I was about four or five, then moved with my parents and brother to Buffalo, New York, where I spent the rest of my childhood. I also have two sisters who were born in Buffalo. My brother is a social worker (and a musician), one of my sisters is a children's book editor and the other is an attorney with the Justice Department. I am the oldest child."

"We had many pets: A Weimaraner dog named Count, a basset hound named Whimpy, a cat named Tora (which means tiger in Japanese), a mutt of a dog named Tippy, two Lhasa Apso sisters named Shishi and Niki and a Shitsu (my mother's dog) named Chibi."

"I am now married to an actor/teacher named Darrow Igus, who is a very funny and very wonderful man. We have two children: my daughter Kazumi was named after my mother and is 10 years old and my son, Kenji, is four."

"I started writing children's books because I wanted to create stories for my own children. My book, *When I Was Little*, was the result of listening to a conversation my father was having with my children about what life was like when he was growing up. My next picture book, *Two Mrs. Gibsons*, for Children's Book Press, is a story about my mother and my grandmother, who were the two most wonderful women in the world, they were very different, but they were very much alike too."

"When I don't write children's books, I publish adult books for UCLA Center for Afro-American Studies, where I am the managing editor."

205

Rachel Isadora

Ben's Trumpet
Flossie and the Fox

Rachel Isadora was born in New York City and lives there today. She was a professional ballerina before she became a popular author/artist, but says that music is the art she loves the best. She performed professionally at age 11 and signed a contract with the New York City Ballet at age 17. She drew to release tension from the dancing.

She has illustrated more than a dozen books for children, many of which she also wrote. Among them are the Caldecott Honor Book, *Ben's Trumpet,* and *Opening Night,* a story based on her experience.

Isadora is married to ballet star and author Robert Maiorano, with whom she often collaborates. She is author-artist of *Max* (her first picture book and an ALA Notable Book).

206 Angela Johnson *

The Leaving Morning
When I Am Old With You
Do Like Kyla

Born on father's day in 1961 in Tuskegee, Alabama, Johnson started writing when she was nine years old.

Her parents gave her a diary and she began writing. Poetry was her first love. Johnson feels her picture books are like poetry. Her ideas come suddenly and she writes them down immediately.

Writing has always been a part of her. Today she says she has no choice: she breathes, she writes. Her advice to others is to write all the time.

She eats buttered popcorn and watches old movies. Her house is full of plants in Kent, Ohio.

She has worked as a housekeeper, in summer camp and at a day care center. She thought of becoming a special education teacher.

Ann Jonas

The Quilt

Ann Jonas wrote and illustrated *The Quilt* and *When You Were a Baby,* both Greenwillow Publications. She was born and grew up in New York. She lives in Brooklyn. After graduating from Cooper Union, she worked for many years with her husband, Donald Crews, as a graphic designer.

Her highly acclaimed books also include *Two Bear Cubs, Round Trip,* (one of the New York times Best Illustrated Children's Books of 1983) and *Holes and Peeks.* She and Crews have two daughters.

Brenda Joysmith *

Shake It To The One That You Love The Best

A nationally known artist, Brenda Joysmith began drawing at an early age. Her pastels help her patrons to relive childhood. She was born in Memphis, Tennessee.

Ezra Jack Keats

A Letter to Amy

The son of Polish immigrants, Ezra Jack Keats was born in 1916 in Brooklyn, NY. He died of a heart attack in New York City in 1983. When Keats was a little boy growing up with his parents in East New York and Brooklyn, no one read to him. He grew up with no picture books and did not discover them until he was about 35. His mother encouraged his drawing and painting, even showing off a detailed drawing he did on her kitchen table. She covered it with a tablecloth and showed it off to the neighbors.

From the age of four, he threw himself into his drawing, went to the library as often as he could, and enjoyed playing street games with his neighborhood pals. The tough guys in the neighborhood called him "Doc," asking to see his drawings and listen to his stories.

In 1941, a group of photographs appeared in a magazine showing a little boy about to be given an inoculation. Jack, as he was called, was struck by the child's expression. He cut the photographs out and saved them. The little boy "had such a friendly, open expression of trust" Keats said, "I just loved that little boy."

One evening, 20 years later, he was reminiscing with friends about what they did in the snow when they were children. A few days later, he began to rough out the idea for a book that would become *The Snowy Day,* the first book he both wrote and illustrated himself. Before he started, he hung the magazine photos of that child on his studio wall "... just to get the feel of that wonderful little boy."

He did not want Peter to be a white kid colored brown. He made many studies and sketches of black children. For about a year, Keats went about creating and revising the book. It was published in 1962 and introduced Peter as the hero of this and other books to follow. In 1963, *The Snowy Day* won the Caldecott Medal.

"I wanted to do *The Snowy Day* with a black child as the hero. I felt it was important for black children to have a book whose main character they could identify with. But a snowy day is also a universal experience, equally important to all children."

Keats devoted his life to drawing and painting. He won many prizes for this art, and his paintings appear in many prominent collections. His best friend, Martin Pope, who grew up with him from childhood, is today President of the Ezra Jack Keats Foundation and has provided this author with information about Jack's life.

Though he had no formal art training, he was a muralist during the depression for the Works Progress Administration (W.P.A.). He was a production assistant for "Captain Marvel Adventure" comics. After his discharge from the Army after World War II, Keats spent a year in Paris, painting. Upon his return to New York, while continuing to paint, he entered the field of magazine and book illustration. A children's book editor who admired his work asked him to illustrate a book for children. He never got a story about black people. Peter was created out of his sensitivity to the common needs of all children. It was at that point that Keats found his direction, with the result that his work has appeared in 16 languages.

Keats won many honors, awards and citations during his lifetime. Besides *The Snowy Day* (Viking), which won the Caldecott Medal, *Goggles!* (Macmillan) was a Caldecott Honor Book in 1970, *Hi, Cat* (Macmillan) received the Boston Globe Horn Book Award in 1970 and *The Snowy Day* was included in the State Department's exhibition of graphic art that toured the Soviet Union. *Whistle for Willie* was an ALA Notable Book.

A participant in several important conferences - including the Black Psychiatrists of America Conference on Children's Films, and the White House Conference on Children in 1971 - Keats also attended the conference that helped formulate the idea for the "*Sesame Street*" TV program. He designed five Christmas cards for UNICEF, which raised a half million dollars. In 1974, Keats was guest of honor at the opening of a children's roller skating rink in Tokyo, which has a plaque bearing his name. The rink was built as a result of enthusiasm for roller skating, sparked by his book. *Skates!*

Keats' last book, *Clementina's Cactus*, was published in the fall of 1982, shortly before his death. Ezra Jack Keats was one of the most celebrated author/illustrators working in children's literature.

Phyllis Koinage *

Mcheshi Goes to the Game Park

She studied graphic arts at the Kenya Polytechnic, where she received a diploma and certificate.

Phyllis was the major illustrator in this book.

Lisa Kopper

Jafta
Jafta's Father
Jafta's Mother

Her warm illustrations help to tell how *Jafta* thinks and feels.

Julius Lester *

The Tales of Uncle Remus: The Adventures of Brer Rabbit

Born in St. Louis in 1939, Julius father was a Methodist minister, and the family moved to Kansas and to Tennessee when he was young. His books have been honored with the Newbery Honor Book, Nancy Bloch Award, New York Times list of outstanding books, School Library Journal Best Book, American Library Association Notable Book, Lewis Carroll Shelf Award Winner and finalist for the National Book Award. *To Be a Slave* by Julius Lester was the first Newbery medal Honor Book by a black author.

Lester has been a political activist and served as a field secretary with the Student Non-Violent Coordinating Committee (SNCC) and was head of SNCC's photo department. He went to North Vietnam in 1978 to Cuba with Stokeley Carmichael for the Latin American Solidarity Conference. He taught black history at the New School for Social Research in the 1960's. He earned his degree in English at Fisk University and has four children. Besides writing, Lester has been a folk singer and guitar teacher and worked with Pete Seeger on a Leadbelly record. He lives in Amherst where he teaches at the University of Massachusetts.

Why is he so interested in Southern rural traditions and black folklore? Because, he says, his father was a good storyteller.

207

Hugh Lewin *

Jafta
Jafta's Father
Jafta's Mother

Hugh Lewin is a South African, born in Lydenburg, Transvaal in 1939.

His auto biographical book *Bandit: Seven Years in a South African Prison,* tells of the years he spent in prison as a political prisoner opposed to apartheid.

Living in England, he was concerned his small daughters had no experiences with their homeland. He wrote the *Jafta* series to teach them and share his memories of his childhood in South Africa.

Eric Marlow

Rosa Parks

Illustrator Eric Marlow is the artist for *Rosa Parks* by Eloise Greenfield, published by Thomas Y. Crowell.

This book won the Carter G. Woodson Award.

Bill Martin, Jr.

I Am Freedom's Child

Author of about 200 children's books, Mr. Martin was born in 1916.

He graduated from Kansas State Teachers College and received his Ph.D. from Northwestern University.

Children throughout the world know him for his book *Brown Bear, Brown Bear.*

Jean Marzolo

Pretend You're a Cat

She loves writing and finds it an intriguing challenge. She is interested in children and enjoys writing books that support families.

Born in 1942 in Manchester, Conn., she graduated from the University of Connecticut.

Her interest in children has lead her to jobs in both teaching and publishing.

Judy Wanjiku Mathenge *

Mcheshi Goes to the Market
Mcheshi Goes to the Game Park

Studying for a Bachelor of Education in Fine Arts at Kenyatta University, Judy is a free-lance illustrator.

She worked as part of the team that created these two books.

Cheryl Warren Mattox *

Shake It To The One That You Love The Best

Collecting the songs of her rock musical heritage, Cheryl Warren Mattox hopes to pass the traditions on to future generations.

Emily McCully

MA nDA LA
Black is Brown is Tan

Emily McCully was born in Galesburg, Illinois. She received her BA from Brown University and her MA in art history from Columbia University. She has illustrated more than 50 books for children. She has lived in Brussels and New York, Brooklyn and rural New Hampshire, where she used their house, which was a tavern before the Revolutionary War, as a model for her painting.

Her husband, George, is a professor of Renaissance and Reformation history. McCully is the artist who illustrated *MA nDA LA* and *Black Is Brown Is Tan,* both written by Arnold Adoff.

Gerald McDermott

Anansi the Spider: A Tale from the Ashanti

At age four, McDermott began his art training at the Detroit Institute of Arts. He was born in Detroit in 1941. He "lived" at the institute through early adolescence, receiving encouragement and inspiration.

At ages 9 to 11, he was a child radio actor on "*Storyland.*" This first hand experience of mixing music and sound effects, and an introduction to myths and legends, influences his film making.

He attended the Pratt Institute of Design in New York where he produced his first animated film: "*The Stonecutter,*" a Japanese folktale.

Dr. Joseph Campbell, who McDermott knows personally, has had influence on his work. Campbell's four volume *The Mask of God* and *The Hero with a Thousand Faces,* influences all of his work.

His book *Arrow to the Sun* was awarded the 1975 Caldecott Medal.

Patricia McKissack *
Fredrick McKissack *

Mirandy and Brother Wind
Who is Who
Flossie and the Fox
The Big Book of Opposites

Patricia and Fredrick McKissack are husband and wife and often work as a team writing children's stories. They have often worked with some of the most outstanding artists in the children's book field.

Patricia McKissack was nicknamed "Tiny" as a little girl. Her favorite story was *The Ugly Duckling*. Instead of having someone read to her, she learned to read herself and read to her grandparents, making up her own stories and drawing pictures. The family lived near Nashville, Tennessee.

The family pets in her childhood were dogs, Buster and Smokie and Rags the Cat. A favorite activity for Tiny was going to camp. She also enjoyed riding her bicycle.

Patricia McKissack's relatives were dynamic and skilled story tellers who helped develop her listening and observation skills before she could read or write. On hot summer evenings, her family would sit on the porch and listen to her grandmother tell a hair-raising ghost story, or her mother would recite Dunbar poems or Bible stories.

"Sometimes, we'd get a real treat when my grandfather would dramatize an episode from his childhood, told in the rich and colorful dialect of the deep South. I can still hear him beginning a yarn, saying, 'It was back in nineteen and twenty-seven. I disremember the exact day, but it was long 'bout July, 'cause the skeeters was bitin' whole chunks outa my arms.' As a youngster, I had no idea that my heritage would one day be the springboard for my writing career."

Patricia McKissack discovered reading at about the age of seven and began a lifelong love affair with the printed word. "To me, reading is like breathing; both are essential to life." She grew up, went off to school, majored in English literature, acquired a teaching certificate and she and Fredrick McKissack married right after graduation. "They said the marriage wouldn't last six months, but that was 25 years ago," she said.

With her three children she visited the library, which was "free, air conditioned and quiet," and a good place to learn her trade. She read everything and attended seminars and workshops, sometimes taking the three children with her. She began keeping a journal and joined a literary organization. Her boys became excellent readers and writers.

"My sons grew out of diapers and into size eight shoes. I grew out of size eight jeans and into size twelve business suits. As a teacher, I saw a need for books about black children. Then, after nine years of teaching junior high and senior high English and after earning a master's degree in children's literature, I changed careers and became a children's book editor. Six years later I became a freelance writer. A year later my husband, Fred, joined me, and we've been writing together since then."

Today, Pat McKissack's favorite children's writers are Virginia Hamilton and Eloise Greenfield.
Why does she write? "I write because there is a clear need for books written about the minority experience in America - ficton and non-fiction. I also write for the love of it!"

Sammis McLean

I Been There

Sammis McLean grew up in Cohasset, Massachusetts, a small town south of Boston. After graduating from the Art Institute of Boston, he lived for a time in Paris. Since returning to New York City, He has co-produced several films for "*Sesame Street.*"

McLean loves theater, opera and movies, especially science fiction and fantasy. He is the artist who drew the illustrations for *I Been There*.

Angela Shelf Medearis *

Dancing with the Indians

To increase literacy is a continued effort made by Angela. As a lover of books, she became a free lance writer, publicist and tutor.

Angela used her own family history to write this book. *Picking Peas for a Penny* is another book she wrote about her family.

Austin, Texas is home to Angela, her husband Michael and daughter, Dianna.

Phil Mendez

The Black Snowman

Phil Mendez is author of *The Black Snowman*, illustrated by Carole Byard. He has worked as an animator for Disney Studios and as an advertising artist. *The Black Snowman* is his first book.

209

Barbara Michaels *

Apples on a Stick

Barbara Michaels is editor and collector with Bettye White, of *Apples on a Stick*.

Barbara Mitchell

A Pocketful of Goobers

Barbara Mitchell is the writer of *A Pocketful of Goobers*, a story of George Washington Carver.

Margarie King Mitchell *

Uncle Jed's Barbershop

Her sisters were fascinated by her stories, even the outlandish ones. She constantly made up stories for them.

As a child she loved all books. She had no favorite. She grew up in Holly Springs, Mississippi on her grandparents' farm. Her grandmother read to her. She loved to go for walks on the farm and dream about the far-away places she had read about. Reading was her hobby.

Because she could not find books set in history with a moral, Margarie decided to write them herself.

She wrote *Uncle Jed's Barbershop* for her son, then six.

She lives with her husband Kevin and son Nelson. You may write to her at :

Suite 1100-335
6763 Highway 6 South
Houston, Texas 77083

Leslie Morrill

Mr. Monkey and the Gotcha Bird

Leslie Morrill is illustrator of numerous books for children. *Mr. Monkey and the Gotcha Bird* and the *Casey Valentine* series are some of them. He lives in Madison, Connecticut.

Margaret Musgrove *

Ashanti to Zulu: African Traditions

Margaret Musgrove was born in 1943 in New Britain, Connecticut. When Musgrove was a child, her mother read stories to her. Her favorite, like the favorite of so many children, was *Charlotte's Web*. She also made up her own stories, living in Plainville, Connecticut, with her parents, sister and brothers.

Childhood pets included Honey, a Mexican Chihuahua; Rover, a mongrel dog and Fluffy, a cat. Her favorite family jaunts were to the beach at Far Rockaway, New York.

But childhood didn't last long for little Margaret. At 14, she was working full time on a tobacco farm in Bloomfield, Connecticut.

As an adult, Musgrove began writing children's books during a class she took in Amherst, Massachusetts.

Musgrove has first-hand African experience from living in Ghana in West Africa in 1969-1970. She loved it so much that she has been back to Africa four times since.

Musgrove is a graduate of the University of Connecticut. She received a Master's degree at Central Connecticut State College and a doctorate in education from the University of Massachusetts.

She has worked in education, as an English teacher in a high school, a college teacher and counselor and as Middle College director at Berkshire Community College in Pittsfield, Massachusetts.

Today, she teaches writing at Loyola College of Baltimore. Her two children are now teenagers. She has so many favorite children's books today that she cannot name them all.

Her work helps all children to read books that overcome the overt and covert racism she finds in children's libraries.

The book, *Ashanti to Zulu: African Traditions*, by Margaret Musgrove, illustrated by Leo and Diane Dillon, was the Caldecott Medal Book for 1977.

Walter Dean Myers *

Mr. Monkey and the Gotcha Bird
Dragon Takes a Wife

Walter Dean Myers was born in Martinsburg, West Virginia. When he lost his mother, he was adopted by the Deans and bears their name proudly. He and his new family moved to Harlem where he grew up. He loved Harlem. Being cold and hungry defined being poor, so he feels he was never poor.

His mama taught him to read at four years old and he read to her while she did housework when he was five. His mama taught him to cook.

He hears nothing wrong with his speech, but his classmates laughed at his garbled words. In fifth grade his teacher told the class they could read their writings to the class. He began writing poems that avoided the sounds that gave him trouble.

Even though he was from a family of storytellers, writing stories or essays was not seen as having practical value for a black child. He did find encouragement, a teacher who felt he was a gifted writer. She gave him a reading list as well. So he went to Central Park to read or write instead of going to school. He is a graduate of Empire State College and received a fellowship from the New Jersey Council of the Arts and a grant from the National Endowment of the Arts.

He spent three years in the army on a strictly vegetarian diet.

He married his first wife and had two children. He and his second wife, Connie, have a son Christopher. He struggled as a writer. His first book *Where Does the Day Go?* won a Council on Interracial Books for Children contest. Bobbs-Merrill Publishing Company hired him as a senior editor. They wanted a black editor. He had no experience editing and was reluctant to take the job.

He learned the business side of books and the profit line. His first book contact was Nikki Giovanni. The job was good for his writing and his awareness of the black image in literature, film and television. He recognized the subtle messages and their effect on black children and he wants his writing to fill the void for black children, telling them about their humanity and history.

James Okello *

Mcheshi Goes to the Market
Mcheshi Goes to the Game Park

As a free lance illustrator, James specializes in figure drawing. He drew Mcheshi, her mother, brother and uncle in this series.

He is continuing his training at the University level in Kenya.

Martin Otieno *

Mcheshi Goes to the Market

Martin's art has been exhibited in Kenya and the USA. He created the batik designs for this book.

He was born in Kisunu. His formal training was taken at the Young Men's Christian Association Institute.

Denise Lewis Patrick *

Red Dancing Shoes

Author of a series of board books, Denise lives in New York City with her husband and two sons.

She was born in Natchitoches, Louisiana. She worked as a children's editor for several national book and magazine publishers after she graduated from Northwestern State University of Louisiana.

Diane Patrick *

Book of Black Heroes Vol. 2:
Great Women in the Struggle

Patrick has written for adults and young readers. She has contributed to "Harambu," a newspaper focusing on the African-American experience, and written two biographies for young readers.

Adults read her in Music Magazine's "Jazz is Jazz."

211

Brian Pinkney *

The Boy and the Ghost
Where Does the Trail Lead?

Brian Pinkney very naturally became a children's book illustrator. He was born in Boston of a children's book family - his mother is a children's book writer and his father is an award-winning children's book illustrator. Drawing was a part of everyday life and Brian began drawing pictures for stories when he was quite young.

When Brian was little, his mother read stories to him. Little Brian's favorite picture book was *Mike Milligan's Steam Shovel*. As a youngster, his hobbies were the Korean art of Tae Kwon Do and drumming, and he loved to go to the beach. He still keeps a pair of drumsticks handy and works out by practicing Tae Kwon Do.

He earned a Bachelor of Fine Arts from Philadelphia College of Art and Master of Fine Arts from the School of Visual Arts in New York. During his graduate years, he taught painting and drawing to underprivileged children at the Children's Art Carnival in Harlem.

His father introduced him into the world of illustration and his first published art was in *Cricket* magazine. He has illustrated several books, including *The Boy and the Ghost* (Booklist Children's Editor's Choice - Ethnic Group, Parents Choice Honor Award for Illustration), *The Ballad of Bell Dorcas* (Parents Choice Honor Award for Story Books, Certificate of Excellence from *Parenting Magazine*), *Harriet Tubman* and *Black History Month*, *A Wave in Her Pocket*, *The Lost Zoo* and *Where Does the Trail Lead?* He has been awarded the National Arts Club Award of Distinction.

Pinkney lived during childhood summers at Cape Cod, and when he read the Albert Burton text for *Where Does the Trail Lead?* he remembered those days. "Suddenly I was back in time... in a daydream, and I was given the opportunity to be there once again."

Where Does the Trail Lead? features his dynamic scratchboard illustrations. He coats a white board with black ink, scratching the ink off with a sharp tool to create the image. Pinkney likes this style because, he says, "it is like sculpting the image as well as drawing it. My work has a lot of energy and requires a sense of movement. I think that scratchboard expresses this best."

Pinkney's favorite projects relate to African-American characters and life. "I'm interested in projects that relate to my life, my heritage, that relate to things I want to know about." He feels that illustrating children's books that feature black characters gives him an opportunity to portray a positive image of blacks, truthful images and not stereotypes. "It helps me to understand my past and my place in society." he says.

Brian Pinkney makes pictures for the child in himself. "That's why I think children enjoy my books: they recognize me as one of their own."

Today, his favorite children's' book is *Abracadabra*. Besides his books, he is also a teacher at the School of Visual Arts. Pinkney and his wife, Andrea Davis Pinkney live in Brooklyn.

Jerry Pinkney *

Pretend You're a Cat
Talking Eggs
Apples on a Stick
Tales of Uncle Remus
Mirandy and Brother Wind
*The Patchwork Quilt**
Half a Moon and One Whole Star

Jerry Pinkney was born in 1939 in Philadelphia. His favorite book was *The Wind in the Willows*, which his mother read to him. Like so many children's authors and illustrators, he began as a child to make up stories and draw pictures.

His father, mother, three sisters and two brothers made up the family. The lived in Philadelphia and Jerry liked to go to his uncle's farm in New Jersey for visits. At home, he enjoyed his goldfish and spent most of the rest of his time drawing from life and enjoying music.

Pinkney earned a scholarship and studied at the Philadelphia Museum College of Arts, did design work for the Boston National Center of the Afro-American Artist and was a visiting critic for the Rhode Island School of Design. As an adult, while working for a design studio, he was assigned his first children's book and has now won many awards. He received gold, silver and bronze medals in the Art Directors clubs of New York and Boston, won the Carter G. Woodson Book Award and drew awards from the American Institute of Graphic Arts. He has earned the Christopher Award, has had books named among the ten best illustrated books by the New York Times. Many reviews of his books have been starred, listing his books as ALA Notable Books, Reading Rainbow Books and Horn Books.

Pinkney created the stunning art for two Caldecott

212

Honor Books, *Mirandy and Brother Wind* (1989) and *The Talking Eggs* (1990). He has received the Coretta Scott King Award for Illustration three times. His work has been selected for exhibition at the International Children's Book Illustration Exhibition at the Bologna Book Fair, the AIGA Book Show, the Society of Illustrators Annual Show and in museums around the country.

Besides children's books, among his other projects have been the design of many United States postage stamps, including two major stamps in the Black Heritage Commemorative Series honoring Harriet Tubman and Martin Luther King, Jr. He has served on the U. S. Postal Service Stamp Advisory Committee. He is a visiting professor of Art at the University of Buffalo and an associate professor of Art at the University of Delaware. Clients have included NASA, IBM, The Negro Ensemble Company and the National Geographic Society.

His favorite book today? *The True Story of the Three Little Pigs*. And what does he recommend for children? "Read as much as possible."

Pinkney and his wife Gloria have four children and three grandchildren. They live in Croton-on-the-Hudson, New York.

James E. Ransome *

Red Dancing Shoes
Do Like Kyla
Uncle Jed's Barbershop

Born in North Carolina, he lived in Rich Square, North Carolina with his grandmother; as a teenager, he moved to New Jersey.

As a child, he had dogs, cats and a duck for pets. He enjoyed playing football, chess, drawing, and watching television. His favorite book was "*A Fly Went By.*"

After being shown a copy of "*The Patchwork Quilt*," illustrated by Jerry Pinkney, James became interested in illustrating children's books.

Do Like Kyla was the first children's book he illustrated.

James' father is a barber who helped others and sacrificed a great deal to own his own shop, James' college tuition was one of these reallocations of funds! So James chose to illustrate *Uncle Jed's Barbershop*. Uncle Jed's features are modeled after James' father-in-law.

He lives with his wife Lesa and daughter Jamie and a dalmatian, Clinton, in New York.

You may write to him at:

> 71 Hooker Avenue
> Poughkeepsie, New York 12601

Christopher Raschka

Charlie Parker Played bebop

Born in Huntingdon, Pennsylvania, he grew up hearing German and English spoken in his home. His mother was from Vienna, Austria; his father from Detroit, Michigan. He also had a brother, a sister and a dog.

Goldfish were his first pets. When he failed to catch any at a contest at the local swimming pool, a man gave him a whole bag. He lived in Detroit until he was ten.

He says being an artist is hard work. He walks, writes, draws, paints, cuts, pastes, drinks tea and then starts all over again.

Chris lives with his wife Lydie, his big cat Alma, his little cat Alaska Wolf Joe and his turtles, Catsmeat and Bingo, in New York City.

Faith Ringgold *

Tar Beach

A painter living in Harlem, Faith Ringgold collaborated with her mother on the soft fabric pieces before working on *Tar Beach*, a quilt painting that incorporates a written story.

Ringgold was born in Harlem and began painting professionally 25 years ago. She gradually moved away from the traditional stretched canvas to make "tankas," paintings on lengths of cloth with frames of fabric. She was influenced to use quilts as a medium for her paintings after hearing her mother's stories of their slave ancestors making quilts as part of their plantation duties.

Tar Beach is her first picture book. Ringgold teaches for half the year at the University of California at San Diego, where she is a professor of Art. She is married to Burdette Ringgold and has two daughters, Barbara and Michelle Wallace.

Melodye Rosales *

Kwanzaa

After illustrating children's books for years, this is the first book she has done on the black experience in America.

213

Robert D. SanSouci

The Talking Eggs

Robert D. SanSouci graduated from St. Mary's College in Moraga, California. He is author of *The Talking Eggs*, a re-told Southern folk tale illustrated by Jerry Pinkney, and has written for both adults and children.

His nickname when he was a boy was Bobby, and he was sometimes called "Sam" from his last name. His favorite story was the *Wizard of Oz*. His favorite picture books, illustrated by Wanda Gag, were *Five Chinese Brothers* or *Millions of Cats*. Bobby lived with his parents, two brothers and one sister in the San Francisco Bay area in Berkeley, California. Pets were dogs, cats, a tortoise, and white rats (briefly). Favorite hobbies were reading and building models. His favorite places to go were the park, the movies and the beach, and he liked to play Cowboys and Indians. Later he liked to play spacemen.

Young Bob's first book was written in second grade and illustrated by his brother Daniel. They made eight copies of the book and distributed it to family members. It was named "Crazy Bang," but somehow Bob transposed the second and third letters and it became known as "Carzy Bang."

As an adult, SanSouci began doing children's books when "my brother Dan (an illustrator) decided (after college) that this was the perfect way to combine our interests in storytelling (me) and illustration (him)." In the past, SanSouci has worked as a bookstore manager, advertising copywriter and editor, but he works only on his writing at present. Today his most recent favorite children's book is *The Frog Prince Revisited*.

Among his many books are *The Legend of Scarface* and *The Song of Sedna*, both illustrated by his brother Daniel SanSouci and both award winners; and, *Short & Shivery: Thirty Chilling Tales*, a Children's Choice Book selected by the International Reading Association and the Children's Book Council for 1988.

A Brian Pinkney illustrated book by Robert SanSouci is *The Boy and the Ghost*. Brian Pinkney also illustrated his *Sukey and the Mermaid*, a rare mermaid story in black folktales, published in 1992.

He lives in Berkeley, California.

Ann Herbert Scott

Sam

She was born in 1926 in Germantown, Philadelphia. She spent earlier years of her life working with urban children in public housing projects and summer camps. Now she lives with her husband, William and their son Peter on the edge of the Sierras in Reno, Nevada. Her husband is a professor of physics at the University of Nevada.

James Seward

Harriet Tubman

James Seward is the artist who painted the inside illustrations for *Harriet Tubman* (Julian Messner), augmented by additional authentic illustrations from the Library of Congress, the National Archives and the National Portrait Gallery.

Anna Shelby

We Keep a Store

Anna Shelby is author of *We Keep a Store*, about a little girl who enjoys the fact that her family has a country store. The book is illustrated by John Ward.

Symeon Shimin

Sam
I Am Freedom's Child

Symeon Shimin was born in Russia and came to the United States with his family when he was ten years old. He attended art classes at Cooper Union in New York, but got most of his schooling in museums and art galleries here and in France and Spain.

He was chosen in 1983 to paint a mural in the Department of Justice building in Washington, and became one of the most moving and sought after artists in the publishing world. His works have been exhibited in many major museums.

He illustrated *I Am Freedom's Child* with evocative paintings that all children can identify with.

Paul Showers

Your Skin and Mine

Paul was born in Sunnyside, Washington in 1910. He was married and had twins, a boy and a girl.

He had many jobs connected to newspapers. In 1942-45 he served in the U. S. Army and continued his writing and editing.

He wrote many science books for children. *Your Skin and Mine* was written by Paul Showers in terms that very young children can understand.

Doris J. Sims *

Stop and Go

Doris J. Sims is a professor of Home Economics at the California State University of Los Angeles. Dr. Sims is also the owner and founder of the Academy of Progressive Education Preschool and Elementary School and has taught at the preschool and elementary school levels.

It was her affection and concern for children, especially black children, that prompted the writing of her books, she said. Sims is a specialist in child development and early education, and realized that children need positive experiences to develop high self-esteem and strong egos. *Stop and Go*, for example, one of her books, is a story for children about the invention of the traffic light by a black inventor.

It was her premise that information about black inventors would strengthen the self-concepts of black children and motivate them to excel and achieve. She also found the literature for young children to be lacking in biographical materials. So, as a segment of her doctoral dissertation, she completed writing a series of biographies for young children.

Kathie Billingslea Smith

Harriet Tubman

Kathie Billingslea Smith wrote *Harriet Tubman*, the story of the heroine of the Underground Railroad.

David Soman

The Leaving Morning
When I Am Old With You

This illustrator lives in new York City. He is painting for a new Angela Johnson book, *One of Three*. He is also writing a comic strip.

John Steptoe *

Daddy is a Monster...Sometimes
Stevie
Baby Says
All Us Come Cross the Water
She Come Bringing Me That Little Baby Girl

The late John Steptoe is one of the acknowledged greats in the illustration of children's books.

Born in 1950, John was read to as a child by his mother, growing up in Bedford Stuyvesant in Brooklyn, New York. His favorite hobbies were drawing and reading. He attended the High School of Art and Design in Manhattan and studied with painter Norman Lewis.

Steptoe attended a minority art program in Saxton River, Vermont in 1968 at the age of 17. The director of that program, sculptor John Torres, said that when John was questioned about goals for his art he said without hesitation that he wanted to create books for black children, as there were none with which he could identify when he was a child.

Stevie was Steptoe's first book. He felt it was important to create books in the dialogue which black children speak. He started writing and illustrating it when he was 16 years old. It was published by Harper & Row when he was barely 19. Stevie was described by Publishers Weekly as "rare and beautiful." The society of Illustrators awarded the book its Gold Medal. He is still the youngest artist ever to have received this award.

In his 20 year career, Steptoe illustrated 15 more books, nine of which he also wrote. Two of them, The *Story of Jumping Mouse* and *Mufaro's Beautiful Daughters*, won many other awards, including the Irma Simonton Black Award from the Bank Street College of Education.

Steptoe's executor, Ann Armistead White, said that "it is difficult...to convey... the extent to which John contributed to children of the African-American community. His books contain a powerful message about family life... ." White is one of six people to whom he dedicated *Daddy is a Monster...Sometimes*, with the statement: "To...Ann White...who knew more about getting through fear than I, and who maintained confidence in one who had almost lost it."

At his death in 1989, John Steptoe was making his home with his daughter Bweela, his son Javeka and a nephew, Antoine.

Beatriz Vidal

Bringing the Rain to Kapiti Plain

Beatriz Vidal had a "magical childhood" in a small town in Argentina. Called Beatrice as her nickname, she loved all fairy tales, and particularly enjoyed the pictures in Grimm's fairy tales.

Her father both read to her and told her stories. "My father was a real storyteller, and that made the whole difference in my life, for my childhood was very magical. I always followed my 'bliss,' the need of my soul. It is important that children trust their intuitions, and follow what they really love, for when that happens, doors begin to open in the most miraculous way. This has been my experience. First, the art of life, second, poetry and philosophy, third, the plastic arts, and to earn a living, drawing illustrations."

Beatrice made up stories and drew pictures when she was a child. She also played with her cats and dogs. She began playing piano when she was little.

Where did she like to go? "To the mountains, to discover new places."

How did she start doing children's books? "It happened without having planned it, after years of being a painter." She lives alone and devotes full time to her art. Her favorite children's books today are "Leo Lionni's books, M. Sendak's books, and so forth."

Based on a story that her father told her when she was a child in Argentina, Vidal wrote a story, which she also illustrated, *The Legend of El Dorado*. "This story gave me a lesson in patience and wisdom. First, I showed it to a publisher, who liked it very much, so we signed a contract. But there was something about it which wasn't right. In the meantime, all kinds of unpleasant things began to happen. The person who was to adapt the story couldn't do it due to many personal problems; sickness, even death, happened in her family. We finally broke the contract in a very unpleasant way. The story seemed to be bewitched, so I put it to rest. I understood then that one shouldn't force things, but wait until they are really ripe. The book is now published and the spell is finally over!"

Mildred Pitts Walter *

My Mama Needs Me

Mildred Pitts Walter was born the seventh child in her family in DeRidder, Louisiana, in 1922. She was denied access to public libraries and books when she was a child, and she says that it sharpened her desire to know what and why. Her books reflect the heritage of her American and African communities and family life, teaching positive values.

She loved school from the beginning and worked her way through college. One of her jobs was working in a shipyard in World War II. She was raised to believe she could do anything she wanted to if she set her mind to it. She received her BA in English from Southern University and her MA in Education from Antioch University. She and her husband were activists in the civil rights movement. They were members of CORE. She began teaching in Los Angeles. While she was teaching children, she began writing books because there were so few books for and about the children who were black. Somebody suggested that she write some for them, so she wrote her first book *Lillie of Watts: A Birthday Discovery*.

Later, Walter became a consultant in Boulder and a consultant, teacher and lecturer at Metro State College. Her travels, too, have affected her work. She was a delegate to the African and Black Arts Festival in Nigeria. Her trip to Africa erased the childhood memories of her school lesson about Africa. Her African experience added to her spirit of community, a closeness and unity she had known growing up. She wanted to combine what was powerful from both heritages to teach children so they could have it all.

Since 1969, she has spent most of her time writing. As an educational consultant, she particularly enjoys teaching children about black culture. "My greatest joy is when I see a black child light up when finally there is comprehension that I am the writer, a part of the creation of a book. My having done it seems to say to him, "She did it; I can too!" Knowing children want to learn through play inspired her to write her books. Her books teach positive values children are looking for. They reflect the spontaneity the laughter, the loving and the caring of her heritages.

She is the author of *My Mama Needs Me*, a book about a young boy who has a new baby sister and doesn't know quite what to do about it. It is illustrated by Pat Cummings. In preparation for writing the book, Ms. Walter visited baby clinics in Denver, where she lives. She found that one way a child can help a newborn is to rub the top of the ear, as Jason does in the story, to stimulate the baby's desire to nurse.

Walter and her late husband, Earl Lloyd Walter, had two sons. She is a grandmother.

John Ward *

We Keep a Store

This was John's first book. It was so much work, he swore he would never do another one. He is working on book #6 and books #7 and #8 are waiting in the wings.

As a child he lived in Brooklyn, then his family moved to Roosevelt, Long Island in New York when he was seven. He had a black German Shepard named "Grizzly."

His hobbies were taking his toys apart to see how they worked and roller skating. He played football, dodgeball, tag, coco lerio (spanish tag), and skully (a game played with bottle tops, stuffed with wax.)He drew pictures especially Snoopy®, Woodstock® and other Peanuts® characters, along with Cap'n Cru. :h.

After he learned to read, he read to himself. His favorite book was *Tom Sawyer*.

A children's editor with "vision" saw his portfolio of mostly magazine work, and his career as a children's book illustrator was launched.

John, his wife and cat Pumpkin live at their home. You may write to him at :

> 125 Maryland Ave.
> Freeport, NY 11520

Leila Ward

I Am Eyes - Ni Macho

Leila Ward is author of *I Am Eyes - Ni Macho*, the story of a day in Africa, illustrated by Nonny Hogrogian. Ward has lived in Italy, England and Kenya. It was in Kenya where she found her inspiration for *I Am Eyes - Ni Macho*.

Ward is the author/illustrator of the children's book. *The Flame Tree*, and illustrator of *The Bible* and *Holiday ABCs*. Today she makes her home in the foothills of the Sierra Nevada mountains.

Valerie Wilson Wesley *

Book of Black Heroes, Vol. 2:
Great Women in the Struggle

Executive Editor of Essence magazine is one of the publishing jobs Wesley has. She has written stories and articles for young adults for Essence, Choices, Creative Classroom and Scholastic News.

She co-authored *Afro-Bits, Book of Black Heroes from A to Z*, which has sold over 100,000 copies.

Bettye White*

Apples on a Stick

Editor and Collector of *Apples on a Stick* with Barbara Michels.

Verna Allette Wilkins *

Dave and the Tooth Fairy

As a mother living in England, Verna was distressed at the literature available for her young son to read.

She started a one-woman campaign for more children's books with black children as the central figure. She wanted self-affirming literature for her children and other black children.

Tamarind Books is Verna's baby and business. It is the result of committment to a purpose. Her books are now distributed throughout the world to be loved by all children.

Vera B. Williams

Cherries and Cherry Pits

Vera B. Williams was born in California. She graduated from Black Mountain College in North Carolina and moved to New York City.

William's book, *A Chair For My Mother*, was a Caldecott Honor Book in 1985, winner of the Boston Globe-Horn Book Award for outstanding illustration. It was her first book about Rosa and was followed by two other books about the irresistible heroine, *Something Special for Me* and *Music, Music for Everyone*.

She is also the author and illustrator of *Three Days on a River in a Red Canoe*.

Williams has had a very varied career. She says that she has "worked for peace, done graphic art, school teaching and children-raising (two daughters and a son), has run a bakery and been a cook in schools and restaurants."

217

Jeanette Winter

Follow the Drinking Gourd

When Jeanette Winter was a child, she loved the *Little Match Girl* story by Hans Christian Andersen and all of the D'Aulaire picture books. Her mother and teachers read to her - and she made up her own stories and drew pictures to accompany them.

She lived with her parents in Chicago and drawing was her favorite thing to do. When she went out, her favorite destination was the Saturday matinee at the movies. Little Jeanette also loved to play dolls, hop-scotch and hide-and-seek and to go roller skating.

When she grew up, a natural profession occurred: because she had always loved telling stories with pictures, she began to tell and illustrate children's stories. She has illustrated many children's books based on traditional material, including interpretations of an old nursery rhyme in *Come Out to Play,* a lullaby in *Hush Little Baby* and a tale from the Brothers Grimm in *The Magic Ring.*

She has illustrated many books based on traditional fairy tales, nursery rhymes and lullabies. Winter took her inspiration for *Follow the Drinking Gourd* from a folk song and slave narratives.

Full page paintings accompany the tale of Peg Leg Joe, who moved from plantation to plantation, teaching slaves the song of the "Drinking Gourd." Hidden in the lyrics were the directions to follow rivers and hills to find freedom.

Winter's paintings will make it possible for children easily to find the Drinking Gourd (Big Dipper) in the sky.

Today she admires Beatrix Potter's beautifully illustrated books. She and her husband, the painter Roger Winter, live in Texas and Maine. Their three sons are grown.

218

Camille Yarbrough *

Cornrows

Camille Yarbrough was born in Chicago. Today she is an author, actress, composer and singer who has appeared often on TV and in the theater in a variety of roles. She was a member of both the New York and touring companies of To Be Young, Gifted and Black.

Yarbrough has made a recording of her songs and dialogues, *The Iron Pot Cooker.* She has also been awarded a Jazz/Folk/Ethnic Performance Fellowship Grant by the National Endowment for the Arts. She has been honored with the Unity Award in Media from Lincoln University and Woman of the Month by Essence magazine. She teaches at African Poetry Theater, which is a writing workshop in Queens. Yarbrough is professor of African Dance at the City College of New York.

Appendix

Publishers

The publishers of children's books have been most generous with permissions to use illustrations from the books we have selected in *Children & Books I*. This list serves as our thanks to them as well as a convenient reference for you, the reader.

220

Black Butterfly Children's Books

Big Friend, Little Friend
Daddy and I
First Pink Light
I Make Music
Nathaniel Talking

Writers & Readers Publishing, Inc.
P. O. Box 461, Village Station
New York, NY 10014

Bowmar

I Am Freedom's Child

Carolrhoda Books, Inc.

A Pocketful of Goobers
Jafta
Jafta's Father
Jafta's Mother

Lerner Publications
241 First Avenue North
Minneapolis, MN 55401

Children's Book Press

I Remember "121"
Things I Like About Grandma

6400 Hollis St., Suite 4
Emeryville, CA 94608

Children's Cultu-Lit Book Co.

Stop and Go

3250 Selby Ave.
Los Angeles, CA 90034

Children's Press

Kwanzaa
Martin Luther King, Jr.: A
Man Who Changed Things

Grolier Society
5400 North cumberland Ave.
Chicago, IL 60656

Coward-McCann, Inc.

Cornrows

200 Madison Ave.
New York, NY 10016

Thomas Y. Crowell Junior Books

African Dream
Me and Neesie
My Five Senses
Rosa Parks
Straight Hair, Curly Hair
Your Skin and Mine

10 East 53rd St.
New York, NY 10022

Crown Publishers, Inc.

Tar Beach

225 Park Ave. South
New York, NY 10003

Delacorte Press

Mr. Monkey and the Gotcha Bird

1 Dag Hammarskjold Place
New York, NY 10017

Dial

The Patchwork Quilt

Dial Books for Young Readers

Amazing Grace
Ashanti to Zulu: African
Traditions
Bringing the Rain to Kapiti
Plain
Flossie and the Fox
Jambo Means Hello: Swahili
Alphabet Book
Moja Means One: Swahili
Counting Book
Pretend You're a Cat
Something on My Mind
The Tales of Uncle Remus: The
Adventures of Brer Rabbit
The Talking Eggs
The People Could Fly
Why Mosquitoes Buzz in
People's Ears
Who's in Rabbit's House? A
Masai Tale

Penguin Books USA
375 Hudson Street
New York, NY 10014-3657

Doubleday

I Been There

666 Fifth Ave.
New York, NY 10103

Greenwillow Books

Ben's Trumpet
Bigmama
Cherries and Cherry Pits
The Quilt
Truck
Where are you going Manyoni?

William Morrow & Company, Inc.
1350 Avenue of the Americas
New York, NY 10019

HarperCollins Children's Books

The Baby
Chilly Stomach
Daddy is a Monster...Sometimes
Honey, I lLove and Other
  Poems
A Letter to Amy
MAnDALA
She Come Bringing Me That
  Little Baby Girl
Stevie
Sweet Baby Coming
Willie's Not the Hugging Kind

10 East 53rd St.
New York, NY 10022

Holiday House, Inc.

Dancing With the Indians
A Picture Book of Martin Luther
  King, Jr.

425 Madison Ave.
New York, NY 10017

Holt Rinehart and Winston

All Us Come Cross the Water
Anansi the Spider: A Tale from
  the Ashanti
Everett Anderson's 1-2-3
Everett Anderson's Nine
  Month Long
Everett Anderson's Goodbye

6277 Sea Harbor Dr.
Orlando, FL 32821

Jacaranda Designs, Ltd.

Mcheshi Goes to the Game Park
Mcheshi Goes to the Market

P. O. Box 7936
Boulder, CO 80306

Just Us Books

Book of Black Heroes, Vol. 2 -
  Great Women in the Struggle
Bright Eyes, Brown Skin
When I Was Little

Just Us Books
Suite 22-24
301 Main St.
Orange, NJ 07050

Kane/Miller

A Cat In Search of A Friend
You Be Me, I'll Be You

P. O. Box 529
Brooklyn, MY 11231

Alfred A. Knopf
Knopf Books for Young Readers

Follow the Drinking Gourd
Mirandy and Brother Wind

Random House, Inc.
201 East 50th St.
New York, NY

Lothrop, Lee & Shepard Books

Baby Says
Galimoto
My Mama Needs Me

William Morrow & Company, Inc.
1350 Avenue of the Americas
New York, NY 10019

Macmillan Publishing Company

Half a Moon and One Whole Star

866 Third Ave.
New York NY 10022-0299

McGraw-Hill Book Company

Sam

Blue Ridge Summit, PA
117294-0850

Julian Messner

Harriet Tubman

190 Sylvan Ave.
Englewood Cliffs, NJ 07632

Open Hand Publishing, Inc.

Habari Gani?
Night Feathers

P. O. Box 22048
Seattle, WA 98122

Orchard Books

A Leaving Morning
Do Like Kyla
Charlie Parker Played be bop
Tell Me A Story, Mama
We Keep a Store
When I Am Old With You

95 Madison Avenue
New York, NY 10016

Putnam Publishing Group

Apples on a Stick: The
  Folklore of Black Children
Grandpa's Face

200 Madison Ave.
New York, NY 10016

Scholastic, Inc.

The Black Snowman
Dragon Takes a Wife
Good Night Baby
I Am Eyes - Ni Macho
Josephine's 'Magination: A
  Tale of Haiti
The Real McCoy

555 Broadway
New York, NY 10012-3999

Simon & Schuster, Inc.

Uncle Jed's Barber Shop
A Weed is a Flower: The Life
  of George Washington Carver

Rockefeller Center
1230 Avenue of the Americas
New York, NY 10020

Stewart, Tabori & Chang

Life Doesn't Frighten Me

575 Broadway
New York, NY 10012

Tamarind Limited

Dave and the Tooth Fairy
I Don't Eat Toothpaste
  Anymore!

P. O. Box 296
Camberley Surrey
GU151QW, England

USA Address:
Child's Play
550 Lisbon St.
P.O. Box 821
Lewiston, ME 04240

Tambourine Books

Red Dancing Shoes

William Morrow & Co., Inc.
1350 Avenue of the Americas
New York, NY 10019

Warren-Mattox Productions

Shake It to the One That You
  Love the Best

3817 San Pablo Dam Road, #336
El Sabrante, CA 94803

221

Sources

Records and/or Tapes:

Children of Selma

Songs written by children in Selma., AL
(positive self concept)

Rose Sanders
P. O. Box 1305
Selma, AL 36702-1305

Every Body Cries Sometimes

222

(personal feelings, positive self concept)

Patty Zeitlen, Marcia Berman
Education Activities, Inc.
Freeport, NY 11520

Jambo and Other Call and Response Songs and Chants

Ella Jenkins singing with a group of children

Folkways Records & Service Corp.
43 West 61st St.
New York, NY 10023

Stomp Dance. Vol. 1.

(6 stomp dances of the Muskogee, Seminole, Yachi. They carry a full range of American Indian music)

Indian House   (505) 776-2953
P. O. Box 472
Taos, NM 87571

Stories From the Heart

(songs and stories about African American culture)

Taifa Productions
6155 Wagner St.
St. Louis, MO 63133

Shake It To The One That You Love The Best

(Songs and rhymes)

Warren Mattox
3817 San Pablo Dam Road #336
El Sabrante, CA 94803

Books:

Johnson, James Weldon

(Black National Anthem in story book form)

Lift Ev'ry voice and Sing (1994).
Illustrated by Jan Spivey Gilchrist

Chuck, V., (1971)

Colors Around Me

Afro. Am Publishing Company

Your Local Library

To keep up with the new book and check for additional books, use these at the reference desk:

Bookfinder: A Guide to Children's Literature

A to Zoo: Subject Access to Children's Picture Books

Horn Book - Journal of Book Reviews

Index to Children's Poetry

Songs

Kye Kye Kule

Kye Kye Kule is a very popular chant sung by children all over Ghana. It is sung so often throughout the country that its true meaning and origin are lost. This is an excellent song to use to teach call and response.

Leader: Chorus:

KYE KYE KULE   KYE KYE KULE
(Che Che Koo-leh)   (Che Che Koo-leh)

KYE KYE KOPISA   KYE KYE KOPISA
(Che Che Koh-fee-sah)   (Che Che Koh-fee-sah)

KOFISA LANGA   KOFISA LANGA
(Koh-fee-sah Lahn-gah)   (Koh-fee-sah Lahn-gah)

LANGA TSI LANGA   LANGA TSI LANGA
(Lahn-gah Chee Lahn-gah)   (Lahn-gah Chee Lahn-gah)

KUM ALELE   KUM ALELE
(Koom Ah-leh-leh)   (Koom Ah-leh-leh)

We Shall Overcome

We shall overcome, we shall overcome,
We shall overcome someday

Chorus:
Oh, deep in my heart I do believe
That we shall overcome some day.

We'll walk hand in hand, we'll walk hand in hand.
We'll walk hand in hand, some day.
(repeat chorus)

We are not afraid, we are not afraid,
We are not afraid today,
(repeat chorus)

We shall live in peace, we shall live in peace,
We shall live in peace, some day.
(repeat chorus)

The truth will make us free, the truth will make us free,
The truth will make us free, some day.
(repeat chorus)

We shall brothers be, we shall brothers be,
We shall brothers be, some day.
(repeat chorus)

Lift Every Voice and Sing
(Black National Anthem)

Lift every voice and sing, 'til earth and heaven ring,
Ring with the harmonies of liberty;
Let our rejoicing rise, high as the list'ning skies,
Let it resound loud as the rolling sea.
Sing a song full of the faith that the dark past has taught us,
Sing a song full of the hope that the present has brought us;
Facing the rising sun of our new day begun,
Let us march on 'til victory is won.

Stony the road we trod, bitter the chastening rod,
Felt in the days when hope unborn had died;
Yet with a steady beat, have not our weary feet
Come to the place for which our fathers sighed?

We have come over a way that with tears has been
    watered;
We have come, treading our path through the blood of the
    slaughtered;
Out from the gloomy past, 'til now we stand at last
Where the white gleam of our bright star is cast.

God of our weary years, God of our silent tears,
Thou who hast brought us thus far on the way;
Thou who hast by Thy might, led us into the light,
Keep us forever in the path, we pray.

Lest our feet stray from the places, our God, where we met
    Thee,
Lest our hearts, drunk with the wine of the world, we
    forget Thee;
Shadowed beneath Thy hand, may we forever stand,
True to our God, true to our native land.

Lift Every Voice and Sing was written by the noted Negro poet and civil rights leader, James Weldon Johnson. It was originally intended for use in a program given by a group of Jacksonville, Florida school children to celebrate Lincoln's birthday. Inasmuch as its words tend to convey a sense of birthright and heritage, it is often referred to as the "Negro National Anthem," and sung at the opening of various public gatherings.

Dr. Martin Luther King, Jr. Rap

Dr. Martin Luther King, Jr.
He was a good man.
He sang in a choir.
He prayed for the children.

Dr. Martin Luther King, Jr.
He died in a hotel
Somebody shot him.
We was mad.
We was sad.

Dr. Martin Luther King, Jr.
His name is on the street sign.
Because he died.
He wanted the children to be friends.

Authors: Three, Four and Five-Year-Old children at Lockhart Elementary School, Tampa, Florida

223

Reprinted by permission from Children & Books I © 1994, Patricia B. Moll, 4104 Lynn Ave., Tampa, Florida 33603

Coretta Scott King Book Awards

1994 **Toning the Sweep.** Angela Johnson.
Soul Looks Back in Wonder. Illus. by Tom Feelings

1993 **The Origin of Life on Earth.** David A. Anderson. Illus. by Kathleen Atkins Wilson.
The Dark Thirty. Patricia McKissack.

1992 **Now Is Your Time.** Walter Dean Myers.
Tar Beach. Faith Ringgold.

1991 **Aida.** Leontyne Price. Illus. by Leo and Diane Dillon.
The Road to Memphis. Mildred Taylor.

1990 **Nathaniel Talking.** Eloise Greenfield.
A Long Hard Journey: The Story of the Pullman Porters. Patricia McKissack and Fredrick McKissack.

1989 **Mirandy and Brother Wind.** Patricia McKissack. Illus. by Jerry Pinkney.
Fallen Angels. Walter Dean Myers.

1988 **Friendship.** Mildred D. Taylor. Illus. by Max Ginsburg.
Mufaro's Beautiful Daughters: An African Tale. John Steptoe.

1987 **Justin and the Best Biscuits in the World.** Mildred Pitts Walter. Illus. by Catherine Stock.
Half a Moon and One Whole Star. Crescent Dragonwagon. Illus. By Jerry Pinkney.

1986 **The People Could Fly: American Black Folktales.** Virginia Hamilton. Illus. by Leo and Diane Dillon.
The Patchwork Quilt. Valerie Flourney. Illus. by Jerry Pinkney.

1985 **Motown and Didi: A Love Story.** Walter Dean Myers.

1984 **Everett Anderson's Goodbye.** Lucille Clifton. Illus. by Ann Grifalconi.

1983 **Sweet Whispers, Brother Rush.** Virginia Hamilton.
Black Child. Peter Magubane.

1982 **Let the Circle be Unbroken.** Mildred D. Taylor.

1981 **This Life.** Sidney Poitier.
Beat the Story-Drum, Pum-Pum. Ashley Bryan.

1980 **The Young Landlords.** Walter Dean Myers.
Cornrows. Camille Yarbrough. Illus. by Carole Byard.

1979 **Escape to Freedom: A Play About Young Frederick Douglas.** Ossie Davis.
Something on My Mind. Nikki Grimes.

1978 **Africa Dream.** Eloise Greenfield.

1977 **The Story of Stevie Wonder.** James Haskins.

1976 **Duey's Tale.** Pearl Bailey.

1975 **The Legend of Africania.** Dorothy W. Robinson. Illus. by Herbert Temple.

1974 **Ray Charles.** Sharon Bell Mathis.

1973 **I Never Had It Made.** John Roosevelt Robinson. Illus. by Alfred Duckett.

1972 **Seventeen Black Artists.** Elton C. Fax.

1971 **Black Troubadour.** Charlemar Rollins.

1970 **Martin Luther King, Jr.: Man of Peace.** Lillie Patterson.

Reprinted by permission from Children & Books I © 1994, Patricia B. Moll, 4104 Lynn Ave., Tampa, Florida 33603

NASA PHOTO

Obtaining a NASA Satellite view of Africa

Write to:
National Aeronautics and Space Administration
Washington, D.C. 20564

Things I Like About Grandma

Invitation to Grandma Day

Teacher's Letter to go with Invitation to Grandma Day

*Dear*_____:

    Our class is having a Share Someone Special Time.

226   *_____ has decided you are the person _____would like to share.*

    Please try to come for this very important sharing time. _____ will be very proud to have you in our classroom.

    If, for some reason, you cannot attend, please give _____ something about you to share with the others. A photograph, a favorite personal item, a story or something that _____ thinks is special about you.

    We would be happy to make arrangements for you to come at another time. Please feel free to visit our classroom at any time.

Sincerely,

_____

Sharing Day

       Date_____Time _____ Place _____

Sharing Week

       Your Day _____ Time _____Place _____

Permission to reprint from Patricia B. Moll, © 1994

Africa Dream

Letter to Parents

Dear_____:

      We have read the book, *Africa Dream*. The child in the book dreams of being in Africa with her long-ago relatives.

      Each child in our class is going to make a picture of a dream. The dream will be of his/her long-ago relatives.

      Please help your child fill in the Family History form.

      If you have any photographs we can copy, please send them. Or, if you can get them copied, that would be helpful.

      We would also like some pictures of the country that the long-ago relative lived in. Please look through your magazines and junk mail for any pictures that might be appropriate and send them along.

      This will be a project of many days. As always, we could use your help in the classroom.

      If you have any items from your relatives that the children can touch, please bring them in. Thank you.

Sincerely,

_____(sign your name here)

227

Family History Form   Child's Name:_____

My present family. (please list everyone living in the house with you and relatives, natural and adopted, that you see on a regular basis.)

Places my relatives live. (Give names, cities and countries.)

Long-ago relatives. (Include any information you have, no matter how sketchy. Give any places and names you know.)

The idea behind the picture your child will make is for your child to learn something about his family history. You may know your great grandfather lived in China. You may know your mother lived in Paris, Georgia. Whatever you know will be important to your child's dream picture.

I Lost A Tooth/ I Grew A Tooth

NAME	Incisor		Incisor		Incisor		Incisor		Canine		Canine		Molar		Molar		Molar		Molar	
	Out	In	Out	In	Out	In	Out	In	Out	In	Out	In	Out	In	Out	In	Out	In	Out	In

228

My Teeth

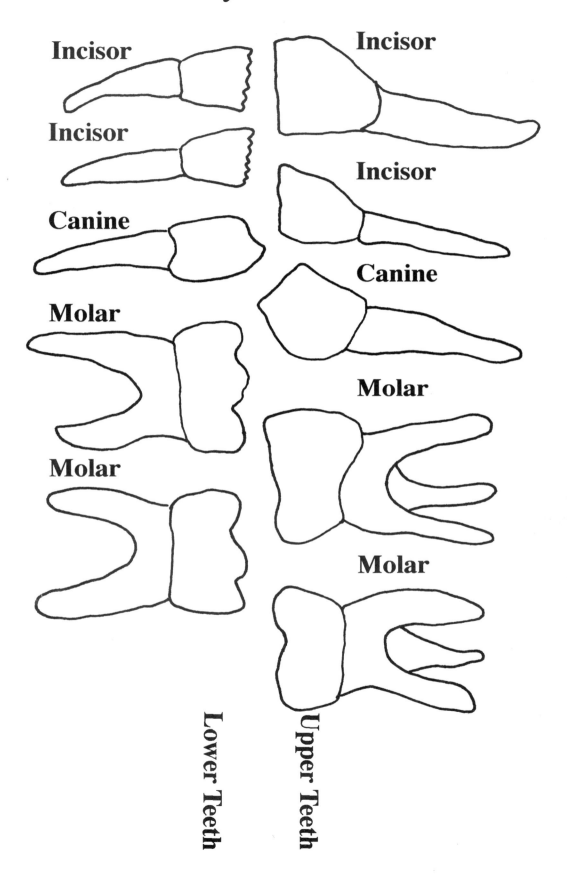

Incisor

Incisor

Incisor

Incisor

Canine

Canine

Molar

Molar

Molar

Molar

Molar

Lower Teeth

Upper Teeth

Index
(By Subject)

Africa
Africa Dream, 110
All Us Come Cross the Water, 112
Ashanti to Zulu, 190
Black Snowman, The, 116
Cornrows, 120
Jambo Means Hello, 186
Ma nDA LA, 84
Mcheshi Goes to the Game Park, 176
Mcheshi Goes to the Market, 174
Moja Means One, 182

Animals
Anansi the Spider, 178
Bringing the Rain to Kapiti Plain, 188
Cat In Search of a Friend, A, 146
Flossie and the Fox, 42
I Am Eyes - - Ni Macho, 166
Pretend You're a Cat, 34
Talking Eggs, The, 46
People Could Fly, The, 138
Who's In Rabbit's House?, 184
Why Mosquitoes Buzz in People's Ears, 180

Brother/Sister
Baby, The, 14
Baby Says, 24
Black Snowman, The, 116
Cornrows, 120
Do Like Kyla, 52
My Mama Needs Me, 74
Sweet Baby Coming, 12
Tar Beach, 118

Expressing Feelings/Growth
Africa Dream, 110
All Us Come Cross The Water, 112
Ben's Trumpet, 100
Bright Eyes, Brown Skin, 26
Chilly Stomach, 156
Cornrows, 120
Everett Anderson's Goodbye, 70
Letter To Amy, A, 148
Me and Nessie, 154
Sam, 76
Stevie, 150
Black Snowman, The, 116
Leaving Morning, The, 32
You Be Me, I'll Be You, 158
Willie's Not the Hugging Kind, 58

Fathers
Daddy is a Monster...Sometimes, 56
Everett Anderson's 1-2-3, 66
Everett Anderson's Goodbye, 70
Jafta's Father, 172
My Daddy and I, 16
You Be Me, I'll Be You, 161

Family History
Africa Dream, 110
All Us Come Cross the Water, 112
Bigmama's, 72
Cornrows, 120
Dancing With The Indians, 140
Josephine's 'magination, 142
Kwanzaa, 114
Mirandy and Brother Wind, 44
Patchwork Quilt, The, 78
Tar Beach, 118
Things I Like About Grandma, 62
Uncle Jed's Barbershop, 128
We Keep A Store, 59
When I Am Old With You, 64

Famous People
Weed Is A Flower, A, 130
Picture Book of Martin Luther King, Jr., A, 136
Book of Black Heroes Vol. 2.
   Great Women in The Struggle, 124
Charlie Parker Played be bop, 136
Harriet Tubman, 127
Rosa Parks, 126
Stop and Go, 132

Grandparents
Bigmama's, 72
Cornrows, 120
Dave and the Tooth Fairy, 82
Patchwork Quilt, The, 78
Talking Eggs, The, 46
Things I Like About Grandma, 62
Uncle Jed's Barbershop, 59
When I Am Old With You, 64

Humor
Apples on a Stick, 41
Baby Says, 24
Daddy Is A Monster...Sometimes, 56
Dave and the Tooth Fairy, 82
I Don't Eat Toothpaste Anymore!, 28
Tales of Uncle Remus, 48
Things I Like About Grandma, 62

Imagination
Amazing Grace, 102
Weed is a Flower, A, 130
Charlie Parker Played be bop, 136
Dave and The Tooth Fairy, 82
Flossie and The Fox, 42
Follow The Drinking Gourd, 122
Half a Moon and One Whole Star, 96
Harriet Tubman, 126
I Been There, 90
I Make Music, 18
Josephine's 'magination, 142
Life Doesn't Frighten Me, 86

Me and Neesie, 154
Mirandy and Brother Wind, 44
Mr. Monkey and the Gotcha Bird, 94
People Could Fly, The, 138
Quilt, The, 36
Red Dancing Shoes, 98
Stop and Go, 132
Tales of Uncle Remus, 48
Talking Eggs, The, 46
Tar Beach, 118
Truck, 30
Uncle Jed's Barbershop, 128
You Be Me, I'll Be You, 158

Math
Big Friend, Little Friend, 20
Dave and the Tooth Fairy, 82
Good Night Baby, 22
Moja Means One, 182
Stop and Go, 132

Mothers
Bigmama's, 72
Book of Black Heroes, Vol. 2, 124
Cornrows, 120
Jafta's Mother, 164
Josephine's 'magination, 140

Music
Amazing Grace, 102
Ben's Trumpet, 100
Charlie Parker Played be bop, 136
Dancing With The Indians, 140
Follow the Drinking Gourd, 122
I Make Music, 18
Red Dancing Shoes, 98
Shake It To The One You Love The Best, 40

Naptime
Good Night Baby, 22
Half a Moon and One Whole Star, 96
Quilt, The, 36

Personal Feelings
Amazing Grace, 102
Bright Eyes, Brown Skin, 26
Chilly Stomach, 156
Everett Anderson's 1-2-3, 66
Jafta, 168
Mirandy and Brother Wind, 44
My Five Senses, 162
Nathaniel Talking, 92
People Could Fly, The, 138
Picture Book of Martin Luther King, Jr., A, 134
Red Dancing Shoes, 98
Rosa Parks, 126
Something On My Mind, 104
Straight Hair, Curly Hair, 160
Tar Beach, 118
Your Skin and Mine, 161

Rhymes
Apples on a Stick, 41

Bright Eyes, Brown Skin, 26
Honey, I Love, 88
I Am Freedom's Child, 108
Life Doesn't Frighten Me, 86
Ma nDA LA, 84
Nathaniel Talking, 92
Shake It To The One That You Love The Best, 40
Something On My Mind, 104

Science
Book of Black Heroes, Vol. 2, 124
Bringing the Rain to Kapiti Plain, 188
Cherries and Cherry Pits, 152
Dave and The Tooth Fairy, 82
Good Night Baby, 22
Half a Moon and One Whole Star, 96
I Am Eyes - - Ni Macho, 166
Mirandy and Brother Wind, 44
Mr. Monkey and The Gotcha Bird, 94
My Five Senses, 162
Quilt, The, 36
Stop and Go, 132
Straight Hair, Curly Hair, 160
Truck, 30
Weed is a Flower, A, 130
Your Skin and Mine, 161

Self-Expression
Follow the Drinking Gourd, 122
Honey I Love, 88
I Am Freedom's Child, 108
I Make Music, 18
Life Doesn't Frighten Me, 86
Nathaniel Talking, 92
Picture Book of Martin Luther King, Jr., A, 134
Rosa Parks, 126
Something On My Mind, 104
Tar Beach, 118

Tales
Anansi the Spider, 41
Bigmama's, 72
Bringing the Rain to Kapiti Plain, 188
Cornrows, 120
Dancing With The Indians, 140
Flossie and The Fox, 42
Harriet Tubman, 127
I Been There, 90
Josephine's 'magination, 142
Mirandy and Brother Wind, 44
Mr. Monkey and The Gotcha Bird, 94
People Could Fly, The, 138
Tales of Uncle Remus, 48
Who's in Rabbit's House?, 184
Why Mosquitoes Buzz in People's Ears, 180

Transportation
Follow The Drinking Gourd, 122
Harriet Tubman, 126
I Been There, 90
Mcheshi Goes to the Game Park, 176
Stop and Go, 132
Truck, 30

Index
(Alphabetical by Title)

Africa Dream (1977), Eloise Greenfield, Crowel - 110
All Us Come Cross The Water (1973), Lucille Clifton, Holt Rinehart & Winston - 112
Amazing Grace (1991), Mary Hoffman, Dial Books for Young Readers - 102
Anansi the Spider (1972), Gerald McDermott, Holt, Rinehart & Winston - 178
Apples on a Stick (1983), Barbara Michels, Putnam - 41
Ashanti to Zulu (1976), Margaret Musgrove, Dial - 190

Baby, The (1994), Monica Greenfield, HarperFestival - 14
Baby Says (1988), John Steptoe, Lothrop, Lee & Shepard - 24
Ben's Trumpet (1979), Rachel Isadora, Greenwillow - 100
Big Friend, Little Friend (1991), Eloise Greenfield, Black Butterfly Children's Book - 20
Bigmama's (1991), Donald Crews, Lothrop, Lee & Shepard - 72
Black Snowman, The (1989), Phil Mendez, Scholastic - 116
Book of Black Heroes, Vol. 2, Great Women in The Struggle (1991), Just Us Books - 124
Bright Eyes, Brown Skin (1990), Cheryl Willis Hudson and Bernette G. Ford, Just Us Books - 26
Bringing the Rain to Kapiti Plain (1981), Verna Aardema, Dial - 188

Cat In Search of a Friend , A (1986), Meshack Asare, Kane/Miller - 146
Charlie Parker Played be bop (1992), Christopher Raschka, Orchard - 136
Cherries and Cherry Pits (1986), Verna Aardema, Greenwillow - 152
Chilly Stomach (1986), Jeanette Caines, HarperCollins - 156
Cornrows (1979), Camille Yarbrough, Coward-McCann - 120

Daddy is a Monster...Sometimes (1980), John Steptoe, J. B. Lippincott - 56
Dancing With The Indians (1993), Angela Shelf Medearis, Holiday - 140
Dave and the Tooth Fairy (1993), Verna Allette Wilkins, Tamarind - 82
Do Like Kyla (1990), Angela Johnson, Orchard - 52

Everett Anderson's 1-2-3 (1977), Lucille Clifton, Holt Rinehart & Winston - 66
Everett Anderson's Goodbye (1978), Lucille Clifton, Holt Rinehart & Winston - 70
Everett Anderson's Nine Month Long (1983), Lucille Clifton, Holt Rinehart & Winston - 68
Flossie and the Fox (1986), Patricia C. McKissack, Dial - 42
Follow the Drinking Gourd (1988), Jeanette Winter, Knopf - 122
Good Night Baby (1992), Cheryl Willis Hudson, Just Us Books - 22

Half a Moon and One Whole Star (1986), Crescent Dragonwagon, Macmillian - 96
Honey I Love (1978), Eloise Greenfield, HarperCollins - 88
I Am Eyes - - Ni Macho (1978), Leila Ward, Scholastic - 166
I Am Freedom's Child (1970), Bill Martin, Jr., Bowman - 108
I Been There (1982), Northern J. Calloway, Doubleday - 90
I Don't Eat Toothpaste Anymore! (1993), Karen King, Tamarind - 28
I Make Music (1991), Eloise Greenfield, Black Butterfly Children's Books - 18

Jafta (1981), Hugh Lewin, Carolrhoda - 168
Jafta's Father (1981), Hugh Lewin, Carolrhoda - 172
Jafta's Mother (1981), Hugh Lewin, Carolrhoda - 170
Josephine's 'magination (1973), Arnold Dobrin, Scholastic - 142
Jambo Means Hello (1974), Muriel Feelings, Dial - 186

232

Reprinted with permission from Children & Books I © 1994, Patricia B. Moll, 4104 Lynn Ave., Tampa FL 33603

Kwanzaa(1990), Deborah M. Newton Chocolate, Children's Press - 114

Letter to Amy, A, (1968), Ezra Jack Keats, HarperCollins - 148
Leaving Morning, The (1992), Angela Johnson, Orchard - 32
Life Doesn't Frighten Me (1993), Maya Angelou, Stewart, Tabori & Chang - 86

Ma nDA LA (1971), Arnold Adoff, HarperCollins - 84
Mcheshi Goes to the Game Park (1992), Jacaranda - 176
Mcheshi Goes to the Market (1991), Jacaranda - 174
Me and Neesie (1975), Eloise Greenfield, Thomas Y. Crowell Company - 154
Mirandy and Brother Wind (1988), Patricia McKissack, Knopf - 44
Moja Means One (1971), Muriel Feelings, Dial - 182
Mr. Monkey and The Gotcha Bird (1982), Walter Dean Myers, Delacorte - 94
My Daddy and I (1991), Eloise Greenfield, Black Butterfly Children's Books - 16
My Five Senses (1989), Aliki, Crowell - 162
My Mama Needs Me (1983), Mildred Pitts Walter, Lothrop, Lee and Shepard - 74

Nathaniel Talking (1988), Eloise Greenfield, Black Butterfly Children's Books - 92

Parks, Rosa (1973), Eloise Greenfield, Crowell - 126
Patchwork Quilt, The (1985), Valerie Flourney, Dial - 78
People Could Fly, The (1986), Virginia Hamilton, Dial - 138
Picture Book of Martin Luther King, Jr, A (1989), David A. Adler, Holiday House - 134
Pretend You're a Cat (1990), Jean Marzollo, Dial - 34

Quilt, The (1984), Ann Jonas, Greenwillow - 36

Red Dancing Shoes (1993), Denise Lewis Patrick, Tamborine - 98

Sam (1967), Ann Herbert Scott, McGraw Hill - 76
Shake It To The One That You Love The Best (1989), Cheryl Warren Mattox, Warren-Mattox Prod. - 40
She Come Bringing Me That Little Baby Girl (1974), Eloise Greenfield, HarperCollins - 60
Something On My Mind (1978), Nikki Grimes, Dial - 104
Stevie (1969), John Steptoe, HarperCollins - 150
Stop and Go (1980), Doris Sims, Cultu-Lit Book Company - 132
Straight Hair, Curly Hair (1966), Augusta Goldin, Crowell - 160
Sweet Baby Coming (1994), Eloise Greenfield, HarperFestival - 12

Tales of Uncle Remus (1987), Julius Lester, Dial - 48
Talking Eggs, The (1989), Robert D. San Souci, Dial - 46
Tar Beach (1991), Faith Ringgold, Crown - 118
Things I Like About Grandma (1992), Francine Haskins, Children's Book Press - 62
Truck (1980), Donald Crews, Lothrop, Lee and Shepard - 30
Tubman, Harriet (1988), Kathie Billingslea Smith - 126

Uncle Jed's Barbershop (1993), Margaree King Mitchell, Simon & Schuster - 128

Weed is a Flower, A (1988), Aliki, Simon & Schuster - 130
We Keep A Store (1990), Anne Shelby, Orchard - 54
When I Am Old With You (1990), Angela Johnson, Orchard - 64
Who's In Rabbit's House (1977), Verna Aardema, Dial - 184
Why Mosquitoes Buzz in People's Ears (1975), Verna Aardema - 180
Willie's Not the Hugging Kind (1989), Joyce Durham Barrett, HarperCollins - 58

You Be Me, I'll Be You (1990), Pili Mandelbaum, Kane/Miller - 158
Your Skin and Mine (1965), Paul Showers, Crowell - 161

Reprinted with permission from Children & Books I © 1994, Patricia B. Moll, 4104 Lynn Ave., Tampa FL 33603

Additional Books

Adair, G., (1989), *George Washington Carver;* Chelsea House Publishers, New York.

Adoff, A., (1973), *Black is Brown is Tan;* Harper Trophy, New York.

Bryan, A., (1994), *The Story of Lightning and Thunder;* Anteneum, New York.

    (1992), *Sing to the Sun;* HarperCollins, New York.

    (1977), *The Dancing Granny;* Anteneum, Hartford.

    (1986), *Lion and the Ostrich Chicks;* Anteneum, New York.

    (1985), *The Cat's Purr;* Macmillan, New York.

Caines, J., (1988), *I Need A Lunch Box;* HarperCollins, Singapore.

    (1982), *Just Us Women;* HarperCollins, New York.

    (1973), *Abby;* HarperCollins, New York.

    (1977), *Daddy;* HarperCollins, New York.

Church, V., (1971), *Colors Around Me;* Afro-am Publishing Company, Illinois.

Clifton, L., (1973), *The Boy Who Didn't Believe in Spring;* Dutton, New York.

    (1992), *Three Wishes;* Doubleday, New York.

Crews, D., (1992), *Short Cut;* Greenwillow Books, New York.

Cummings, P., (1991), *Clean Your Room, Harvey Moon;* Bradbury, New York.

    (1986), *C.L.O.U.D.S.;* Lothrop, New York.

Dee, R., (1988), *Two Ways to Count to Ten: A Liberian Folktale;* Holt, New York.

Ellis, V. F., (1993), *Land of the Four Winds;* Just Us Books, New Jersey.

Feelings, M., (1990), *Zamani Goes to Market;* Africa World Press, New Jersey

Feelings, T., (1993), *Soul Looks Back in Wonder;* Dial Books, New York.

    (1993), *Tommy Traveler in the World of Black History;* Black Butterfly Children's Books, NY

Fields, J., (1988), *The Green Lion of Zion Street;* McElderry, New York.

Gilchrist, J. S., (1993), *Indigo and Moonlight Gold;* Black Butterfly Children's Books, New York.

Giovanni, N. (1980), *Vacation Time; Poems for Children;* William Morrow & Co., New York

Greenfield, E., (1991), *First Pink Light;* Black Butterfly Children's Books, New York.

    (1980), *Grandma's Joy;* Philomel, New York.

    (1988), *Grandpa's Face;* Philomel, New York.

    (1990), *Night on Neighborhood Street;* Dial Books for Young Readers, New York.

    (1991), *My Doll, Keshia;* Black Butterfly Children's Books, New York.

    (1988), *Under the Sunday Tree;* HarperCollins, New York.

    (1993), *William and the Good Old Days;* HarperCollins, New York

Grimes, N., (1993), *From A Child's Heart;* Just Us Books, Orange, New Jersey.

Hartman, W., (1993), *All the Magic in the World;* Dutton Children's Books, New York.

Haskins, F., (1991), *I Remember "121";* Children's Book Press, San Francisco., California.

Haskins, J., (1989), *Count Your Way Through Africa;* Carolrhoda, Minneapolis.

Howard, E. F., (1991), *Aunt Flossie's Hats...and Crab Cakes Later;* Clarion, New York.

Hudson, C. W., (1992), *Good Morning Baby;* Scholastic, New York.

    (1987), *Afro-bets, ABC Book;* Just Us Books, Orange, New Jersey.

    (1987), *Afro-bets, 123 Book;* Just Us Books, Orange, New Jersey.

Hudson, W., (1991), *Jamal's Busy Day;* Just Us Books, Orange, New Jersey.

    (1993), *Pass It On, African American Poetry for all Children;* Scholastic, New York

Hughes, L., (1969), *Don't You Turn Your Back;* Knopf.

    (1994), *"An ABC Book";* (This is new, ask your bookseller).

234

Igus, T., (1992), *When I Was Little;* Just Us Books, Orange, New Jersey

Isadora, R., (1992), *Over the Green Hills;* Greenwillow Books, New York

Johnson, A., (1989), *Tell Me a Story, Mama;* Orchard Books, New York

    (1994), *The Girl Who Wore Snakes;* Orchard Books, New York

Johnson, D., (1992), *The Best Bug to Be;* Macmillan, New York

    (1991), *What Kind of Baby Sitter is This?;* Macmillan, New York

    (1994), *Now Let Me Fly: The Story of a Slave Family;* Scholastic, New York

Johnson, J. W. & Johnson, J. R., (1994), *Lift Every Voice and Sing;* Illustrated by Jan Spivey Gilchrist

Koplow, L., C.S.W., *Tanya and the Tobo Man: A Story for Children Entering Therapy;*
    Magination Press: 19 Union Square West, 8th Floor, New York, NY 10003

Lester, J., (1988), *More Tales of Uncle Remus;* Dial Books, New York.

    (1990), *Further Tales of Uncle Remus;* Dial Books, New York.

    (1989), *How Many Spots Does A Lepord Have? and Other Tales;* Scholastic, New York.

    (1994), *John Henry;* Illustrated by Jerry Pinkney

Lillegard, D., (1987), *My First Martin Luther King Book;* Children's Press, Chicago.

McClester, C., (1990), *Kwanzaa, Everything You Always Wanted to Know But Didn't Know Where to Ask;*
    Gumbs & Thomas Publishers, Inc., New York.

McKissack, P. C., (1992), *The Dark Thirty: Southern Tales of the Supernatural;* Alfred A. Knoff, New York

    (1992), *A Million Fish...More or Less;* Alfred A. Knopf, New York.

    (1989), *Nettie Jo's Friends;* Knopf, New York.

Mathis, S. B., (1991), *Red Dog/Blue Fly;* Football Poems; Illustrated by Jan Spivey Gilchrist, Viking Press,

Medearis, S., (1994), *Our People;* Macmillan, New York

Mitchell, B., (1986), *A Pocketful of Goobers*; Carolrhoda Books, Minneapolis.

Mitchell, R. P., (1993), *Hue Boy;* Dial Books for Young Readers, New York.

Morninghouse, S., (1992), *Habari Gani? What's the News? A Kwanzaa Story;* Open Hand Publishing,
    Seattle, WA

    (1989), *Nightfeathers;* Open Hand Publishing, Seattle, WA.

Myers, W. D., (1994), *Dragon Takes A Wife*, Scholastic, New York.

    (1993), *Brown Angels, An Album of Pictures and Verse;* HarperCollins, New York.

Nabwire, C., (1988), *Cooking the African Way;* Lerner Publications Co.,, Minneapolis.

Onyefulu, I., (1993), *A is for Africa*; Cobble Hill Book

Pinkney, A. D., (1993), *Seven Candles for Kwanzaa;* Dial Books, New York.

Pinkney, B., (1994), *Max Found Two Sticks;* Simon & Schuester, New York.

Pinkney, G. J., (1992), *Back Home;* Dial Books for Young Readers, New York.

Ringgold, F., (1992), *Aunt Harriet's Underground Railroad in the Sky;* Crown Publishers, Inc., New York.

    (1993), *Dinner at Aunt Connie's House;* Hyperion Books.

Sankofa, D. A., *The Origin of Life on Earth, an African Creation Myth;*
    Sights Productions, P. O. Box 101, Mt. Airy, MD 21771

Schlank, C. H., (1990), *Martin Luther King, Jr., A Biography for Young Children;* Gryphon House,Maryland.

Slier, D., (1991), *Make a Joyful Sound: Poems for Children by African American Poets;* Checkerboard Press, NY.

Steptoe, J., (1983), *Jeffrey Bear Cleans Up His Act.;* Lothrop, Lee & Shephard, New York.

    (1987), *Mufaro's Beautiful Daughters: an African Tale;* Lothrop, Lee & Shepard, New York.

    (1984), *The Story of Jumping Mouse;* Lothrop, Lee & Shepard, New York.

    (1971), *Train Ride;* HarperCollins, New York.

Stock, C., (1993), *Where are you Going Manyoni?;* Morrow Junior Books, New York.

Strickland, D. and Strickland, M., *Families; Poems Celebrating the African American Experiences*

Taylor, M. W., *Harriet Tubman Anti-slavery Activist;* Chelsea House Publisher, New York.

Thomas, J. C., (1993), *Brown Honey in Broomwheat Tea;* HarperCollins, New York.

Walker, M., (1980), *Ty's One-Man Band;* Four Winds, New York.

Williams, K. L., (1990), *Galimoto;* Mulberry Books, New York.

Williams, S., (1994), *Working Cotton;* Harcourt, Brace, Jaovaovich, Orlando, Florida

Bibliography

Beckman, Carol, Roberta Simmons, Nancy Thomas, 1982, *Channels to Children.* Colorado Springs, Colorado.

Bensen-Hale, Janice E., 1982, *Black children: Their Roots, Culture and Learning Styles.* Baltimore: Johns Hopkins University Press.

Bettelheim, Bruno, 1989, *The Uses of Enchantment.* New York: Vintage Books.

Bredkamp, Sue (ed.), 1987, Developmentally Appropriate Practice in Early Childhood Programs Serving Children Birth Through Age 8. Washington, D.C.: NAEYC.

Cooperative Children's Book Center. Third Edition, *Multicultural Literature for Children and Young Adults.* University of Wisconsin, Madison.

Cooperative Children's Book Center. 1991, *The Multicolored Mirror: Cultural substance in Literature for Children and Young Adults.*

Derman-Sparks, Louise, 1989, *Anti-Bias Curriculum Tools for Empowering Young Children.* Washington, D.C.: NAEYC.

Hale, Janice, 1991, *"The Transmission of cultural Values to Young African American Children," Young Children,* V.46 No.6, September 1991.

Harris, V., Editor, 1992,, *Teaching Multicultural Literature in Grades K-8.* Christopher-Gordan.

Hopson, Darlene .D., Derek S. Hopson, 1990, *Different and Wonderful,* New York: Prentice Hall Press.

Johnson, Barbara, 1978, *Cup Cooking.* Lake Alfred, Florida: Early Educators Press.

Kohl, Mary Ann, 1989, *Mudworks.* Bellingham, Washington: Ring Publishers.

Krementz, Jill, 1988, *How It Feels When A Parent Dies.* New York: Alfred A. Knopf.

Levine, L., 1977, *Black Culture and Black Consciousness.* New York: Oxford University Press.

Lewis, Linda, Michelle Miller, Sandra Riggs, Cathy Stewart, 1990, *Let's Pretend Together,* Des Moines, Iowa: 4217 Lincoln Avenue, 50130.

Lorton, Mary Baratta, 1976, *Mathematics Their Way.* Menlo Park, California: Addison-Wesley Publishing Company.

Manna, A.L. & Brodie, C.S. Editors, 1993, *Many Faces, Many Voices: Multicultural Literary Experiences for Youth.*

Moll, Patricia Buerke, 1975, *Children & Scissors.* Tampa, Florida: Hampton Mae Institute.

Piaget, Jean, 1952, *The Origins of Intelligence in Children.* New York: International Universal Press.

Raines, Shirley A. and Robert J. Cansby, 1989, *Story Stretchers,* Mount Rainer, Maryland: Gryphon House.

Rollock, Barbara, 1992, *Black Authors and Illustrators of Children's Books: A Biographical Dictionary, Second Edition.* New York & London: Garland Publishing Inc.

Simon, Sidney, 1976, *Caring, Feeling, Touching.* Niles-Illinois: Argus Communications.

Sims, R., 1982, *Shadow & Substance: The Afro-American Experience in Contemporary Children's Fiction.* NCTE.

Smith, Charles A., 1989, *From Wonder to Wisdom.* New York: NAL Books.

Spencer, M.B., G. Brookins and W. Allen (eds.), 1985, *Beginnings: The Social and Affective Development of Black Children.* Hillsdale, New Jersey: Lawrence Erlbaum.

Strickland, Dorothy S. (ed.), 1982, *Listen Children, An Anthology of Black Literature,* Bantam Books, New York.

Trelease, Jim, 1994, *The New Read Aloud Handbook.* New York, Penguin.

Williams, Robert A., Robert E. Rockwell, Elizabeth A. Sherwood, 1987, *Mudpies to Magnets.* Mount Ranier, Maryland: Gryphon House, Inc.

Wishik, Cindy S., 1982, *Kids Dish It Up Sugar Free.* Port Angeles, Washington: Peninsula Publishing Inc.

Children & Books I
Second Edition

introduces you to the best of 86 children's story books
featuring Black children from America, England and Africa as main characters.
Moll has selected 25 new books for the Second Edition.
All of the story books were written or illustrated by African-Americans,
or are about African culture, customs and folklore.
In addition, authors and illustrators of African heritage who live in
England, Kenya and South Africa are also included.
Moll has suggestions for the presentation of each book and follow-up activities
for use throughout the curriculum.

$14.95

Children & Scissors, A Developmental Approach
Third Edition

was Moll's first book. Thirteen sequential steps for learning the art
of cutting, including gluing, pasting, free cutting and line cutting, are presented.
Common problems are identified and classroom-tested solutions are suggested.
There are 87 sequential cut and paste activities which are open ended and
guide teachers to encourage children to explore with their materials.
The book gives instructions for teachers on developmental growth through
process and encourages children to control and define their own product.

$14.95

**Contact your local
School Supply Dealer,
Children's Bookstore**

or call or write:

**Patricia B. Moll
4104 Lynn Avenue
Tampa, Florida 33603-3421
813 238-2221**

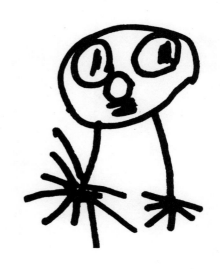